Addiction, Attachment, Trauma, and Recovery

The Norton Series on Interpersonal Neurobiology
Louis Cozolino, PhD, Series Editor
Allan N. Schore, PhD, Series Editor, 2007–2014
Daniel J. Siegel, MD, Founding Editor

The field of mental health is in a tremendously exciting period of growth and conceptual reorganization. Independent findings from a variety of scientific endeavors are converging in an interdisciplinary view of the mind and mental well-being. An interpersonal neurobiology of human development enables us to understand that the structure and function of the mind and brain are shaped by experiences, especially those involving emotional relationships.

The Norton Series on Interpersonal Neurobiology provides cutting-edge, multidisciplinary views that further our understanding of the complex neurobiology of the human mind. By drawing on a wide range of traditionally independent fields of research—such as neurobiology, genetics, memory, attachment, complex systems, anthropology, and evolutionary psychology—these texts offer mental health professionals a review and synthesis of scientific findings often inaccessible to clinicians. The books advance our understanding of human experience by finding the unity of knowledge, or consilience, that emerges with the translation of findings from numerous domains of study into a common language and conceptual framework. The series integrates the best of modern science with the healing art of psychotherapy.

A NORTON PROFESSIONAL BOOK

Addiction, Attachment, Trauma, and Recovery

The Power of Connection

Oliver J. Morgan

W. W. NORTON & COMPANY

Independent Publishers Since 1923

Note to Readers: Standards of clinical practice and protocol change over time, and no technique or recommendation is guaranteed to be safe or effective in all circumstances. This volume is intended as a general information resource for professionals practicing in the field of psychotherapy and mental health; it is not a substitute for appropriate training, peer review, and/or clinical supervision. Neither the publisher nor the author(s) can guarantee the complete accuracy, efficacy, or appropriateness of any particular recommendation in every respect.

As of press time, the URLs displayed in this book link or refer to existing sites. The publisher and author are not responsible for any content that appears on third-party websites.

For information about permission to reproduce selections from this book, write to Permissions, W. W. Norton & Company, Inc., 500 Fifth Avenue, New York, NY 10110

For information about special discounts for bulk purchases, please contact W. W. Norton Special Sales at specialsales@wwnorton.com or 800-233-4830

Manufacturing by Lake Book Manufacturing, Inc.
Production manager: Katelyn MacKenzie

Library of Congress Cataloging-in-Publication Data

Names: Morgan, Oliver J., author.
Title: Addiction, attachment, trauma, and recovery : the power of connection / Oliver J. Morgan ; foreword by Louis Cozolino.
Description: First edition. | New York, NY : W.W. Norton & Company, [2019] | Series: A Norton professional book | Includes bibliographical references and index.
Identifiers: LCCN 2019016055 | ISBN 9780393713176 (hardcover)
Subjects: LCSH: Substance abuse—Treatment. | Addicts—Counseling of. | Addicts--Rehabilitation.
Classification: LCC RC564 .M6626 2019 | DDC 362.29--dc23
LC record available at https://lccn.loc.gov/2019016055

W. W. Norton & Company, Inc., 500 Fifth Avenue, New York, N.Y. 10110
www.wwnorton.com

W. W. Norton & Company Ltd., 15 Carlisle Street, London W1D 3BS

In my life,
families have arisen when I needed them.
The Society of Jesus (Jesuits) when I was seventeen.
Alcoholics Anonymous in my mid-thirties.
Ellen and the kids in my fifties and beyond.
Thank you!

Contents

Foreword

WE ARE PAST A TIME in the mental health profession when simple solutions and strategies are satisfactory in any specialty area, especially addiction and recovery. Therapists and clients live within a society which influences us in every possible manner. None of us doubt that the long-standing addiction epidemic in the inner cities is related to cultural and economic marginalization and prejudice. It is just as clear that the current epidemic of addiction among people in suburban and rural communities is associated with the painful transition from industrial to technology-based economies. Addiction is not just a diagnosis, it's a symptom of something bigger.

The emergence of social neuroscience in the 1970s started the exploration of the brain as a social organ. We have discovered that our brains consist of a government of systems which are interwoven, integrated, and shaped during development through experience-dependent processes. And like our brains, we too live in a government of relationships which trigger our genetic expression, build our neural circuitry, and modulate our biochemistry. Over the last twenty years, those of us who work in the area of Interpersonal Neurobiology (IPNB) have explored these and many other fields of scientific study to try and make sense of the vast complexity of human behavior and experience.

Two decades into the twenty-first century, we need clinician-theorists who are capable of multidisciplinary integration, synergistic thinking, and therapeutic sophistication. Enter Oliver Morgan. Combining his decades of clinical experience with an array of new findings and insights, Dr. Morgan expands the fields of Interpersonal Neurobiology and Social Ecology into the treatment of addiction. He does not shy away in the face of complexity, rather, he embraces it in a very human and understandable manner. In his openness about his personal struggles with addiction, he provides us with a living window to the thoughts, feelings, and struggles that all need to be addressed for successful treatment.

Each belief about addiction, from it being a medical disease, to a failure of character, to an individual choice, lacks a coherent understanding of the heterogeneity and complexity of human experience and addiction. Each perspective may be relevant, but certainly not to the exclusion of the others.

From the perspective of IPNB, experience is a consequence of our genetic history, epigenetic processes of gene expression, the history of our social relationships, the quality of our connections with others, and our ability to both connect to the group mind and contribute to our tribe. These and many other human processes lead to the experience of an individual who either builds a generative life, or participates in its destruction. Dr. Morgan focuses on an important aspect of addiction, an estrangement from the group mind and feeling disconnected from others, making addiction a symptom of the pain of loneliness and separation—he is on to something very important.

In the following pages, Dr. Morgan will explore the relationship between the brain, attachment, and trauma to learn about their central role in the successful treatment of addiction. It is time to build on the successes of past treatment modalities and expand them to include new findings and insights. There is no doubt that an appreciation of the brain helps us to understand the entire range of human behavior. The expanding appreciation of the contribution of meditation and mindfulness to mental health is increasingly a component of all forms of treatment.

In my experience treating those with substance abuse, what has always struck me is how many of my clients have been insecurely attached or felt as if they were unconnected to others long before addiction reared its head. Research in attachment and social neuroscience support Dr. Morgan's belief that, "Disconnection is intolerable for human beings. From deep within our evolutionary past, it signals an extreme threat to survival." We do anything to avoid the dread of separation; from staying in abusive relationships, to sacrificing all we have worked for by medicating the terror. We all strive for embeddedness and when this fails, we look for substitutes—whatever form they may take. The problem with substitutes for love and connection is that there is never enough.

Louis Cozolino
Los Angeles, California
2019

Preface

"Alcohol ruined me financially and morally, broke my heart and the hearts of too many others. Even though it did this to me, and it almost killed me, and I haven't touched a drop of it in seventeen years, sometimes I wonder if I could get away with drinking some now. I totally subscribe to the notion that alcoholism is a mental illness because thinking like that is clearly insane."

—CRAIG FERGUSON

TODAY, I AM CLEAN AND SOBER and have been for some time. But it wasn't always that way. I have been rescued from myself more than once, pulled out of the pit of addiction and compulsive behavior. As a 12-step sponsor once said to me, "You're a *real* one." Over the years I have wondered, both personally and professionally, why these issues are part of my life. Where does my compulsive way of living and the addictions it breeds come from? How did addiction become so embedded in me?

These have been tantalizing personal questions in my life ever since I realized that my maternal grandfather and all three of my uncles on both sides of the family died from addiction. Professionally, as a mental health and addiction counselor, as well as a supervisor and professor of counseling, it has been incumbent on me to explore the roots of my own thinking and behavior. Consequently, I was curious about my inclination to excess, but never more so than when I was sitting in detox, disheveled and trying to figure out how I got there. That was over 30 years ago, but seems as fresh as yesterday. Was I destined to follow my ancestors' path and become one more statistic, I wondered? Was addiction eventually going to kill me, too?

As I have taught and trained numerous addiction and mental health counselors over the years, I have tried to understand these questions, the intricacies of this disorder, and the circuitous pathways that led me to a mental health career. Understanding is, of course, therapeutic in its own right. It continues to help in my own addiction recovery and search for life balance. It is helping me to be a better parent and spouse. And, I hope, it is helping me to teach and guide a new generation of mental health and addiction counselors. This book is an extension of that work.

In the 1980s and 1990s, I consulted about drugs and compulsions with a number of schools and colleges, parent groups, and peer-based prevention programs, as well as participating in panel discussions on campuses and the local PBS station. Looking back, I'm embarrassed at how primitive and narrow our understanding was about it all. In 1990, I came to my university, in the midst of writing a doctoral dissertation about the experience of recovery, as narrated to me by a group of long-recovering alcoholics and drug addicts (Morgan, 1992, 1995a), and I was given control over our state-approved curriculum of alcohol and other drug courses. This launched a career in which I have published over 30 peer-reviewed articles and chapters as well as two books in addiction studies (Morgan & Jordan, 1999; Morgan & Litzke, 2008). As a person in long-term recovery myself, I am grateful for these opportunities to make a contribution.

As the reader can see, I have spent many years of my life studying addiction. In all that time, perhaps the deepest insight I have is echoed in the recent words of journalist Johann Hari: "The opposite of addiction is not sobriety, it's connection."[1] When I first heard it, this phrasing caught me up short. The insight was breathtaking. Nevertheless, the more I study and learn about addiction, the more I believe it to be true. A goal of this book is to lay out *why* this is so and *what it might mean* for those of us who struggle on behalf of addicts every day.

Connection and a sense of belonging, of community and common purpose, are foundational first principles in human development as well as in recovery, and can serve both as an antidote to, and inoculation against, addiction. As we confront the current public health crisis of addiction—made more concrete by the ongoing opioid crisis—we need to consider community and connection as essential healing strategies. They can also help us to address a host of other problems that plague our times. The absence of these very same experiences can be the catalyst for a multitude of life struggles.

HOW DID I GET HERE?

Listening to addiction and mental health professionals—through multiple research interviews with addicts and recovering persons over the years and through many counseling sessions with them and those who love them—I have tried to learn about addiction. Teaching a variety of students, of all ages and varied experiences, I have explored addiction and been humbled. Perhaps you have a similar experience.

There have been times when I thought, "I've got this. Addiction is . . . [*a moral weakness, a choice, an inherited vulnerability, a chronic relapsing disorder, a disease . . . plug in your favorite theory or approach*]." And then something happens and I'm no longer so sure. Maybe I've come up against someone's unfathomable choice ("He did *what*!?"), or maybe I've seen again the depths to which someone sinks ("Oh no, not *that*!"). Maybe a new model emerges with fanfare and the trappings of scientific certainty, and it seems to offer a more complete understanding than what I previously had ("*Now* I get it."). Maybe I re-experience the aftershocks of my own addictions, and even though I'm in recovery for many years, I feel the lure of the monster rise again. Something happens, and all of a sudden I'm no longer so sure about my way of thinking. What I thought was certain now seems incomplete . . . and a little off.

In recent years, I've had several of these experiences, and they have forced me to look anew at long-held beliefs about addiction and human beings. Studying addiction, after all, brings one face to face with core elements of our shared humanity. As a result, I began a multiyear personal project to examine, and where needed revise, my own view of addiction and recovery. I began this project thinking that I would write a book that integrated different sciences into a synthesis about addiction and the challenges it poses. Knitting together clues from attachment theory, neurobiology, family systems, and trauma studies, I discovered some useful and fresh ways of thinking. I learned that a new hybrid and integrative science called "interpersonal neurobiology" (IPNB) offered the kind of cohesive perspective I was searching for. The discerning reader will see throughout this book that IPNB does offer a robust and muscular picture of what is happening in addiction.

As time went on, however, and I followed the clues that were emerging in my research, my thinking expanded even further and I began to examine sociological, socioeconomic, and cultural literature on the fragmentation of modern society and the experience of cultural dislocation that inevitably follows. I began to see that there are pockets of poor health, addiction, and economic despair that seem to cluster by geography or ZIP code.[2] Addiction is not just about individuals, or genetics, or neurochemistry. I saw a wider ecology of relationships and connections enfolding individuals' addictive experiences (Alexander, 2008/2011). My view of addiction as a symptom and direct result of larger social and cultural forces began to envelop equally valid insights into the neurobiological, attachment- and trauma-related factors that also lead to harmful and addictive use. These domains mutually trigger and reinforce one another. Earlier insights nested within this more expansive framework. A new way of conceptualizing addiction and the tasks of recovery slowly dawned on me.

I offer this framework below as a fresh way to understand addiction and address the current addiction crisis. The framework integrates interpersonal neurobiology and what I call social ecology. Some provocative learning experiences are presented within the book as case studies and as personal life events. These experiences were triggers for my own project and were pivotal for my personal reexamination. The case studies inside are all true and accurate, as best I could recreate them. Some are from memory, while others are recounted from my clinical notes. Naturally, the names and details are changed and identities disguised to protect the privacy and anonymity of former clients. Where necessary, I use specific details with permission, and sometimes several cases are merged to enrich the description. The fundamentals of these stories, however, are authentic and revealing. Personal stories are also told from memory, as I believe they happened, and contain recollections from family members who were there. These presentations are similar to the way I teach, using illustrative materials from counseling practice or my own life as ways to explain or further a point.

WHY THIS BOOK?

The focus of this book will be addiction and recovery. I have found interpersonal neurobiology (IPNB) and social ecology (SE) to be twin perspectives that can assist in deeper understanding. Like the dual lenses in a pair of binoculars, when aligned together, these two frames of reference can help us to see farther and with clarity. These perspectives come together in an approach to counseling that I call "attachment-sensitive counseling." The outline of this approach is presented inside.

Sitting quietly at home one day, I realized that I wanted to share what I was learning with the colleagues, young professionals, and supervisees I had taught and written for over the course of my career. So much new information is emerging—much of it developed in my lifetime—and it begs for a synthesis. New insights across disciplines are coming together. They complement and deepen some of what we already know and replace some of it, too. Working across disciplines and finding common ground between divergent viewpoints is now a method of scientific inquiry in its own right and has given us exciting new ways to imagine the world and how things work. This way of thinking, called "consilience" (Wilson, 1998), opens new pathways forward.

A consilient approach attempts to see a seamless web of causes and effects, pulling together several sciences (and even humanities) into a multifocal and unified view. Emphasis is placed on the connections of ideas and disciplines. With this kind of thinking, providers and scholars can feel the approach of a new model or paradigm within multiple fields of inquiry, including addiction studies, once we are willing to open the limits and boundaries of our thinking and look across different areas of knowledge. Fresh insights have the power to expand and revitalize what we know and how we practice. I want to share these new ideas with you. Others, such as struggling clients, their loved ones, and the public may benefit as well.

Throughout the book, I present what we are learning about human development, addiction, recovery, and social ecology from a variety of viewpoints. Attachment, neurobiology, family systems, as well as trauma and adversity interact from the very beginning and throughout our lives; they create the conditions, internal to the individual and surrounding the person, which can lead to addiction as well as many other conditions that bedevil human living and public health.

From this perspective, addiction is not so much an individual misfortune as it is a result and a symptom of larger conditions. Those struggling with substance-related and addictive disorders may be harbingers of deeper social dangers.

I have come to the conclusion that addiction studies may benefit from such a new, integrated, and consilient paradigm and new metaphors that can better express what science and experience try to teach us about addiction and recovery. The perspective offered by interpersonal neurobiology, augmented with social ecological perspectives, will guide us.

Welcome aboard.

Introduction

"Addiction is a primary, chronic disease of brain reward, motivation, memory and related circuitry. Dysfunction in these circuits leads to characteristic biological, psychological, social and spiritual manifestations. This is reflected in an individual pathologically pursuing reward and/or relief by substance use and other behaviors."

AMERICAN SOCIETY OF ADDICTION MEDICINE

"The idea that addiction is a disease is the greatest medical hoax since the idea that masturbation would make you go blind. This is not to say that the behaviors people now fashionably regard as symptoms of addiction are non-existent. . . . Calling human pursuits diseases tells us more about the diagnostician than it does about the persons being diagnosed."

JEFFREY SCHALER

THERE HAS ALWAYS BEEN some controversy in the field of addiction studies, but more recently discussions have become quite polarized, often generating more heat than light.

On one side we have those who advocate for the position that *addiction is an acquired, chronic, relapsing disease of a hijacked brain.* Advocates tell us that under the impact of drugs or compulsive behaviors such as gambling or Internet gaming, personal choice is limited in vulnerable individuals. Drug use and behavioral actions become compulsions and are not under conscious control. Psychoactive drugs and compulsive behaviors, mixed with vulnerabilities in individuals, are the culprits here.

There is much to recommend this view. Clearly, alcohol, nicotine, and other drugs as well as compulsive behaviors have psychoactive effects. On its face, addiction involves the brain, a chronic course, relapse, and a process that resembles abduction. The labeling of addiction as a disease relieves some of the shame and stigma felt by addicts, but it also raises a number of thorny and troubling issues (Satel & Lilienfeld, 2017). This is the current and dominant model of addiction espoused by many of our most respected addiction scientists, treatment professionals, and scholars (Volkow, Koob, & McLellan, 2016; Volkow & Koob, 2015). It is the view that guides much of our public policy and research funding (U.S. Department of Health and Human Services, 2016). Many in the media and pop culture champion this model. But the common man or woman finds it difficult to accept at face value.

On the other side is a chorus of respected scholars, treatment providers, and advocates for an opposing and vocal minority view, namely that *addiction is a choice and not a disease.* It is voluntary behavior akin to adopting a religious belief system or falling in love, but more harmful, a willful dedication and commitment that leads to self-destruction (Heyman, 2010; Schaler, 2002). This view is directly opposed to any analysis of addiction's "compulsiveness" that excludes an individual's sovereign choice to use. People are held accountable. This view also tends to be hostile to any kind of mutual help or 12 Step engagement. "Empowering the self" is its mantra, not "powerlessness" or reliance on higher powers. This makes it controversial in addiction treatment circles that, more often than not, have some loyalty to Alcoholics Anonymous and related programs.

More recently, a new perspective has emerged that builds on elements of the choice model, but underlines *addiction as a learned behavior.* The advocates of this model emphasize that the brain is changing all the time, adapting to the living world, and altering itself as circumstances demand.

Neuroplasticity is highlighted, and adaptive learning is understood to involve motivation, desire, and repetition as well as reward, mechanisms that become routinized and stable over time (Lewis, 2013, 2015; Szalavitz, 2016). An impulsive search for pleasure or relief ("liking") is replaced, so the model goes, by a continuing and compulsive repetition of increasingly automated learned behavior ("wanting") that is difficult to relinquish.

Disease, choice, learning: There is some truth in each point of view. However, what is striking in all these depictions of addiction is the singular attachment to individualized representations of the human person. Disease, choice, and learning are primarily conditions of the individual and by extension his or her near relationships such as family, kinship, or close friendship networks. And yet, any view of human persons that ignores our essentially social, systemic, and thoroughly embedded nature—that is, our deep ties to diverse connections and social ecologies—can only be a partial picture of reality.

I have become weary of the back-and-forth, frustrated by our limited vision, and I believe that I have found another way. There is more consensus than we know or are willing to admit, and we need to move beyond sterile debates to focus on a more comprehensive paradigm. This book attempts to meet that need. It (a) incorporates the newest information and the latest science; (b) provides scaffolding for what is already known and helps to integrate new knowledge; (c) provides fresh methods and perspectives for helping persons struggling with addiction and other chronic illnesses; and (d) fosters hope for the tasks of recovery and mental health care.

Do we really need another book, another model of addiction? This is not just another approach, something new and unconventional. Taking the best insights of our biological *and* social sciences, and integrating those ideas with leading-edge work in attachment, trauma, and systems thinking, the book provides a new and more comprehensive synthesis. I fold previous models into a wider frame by placing the biological sciences (disease, neurobiology) and social psychology (choice, learning) of addiction within the wider perspective of interpersonal neurobiology, while embedding it within a broader human ecology. This perspective allows us to see the true worth of previous models and appreciate the unique contributions of each. Combining insights and methods across disciplines, a new synthesis is emerging in other areas of investigation, such as the mental health and trauma recovery movements. This book presents a similar, consilient model of addiction.

COMPETING MODELS

I am increasingly uncomfortable with the guiding metaphors of the *disease model* of addiction, defined as a chronic relapsing disease of a brain that has been hijacked by the use of substances and compulsive behaviors. The term *disease* speaks to an understanding and interventions that emerge from a one-sided medical model, while *hijacking* has criminal justice implications and places the responsibility for addiction in the wrong place, namely on the drugs or activities themselves. Addiction, however, is not a criminal or even a medical problem only. And while it would be a mistake to disregard the growing evidence that is emerging from neuroscience and biomedicine about the role of the broken brain in addiction, neurobiology cannot be the whole story (Kalant, 2009; Satel & Lilienfeld, 2013a & b, 2017).

Why? Contrary to popular belief, every single day some people who struggle with the disease of addiction wake up and say, "That's it." In the parlance of Alcoholics Anonymous, they arrive at that point where they are "sick and tired of being sick and tired." They reach a "moment of clarity" (Lawford, 2010). This is a challenge for the medical disease model: How does a truly hijacked brain make this choice? Addicts do not act like "automata"; they do retain some control. Neuroscientist Kent Berridge of the University of Michigan writes: ". . . addictive urges are not entirely uncontrollable . . . they can be controlled, at least for a short while, and sometimes for longer if the stakes are high enough and clear enough" (quoted in Holton & Berridge, 2013 p. 241). We have, in fact, known this for a long time. People struggling with addiction often find a pathway out. Newly awakened addicts do follow through with the initial decision to stop. This happens a lot more often than the prevailing disease narrative would lead one to believe. I was fortunate to begin my academic career collecting the stories of alcoholics and addicts who arrived at clarity (Morgan, 1992, 1995a). Without knowing it at the time, I was learning about the central "paradox at the heart of addiction":

"How can the capacity for choice coexist with self-destructiveness?" (Satel & Lilienfeld, 2013, p. 54).

Alternatively, rhetoric about addiction as *a voluntary choice* also makes me uncomfortable. Speaking about *choice* carries pejorative implications about addicts as "bad actors," unwilling to curtail destructive behavior, or weak-willed characters unable to follow through with resolve. Nevertheless, this viewpoint should not be dismissed out of hand. The choice model keeps (inconveniently) reminding us that there *is* an element of choice in the use of chemical or behavioral "comforters"; addicts do not lose all their goal direction and executive functions or stop being moral agents just because they are addicted. Given sufficient incentive, for example, research (Alexander, 2014; Hart, 2014; Lewis, 2015) shows that some do seem able to regulate or moderate their use, at least at certain times. It is also true that persons struggling with harmful use or addiction are able to perform admirably in other areas of living. Their supposedly hijacked brains seem able to function well enough in those areas. And then there is that pesky fact about those—a *majority* of addicts and harmful users, it turns out—who stop or moderate use on their own and enter a form of "natural recovery" without formal intervention or treatment (Heyman, 2010; Klingemann, Sobell, & Sobell, 2010). It turns out that this is much more common than we previously believed (Granfield & Cloud, 1996; Kubicek, Morgan, & Morrison, 2002).

This is key. It can be challenging to discern whether addicted behavior cannot be controlled or is just uncontrolled. In regard to drug use or participation in compulsive activities, as in so many other areas of living, it is the role of choice and the quality of the choices made where responsibility and accountability reside, and ultimately where one's humanity is on the line. It is, in other words, the degrees of freedom and self-determination available in any particular choice to use, or pattern of using drugs or engaging in compulsive activity that are in question.

Consequently, the choice model has its own challenges to confront. The neurobiology is clear that there are hidden and powerful forces at work outside of the addict's consciousness and choice framework (Childress, 2006; Young et al., 2014). For example, we now know that the brain responds to "unseen" reward cues from the environment, that is, we can be motivated to act with or without awareness of the triggers (Childress et al., 2008). As neuroscience spotlights the neural mechanisms that accompany addictive processes, it is more and more difficult to ignore their role. Clearly some choices to use drugs or cope with stress are influenced, perhaps even compromised, or motivated, by neurological and appetitive factors that are outside of full conscious control. Addicts do not act like robots, mindlessly seeking drugs or pleasure, but neither are they totally free agents, making unfettered rational choices.

How many times in my own addiction did I promise myself on Saturday morning that I would not drink, and yet on Saturday night ended up drunk in Harvard Square? I had resolve in the morning, but during the day other factors piled up, related to (a) stress and loneliness; (b) emotional volatility, particularly around elation or guilt; (c) a general sense of personal dis-ease (poverty of spirit) with my life; (d) fantasies of relaxation; (e) overinflated misperceptions of my ability to manage alcohol use; (f) forgetfulness about the likely consequences on the other side of intoxication; coupled with (g) the triggers of seeing bottles of booze and smelling the spirits inside. These shifting experiences, mediated by a variety of neural and psychological structures, but coming only vaguely into sight, all conspired to weaken my initial resolve and added up to another instance of drunken choices, even before alcohol ever touched my lips. Did I make a choice to drink or use under those circumstances? Yes, but what kind of choice was it?

Clearly, learning and repetition, as well as changes in brain structure and function, also have roles to play in addiction. As opposed to disease or choice, I am more comfortable with metaphors of neuroplasticity and learned behavior as depictions of addictive conduct. However, this is also a view limited by its individualized perspective. It can only partially account for our deeply social, cultural, and ecological nature. Consequently, this perspective ultimately leaves me cold as well.

If we free ourselves of the metaphors (disease, hijacking, choice, learned behavior) that limit our view, perhaps we can raise the question—not whether addiction is a neurobiological and behavioral disorder, but whether it is *only* such a disorder.

WHAT'S MISSING?

There is a larger issue that goes beyond any particular individual and reaches into the social ecology, and even the natural environment that encircles us. We are speaking here of social, political, cultural, and economic fragmentation and the stresses they place on all of us. More deeply still, we are speaking of the *fracturing of meaning and spiritual purpose* that keeps us afloat as individuals and societies (Alexander, 2008/2011).

Broken ecologies of meaning, purpose, and belonging create an empty vacuum at the center of living. Fragmentation and disconnection often collude with experiences of adversity and trauma that take up residence in people's experience. Societal fragmentation and fracturing of meaning lead to experiences of dislocation, estrangement, and disconnection from one another (Badenoch, 2018). Individuals and relationships suffer. Alienation and suffering from around the world exacerbate the burden of stress. Professor Bruce K. Alexander calls this "poverty of the spirit."

Disconnection is intolerable for human beings. From deep within our evolutionary past, it signals an extreme threat to survival. Infants and children cannot survive for long without a tribe or clan to protect and nurture them. Throughout our lives, without connection to others of our kind, we are left alone in the dark. Marginalization or exclusion from the social group sets off alarm bells in several neural areas that signal pain, physical or emotional, and may be implicated in drug craving (Heilig, Epstein, et al., 2016). Furthermore, within the ecology of their clan, children learn their place and assert their social role. They discover an identity, a sense of mission and purpose that helps them to belong.

Alienation or separation from others, on the other hand, create a deep need for setting things right, for coping, for reconnection or, when absolutely necessary, it triggers settling for counterfeit connection with anything that will help to calm our anxieties, even with substitutes that only partially suffice. This can become the royal road to harmful use and addiction.

This is something that all three models—disease, choice, and learning—miss. This should not be a surprise; these models focus on what happens to the individual addict. There is a wider view, however, that is often given short shrift.

> Addiction in the modern world can be best understood as a
> compulsive lifestyle that people adopt as a desperate substi-
> tute when they are dislocated from the myriad intimate ties
> between people and groups—from the family to the spiritual
> community—that are essential for every person in every type
> of society.... Even the most harmful substitute lifestyles
> serve an adaptive function (ALEXANDER, 2001, PP. 1, 4).

There is an *adaptive function* for which substance use and compulsive activities seem ideally suited (Alexander, 2001, 1987; Alexander & Hadaway, 1982). They "have what it takes." Addiction helps people to cope; it serves a purpose. Use or engagement with drugs or compulsive activities may *begin* for a variety of reasons, but they often *continue* and deepen because they are a solution to a problem, long before they become problems in their own right. This is an old story for mental health practitioners: The client's solutions—his or her attempts to cope—often end up as a problem. Failed adaptation is written all over addiction.

Canadian psychologist Bruce K. Alexander has explored the dimensions of this wider perspective in his book, *The Globalization of Addiction* (2011), calling addiction a "substitute lifestyle" that ameliorates the pain of discon-nection. Substitution helps people to tolerate the pain and loss, and because this adaptation is so valuable and deeply driven, people cling to it with "tenacity" (Alexander, 2001, p. 4).

Allied observations are made by sociologist Peter Adams in *Fragmented Intimacy* (2008). *New York Times* best-selling authors Robert Putnam in *Bowling Alone* (2001) and Marc Dunkelman (2014) in *The Vanishing Neigh-bor* similarly explore the breakdown and fragmentation of civil society and the dislocation that ensues. In *Hillbilly Elegy*, best-selling author J. D. Vance (2016) describes the alienation that comes with societal fragmentation and a crisis in culture. Alexander (2001, p. 20) again:

> It is poverty of the spirit . . . that is the precursor of addic-
> tion. The key to controlling addiction is maintaining a soci-
> ety in which psychosocial integration is attainable by the
> great majority of people.

In other words we, as a society, live with the proverbial "hole in the soul." Reconnection and community—"psychosocial integration"—are the antidotes.

POVERTY OF SPIRIT

Mental health and addiction professionals live in the trenches and we often look for new and more complete ways to help. I wrote this book so that you and I would have in our hands the very best that science can teach us today about addiction. What I have learned as I prepared to write this book has opened my eyes to many aspects of the addiction problem and helped me to connect addiction to our deepest human needs. Human relationships and connection are, in the words of martyred Jesuit social psychologist Ignacio Martín-Baró, the sustaining birthplace of "humanization" (Martín-Baró, 1994, p. 109). Addiction is a cry for help—personal, societal, and spiritual—from this deep source. *Humanization*—relational connection and meaning—is the long-term antidote to addiction.

However, if we continue to limit our comprehension to the currently available models of addiction, it is difficult to see how our understanding and effectiveness will grow. Yes, neuroscience and biomedicine can develop new medications to help us with emergency intervention, detoxification, or craving. Social and intervention science may develop new therapies to assist addicts or harmful users with making better choices. We are already seeing some success with retraining and assisting users to choose differently, using mindfulness strategies, cognitive-behavioral techniques, and the like.

What, however, do we do for poverty of the spirit? This is where an examination of the depths of disconnection and social dislocation in our culture may help us to understand more deeply. We need to complement our biological and psychological views of addiction with examination of social ecology. I have come to believe that the "soul" of addiction is lack of connection and belonging. Addiction involves fractured connections and relationships gone awry. Alexander (2001, 2008/2011) and others call for changing the debate in regard to the ills of our society, including addiction. This book is an attempt to help refocus that debate. We must find deeper and more encompassing strategies to address the current public health crisis that is addiction.

The old strategies of law enforcement, treatment, and public education are no longer sufficient.

NESTED LIVING SYSTEMS

As I read through the scientific literature, I keep coming back to the functioning of natural, biophysical, and social systems as a way to organize my thinking and learning. They seem more appropriate than rhetoric about disease, or hijacking, or choice. The metaphors of connection and nested living systems, as a relational and social ecology that is fundamental to human development, can be elaborated in several different ways.

Surrounded by others, we live within a web of connections. Born into a network of relationships, we come to consciousness surrounded by others. This is a critical fact throughout our lives. The relational connections that envelop us leave their imprint on every aspect of our humanity. They build and wire our brains; they provide safety and security. They affect every system in our bodies, neural, hormonal, immunological (Badenoch, 2018). They help to structure and populate our inner psychosocial worlds as well as our relationships. They nurture and support our bodies and spirits. Our connections tether us to life.

Our lives unfold as active partners with other persons who are organized into systems—families, neighborhoods, schools, churches, and so on—that surround each individual with circles of influence and strength. Each individual person nests within these circles of influence; interactions within these circles shape us as human beings (Bronfenbrenner, 1981, 2004). These circles impact the life of each person, *and* each person has a powerful impact on the surrounding systems. The circles interpenetrate and interact with one another. These influences are a two-way street at all times, energetically and mutually affecting one another, but this ecological fact is often forgotten.

We are not only related to systems and connections externally, we are also composed of living systems and intimate connections internally. That is, just as persons are located within ever-widening social spheres of influence, our internal systems—neurons function within pathways and circuits, which are organized and linked into larger and interconnected brain structures, which are also linked to larger organ systems—harbor complex and nested links as well. These internal and external spheres of influence are mutually interactive. Neurons are affected by politics, genes are affected by environment.

We discover and shape our life's meaning within this holistic nested network of relationships, external and internal. Without living connections to those around us, without lively connections within, we wither and die *or* we seek substitute connections that temporarily satisfy our needs. Addiction is not just about neurons, or genes, or broken brain functioning; all these elements are nested within a human organism that is itself nested within a social ecology of interpersonal connections (families, friends, kinship networks) and fragmented systems (neighborhoods, societies), and also within a natural ecology that is stressed and under threat (climate change, environmental degradation). Living in a world and at a time when conflicts among peoples seem so menacing, compounded by climate, population growth, and other natural crises, all creates stresses to the fabric of human society, attenuating the connections among us and fragmenting any solid foundation for living calmly, productively, and in balance with all around us. Existence becomes dislocated.

In the face of dislocation, humans will adapt and substitute addictive self-medication, chemical comfort, and behavioral distraction. Having found an essential purpose in response to a variety of stressors, the addictive process then feeds on itself and becomes a runaway process, an intense, substitute relationship with both an object of false connection (drug or activity) and the runaway process of intoxication. Addiction, however, is also a perverted and jealous relationship. It will eventually crowd out any other relationship that is potentially healthy.

Spiritual poverty and alienation result, underlying many contemporary problems. They remain, however, largely hidden elements in our lives. A truly human science of addiction must account for these levels and layers of connection and relationship. Recovery is a restoration to connection, to meaningful and life-giving relationships.

PREVIEW

To begin the discussion, Chapters 1 and 2 examine the case of "Joe" in some detail. Joe's experience of childhood adversity (developmental trauma) initiated a lifetime of futile searching for connection. Trauma is often an essential relationship disruption and intimate experience of disconnection and fragmentation. As we explore his experience, we will look behind the curtain at the neurobiological, psychological, and social impacts of adversity and attachment ruptures. These chapters are a thought experiment into the interpenetration of psychosocial experience in the form of childhood adversity with hidden neurobiological systems of stress response as well as reward/motivation. Ecological factors are also involved, and disconnection is the result.

While I do not believe that episodes of trauma underlie every addict's lifestyle, it is clear to me that adversity and toxic stress are ubiquitous and play *at least as significant a role* in addiction as neural hijacking by drugs. In fact, it may be just as true to say that the "hijacking" in addiction comes from childhood adversity or later trauma as from any other source. Add to this the social ecological stress that surrounds us all, and the substitute relationships we utilize to regulate ourselves, and we have a highly potent and volatile mix of predisposing vulnerabilities that often remain hidden from view.

The chapters that follow tease out relevant elements for closer examination. Chapters 3 and 4 cover basic facts and myths about addiction. Chapter 3 discusses the population of addicts with its varied experiences, and the process by which someone falls into an addicted lifestyle. Chapter 4 looks at the brain and lays out the five primary neural systems implicated in addiction: reward/motivation, stress response, self-regulation, attachment/affiliation, and pain response. In both chapters we explore effective ways to initiate a counseling relationship that can address addiction and harmful use.

Chapter 5 examines the fundamental experience of attachment and the role it plays in human development and addiction. Attachment and attunement ground our humanity. Attachment successes set the stage for wellness; failures are responsible for vulnerability to addiction, as well as other troubling life challenges.

Chapters 6 and 7 explore the roles of stress, adversity, and trauma in the predisposition to addiction. Stress and trauma are the hidden engines underneath many of the societal and cultural health hazards we face, including chemical and behavioral addictions. "Adverse childhood experiences," or ACEs, are a concrete example.

Chapter 8 lays out a model of addiction recovery. Examining the dynamics of recovery and calling for transformation of the current systems for initiating and maintaining recovery, this chapter calls for a reconceived and revitalized "recovery-oriented system of care." Recovery and healing must reach into the ecology and society that surround us, as well as providing responsive care for addicts, harmful users, and their families.

Chapter 9 looks more deeply at social ecology and poverty of spirit. What happens when connections fail? The challenge of social and cultural disconnection is critical to vulnerability for substance use disorders.

Creating a society of compassion and pushing connection to the forefront continues to elude us. Chapter 10 envisions a new society built on these principles.

We are learning that sustainable long-term recovery, an enduring and passionate interest of mine, is all about the mending of broken connections and the forging of new ones in people's lives. This creates a vital social ecology for addicts and loved ones. A spiritual outlook and lifestyle is the result of our connectedness and vibrant relationships with self, others, and the larger world, as well as a hopeful reengagement with life-giving meaning. Recovery and spirituality are all about connection. We must find ways to increase community, self-compassion, and openness to others (Cozolino, 2010). A process of "attachment-sensitive counseling" for those struggling with addiction and adversity includes these elements.

Below, I present a model, a method, and a mandate. Connection and social ecology are the core of my *model* of healthy development. How these elements converge and interact with the physiological, psychological, and relational aspects of our lives, forming the linkages that keep us alive, is the thread that binds this book together. These links are vulnerable, however, and can be severed or attenuated in multiple ways. When they are, addiction and other "substitutes" are not far behind.

The *method* I espouse is reconnection. Intervention, treatment, and recovery in attachment-sensitive work must focus on root causes if we are to achieve enduring outcomes. Simply addressing drug use or compulsive behavior, while obviously valuable tasks, cannot be the whole story. Addicted persons need communion, reconnection, belonging, and purpose—in short, a reason to get and stay sober—for sustainable recovery. Attachment-sensitive counseling can initiate and sustain a viable recovery.

Once we understand the integrated interpersonal neurobiology and social ecology model in this book, then the tasks of prevention, assessment, treatment, and recovery begin to reveal themselves more fully. The *mandate* becomes clear. This work appeals to my sense of mission and purpose.

We proceed first to look at a clinical case that started my journey of exploration. Then we will proceed step-by-step to look at the different nested concepts that provide insight into addiction. The overall formulation of the book will become clear as we proceed.

I hope you are willing to explore this new paradigm with me.

A Note on Language

MOST OF US IN THE HUMAN SERVICE and counseling professions try to utilize "person-first" language to describe the realities we work with every day. We think of this as a humanistic and ethical imperative. Throughout this book, I will attempt to do the same, but in some of the descriptions within, this has not always been possible. Sometimes, "person-first" can become overly cumbersome. In a few instances, I have had to settle for brevity. I ask the reader to transform my inept usage when it is encountered.

Why the imperative? First of all, not all members of a population are the same. People wrestling with addiction, for example, are diverse and their challenges are unique forms of suffering, rich with personal history. Their pain is individualized and needs to be honored in that way. This fact can be hidden when they are simply referred to as "addicts."

In a similar way, persons coping with or recovering from trauma/adversity/toxic stress can have their unique individuality homogenized when they are referred to as "victims." They can also experience stigma or oppression when labeled with a term that emphasizes passivity and undermines their attempts to live as survivors/thrivers. And again, persons struggling with mental illness experience dismissal and stigma when called, "bipolars," or "schizophrenics," or "borderlines."

When person-first language is eschewed, uniqueness can be passed over, real human suffering and the heroism that confronts it can be missed, false conclusions can be drawn, and people can be stigmatized as "other," separate from and less than "us." There has been too much of this thoughtless usage of terms in mental health for too long.

As this book tries to help practitioners and researchers to see addiction and trauma differently, I hope that it can also help us to see those struggling more completely, humanely, and compassionately.

Addiction, Attachment, Trauma, and Recovery

1

Résumé of an Alcoholic

"The opposite of addiction is not sobriety; the opposite of addiction is connection."

JOHANN HARI

"Unlike rats, the cages that make people vulnerable to addiction are often invisible."

BRUCE K. ALEXANDER

"Joe" is sitting at the dining room table finishing his homework. His younger sister, 13 years old, is there as well, along with his 9-year-old brother. Joe just turned 16 and he is helping them as needed, offering gentle motivation and encouragement. Mom is upstairs, folding laundry, while the baby sleeps. The house is quiet, holding its breath.

It's Friday afternoon and Joe is trying to get ahead of homework so the weekend isn't so busy. He has felt a bit queasy all day and apprehensive about the coming weekend. While last weekend passed without incident, Joe knows that the family can rarely piece together two calm weekends, and this year has been particularly troubled with dad's difficulties at the office. Something is bound to happen.

All the children hear their father's car pull into the driveway. He's home late from work. They glance apprehensively at one another. Jimmy, the younger brother, anxiously gets out of his seat and heads upstairs. Rachel puts down her pencil and puts on that face she often wears when dad's around, something between "leave me alone" and "I don't give a shit." Listening intently, Joe hears the car door slam shut and his father's muttered curse. His muscles automatically tighten. Joe wants to crawl under the table and hide, but knows that's a useless thought. The last time he did that was years ago, and the result was worse than usual. He knows the weekend has arrived.

Joe's[1] story of harmful use and addiction was long in the making. He struggled with adversity and dysfunction before he ever enlisted the help of chemicals. In this chapter and the next we will examine his story, alternating with commentary to elaborate important themes.

Humans are resolutely social beings. We are born expecting connection with others, anticipating experiences of positive attachment. We are primed for those connections, wired for relationships. In fact, we need those experiences; attachment and attunement provide the context of safety, security, and energy for proper development.

Because of the way we are made and our requirements for development, life surrounds us with an ecology of relationships, community, and culture. We are embedded within relationships and connected to systems and surrounding ecologies for support, nurture, and guidance. Without them, we are truly alone and enter a primal state of deficit and loss.

Adverse and traumatic experiences, especially in childhood, separate us from this shared birthright. Trauma leaves us isolated and fragmented; the hurt penetrates to our bones. Adversity and trauma damage the nourishing experience of safety (Porges, 2017) and become the "original sin" at the center of life.

When Joe hears his father pull into the driveway and slam the car door, the first phase of his body's stress response—the signal of adversity—kicks in. His brain's early warning system alerts other parts of his neural and hormonal systems to approaching danger. Stress pathways mobilize and initiate elaborate processes, releasing a flood of stress chemicals designed to activate the fight-flight-freeze response. Their emergency alerts are imperious and bypass the slower rational and cognitive neural circuits, warning of threats and initiating a response even before Joe is consciously aware of them. This protective mechanism signals danger and helps him to prepare.

Stress surges. Joe feels his heart begin to pound as adrenaline flows and his blood pressure rises; he experiences a rush of nervous energy while blood streams to his muscles, preparing his body to respond. Joe's defenses, neural and psychological, deploy quickly. His attention and memory are enhanced. His body is gathering its resources to meet a threat, and the systems involved and preparations that ensue are the same whether Joe were to anticipate an altercation with his father, or expect a stiff correction from a teacher, or see a predator stalking him in the forest. Energy transfers from less critical systems to focus on the immediate danger; one does not need to digest food or consider reproduction, for example, while facing off against a predator.

This scenario often plays itself out during Joe's childhood and teen years. Between periods of anxious calm, this is his normal. Once the danger or emergency passes, or buffering of the stress occurs, or Joe learns to modulate safety or relaxation, his body is designed to regulate back down, with systems operating like a stress thermostat.

Evolution has given us bodies that can experience safe/not safe in the blink of an eye, without referring to conscious awareness. Structures within the brain and nervous system (extended amygdala, vagal complex) sense environmental and interpersonal safety and respond accordingly. These neural pathways are highly sensitive and support a protective process called *neuroception*, which helps us to shift seamlessly between assessment of threat or safety, and the balancing of their corresponding bodily reactions (Badenoch, 2018; Porges, 2004). This allows us to respond quickly to danger and/or utilize calm for restoration and repair.

For Joe, these pathways helped to navigate the rapidly fluctuating emotional shoals at home. For the attentive counselor, awareness of neuroception can provide a guidepost in the counseling relationship. Client neural systems that sense safety or danger are constantly active. Signals of safety from the counselor (attentiveness, encouraging comments, eye contact, affirmations, curiosity) help the client relax and remain receptive. Criticism, lack of acceptance, or censure can trigger client resistance. Establishing a felt sense of safety and sanctuary is essential in working with traumatized and addicted clients (Badenoch, 2018).

THE SOIL OF ADDICTION

One of the earliest questions asked by those struggling with harmful use of chemicals or addiction is "where did this problem come from?" We know that overall health is usually the result of interactions between genes and environment, between inheritance and nurture, and that some people are vulnerable to harmful use or addiction through genes (about 40 to 60 percent of addiction liability comes through genes); temperament (negative outlook, chronic defensive posture); or by life experience (NIDA, 2012). We also know that alcohol and drug dependence "runs in families" (of course, so does speaking Polish!) and that family history and lifestyle as well as genes can have an impact. In addition, frequent use or abuse of chemicals can itself sensitize brain circuits and reinforce compulsive habits.

In this book, however, I want to focus our attention on *adversity*—individual, communal, ecological—as the often hidden engine underneath harmful use and addiction (Sinha, 2008). Adversity can affect the *individual* who, like Joe, grows up in a toxic family environment with childhood or teenage maltreatment that can predispose for poor health outcomes and addiction susceptibility, or co-occurrence with mental disorders. However, *communal* adversity can also come through family lifestyle. Social influence matters. Having a parent (or two), or a related family member, with an addiction heightens the chances for vulnerability; so does having friends who use (NIDA, 2012). Finally, where a person grows up (location, ZIP code) and the culture that surrounds her or him can create an *ecology* of adversity that predisposes and maintains addiction vulnerability (NIDA, 2012).

Addiction is a multi-determined phenomenon with layers within layers of mutual influences, internal and external, all interacting concurrently, leading to a pathological outcome. It is no more true to say that addiction is simply a brain disease, or a flawed choice, or an experience of learning than it is to say that falling in love is nothing but biochemistry. Rather, many factors are simultaneously involved. On the other hand, it is also true that addiction emerges from adversity. This is not to say that every case of addictive behavior is *caused* by trauma and adversity. Some combination of factors always accompanies addiction. But, most often, adversity and toxic stress are right alongside.

Trauma is the premier predisposing risk factor underneath substance misuse and the hidden, dynamic engine behind addiction (Felitti, 2003).

Of course, an addicted lifestyle itself brings many additional kinds of adversity in its wake. It is important to distinguish instances of adversity between trauma with a "capital T," the result of outright abuse or abandonment, and "little t" trauma, the critical or indifferent home-based relating that can accumulate and cause attachment degradation (Diamond, Diamond, & Levy, 2014).

Counselors working with a client's harmful use of chemicals or resort to compulsive behaviors should be curious about a potential history and impact of adversity. With adversity, the original promise of care and connection—the birthright of safety and security—fails. The individual must find ways to cope and seeks adaptations that then become routine and entrenched into neural, emotional, and behavioral grooves. We call these "substitute relationships."

Joe's story continues.

Later that same evening long ago, after a tense family dinner in front of the TV, Joe helps his mom with the dishes and then goes out with his friends. Just that past summer, they had begun going to the nearby woods and drinking beer around a campfire. As Joe and his friends approach the spot, he feels anticipation building. He looks forward to the relaxation and emotional warmth from the alcohol and camaraderie with his friends. He tells himself that he needs this respite in order to cope with life at home.

When he returns home after midnight, everyone is in bed and the house is quiet. Before going up to bed himself, he goes to his parents' liquor cabinet and pours himself one last drink. He sits in the living room and sighs deeply, letting the quiet roll over him. He sips his whiskey until he feels ready for bed.

For Joe, the trip to the woods with friends and the relaxing action of alcohol are part of an evolving ritual that mitigates the tension and stress from earlier. Joe feels safe among friends and can let down his guard; he is open to calming relationships and utilizes these connections for emotional relief.

Early on, young humans learn that connection and being together with others can be soothing. It can buffer stress. In science terms, regulating our internal states is also co-regulation; attachment and attunement with others are essential for stress relief and self-regulation (Cozolino, 2014). Hanging out with friends is a teenage version of co-regulation, sharing acceptance and safety with others; alcohol or marijuana are often the preferred drug of choice for this kind of fellowship. However, Joe's reward and stress systems are learning in the process; they will remember that relationships and chemicals bring contentment. Over time, this pattern can become both emotionally and neurophysiologically engraved, available for action when needed again. It can become a preferred method of stress relief.

For Joe, these were the all-too-common beginnings of later trouble. At the core were childhood adversity and toxic stress. As all of us do, Joe found ways to manage his emotions and cope with stress through relationships and reliance on others. When stress systems relax their vigilance, people are more open to connection. Add in a relaxing chemical, and the result is almost too good to be true.

Joe has utilized friends and alcohol as a way to cope with spoiled and lost love at home. He is certainly not the first teen to do this, but counseling should explore the extent, circumstances, and intensity of his loss. The pleasurable anticipation Joe feels and expectation of easy familiarity with friends—as well as the calm he feels before bed—are not only behavioral and psychosocial experiences of reward. They are also physiological experiences, mediated by chemicals and activity in his brain and monitored by neuroception. In recent years, we have learned much about the mutual influence of psychosocial experience, neural activity, and embodied emotion.

As Joe heads to the woods with his friends, dopamine—a crucial neurochemical for understanding addiction—is already priming the pump for Joe's evening. Dopamine is the neurochemical most associated with addiction and is also one of the most misunderstood. We need it to experience pleasure and reward. More important, we need it to attach motivation to that reward so that we seek it again. Dopamine is the neurochemical for motivation. This is one of the building blocks of learning—knowing what pleases us isn't much good without wanting to repeat the experience. Dopamine also helps us to anticipate rewarding experiences and then measure if they match up to our expectations. Finally, excess dopamine can oversensitize our neural structures and lay the groundwork for craving, or motivation gone wild.

Let's examine dopamine and its role a bit more closely.

"LIKING" AND "WANTING": A REVISED VIEW OF REWARD

With new research, science is reimagining the role that dopamine plays in the brain-related systems for pleasure, calm, and reward. Clearly, dopamine assists as part of a neurochemical cocktail in marking some experiences and memories with pleasure so that the individual wants to repeat the experiences. However, these normal processes can become distorted by excess. Dopamine, then, is also involved in our relationships to intoxication and addiction, whether to psychoactive drugs or potentially repeatable, compulsive activities such as gambling or gaming. Neurobiologically, dopamine helps to create the "signature brain response" of addiction (Berridge, 2017).

In the early 1990s researcher Kent Berridge and his associates proposed a revolutionary view of dopamine functioning, and identified two different kinds of brain activity that underlie this signature response. They suggested that, while "liking" something often accompanied "wanting" it, these two experiences could become separable under the right circumstances (Berridge & Kringelbach, 2015; Berridge & Robinson, 2016). These are two separate experiences, mediated by different but associated brain systems and neurochemistry.

"Liking" (pleasure, reward) emerges through a small number of interactive "hot spots" in the brain, they discovered. These spots are tiny and anatomically diversified; the system is fragile, easily disrupted, and is shared by a variety of rewards, from food to drugs to social pleasures. Natural opiates, neural cannabinoids, and other pleasure-related chemicals, as well as dopamine, often drive it. "Wanting" (desire, motivation for seeking rewards), however, is located throughout a much larger and more robust neural system, called the mesocorticolimbic dopamine system (MDS), which is mediated largely by dopamine. They named this the system for *incentive salience*, that is, rather than responding primarily to cognitive direction and goals, it responds to reward cues (incentives). Those cues become "attention-grabbing and attractive," marked with emotional and cognitive memory. Cues can become salient, even commanding—described as "irrationally strong motivation urges" by Berridge (2012)—when we are under stress or high emotion. In situations of fear, excitement, or intoxication, pairing cues with dopamine reactivity is a volatile mix. Addiction, they suggested, is not so much about satisfaction or pleasure as it is about runaway, cue-enhanced "wanting" (Berridge & Robinson, 2016, p. 671–672).

Incentive salience and the separation of liking and wanting dynamics in the brain also complement what Berridge and his colleagues came to understand as the *sensitization* of brain systems by many psychoactive drugs. Under the right conditions (including frequent repetition of drug use, at high doses, and in an intermittent schedule), dopamine systems can become *hyper*-re-active to drug cues, situations, and environments, which in turn heightens both incentive salience and intensified drive for acquiring and using drugs, although not necessarily pleasure. The cues and contexts trigger "pulses" of wanting or swelling urges to use that are temporary, often unexpected, and occur outside of conscious awareness, but are powerful nonetheless. (It is important to note that sensitization fuels hyper-*re*-activity to drug cues and contexts, and not necessarily an ongoing state of hyperactivity.). Over time, Joe repeatedly turned to alcohol when celebrating or feeling stressed (repetition), and sometimes in higher doses than expected (high dose), except when he was trying to moderate or slow down use (intermittent schedule). He unintentionally trained his reward systems to react forcefully.

Combined, salience and sensitization are often experienced by users as a state of "needing," as in "I *need* a drink . . . or another hit of heroin . . ." Needing is an extreme, pathological form of intense wanting, triggered by cues and rewards (Berridge & Robinson, 2016; Robinson & Berridge, 2008). In later counseling, for example, Joe could not remember exactly when he switched from "liking" to "wanting" alcohol, but he could identify when he switched to hard liquor almost exclusively. Beer and wine just did not give him the same kick. He needed more.

Sensitization can become enduring and long-lasting, perhaps even permanent. It is believed to be the culprit in fostering cue-triggered compulsion and intense desire to take drugs, and can even initiate those urges that seem to come out of nowhere and leave the struggling addict defenseless (Childress, 2006). While sensitization can occur with other neurotransmitters and neural structures, it is the action with dopamine that appears to enhance drug reactivity and compulsion to use. Pleasure or reward may not be the only or even the most important factor in motivating and maintaining addicting behavior. Predicting a return to these experiences may depend more on the meaning and emotional memory of the experience than on the pleasure it provides. Indeed, as counselors and family members know all too well, addicts will continue to use long after the pleasure and thrill is a distant memory.

Incentive salience and neural *sensitization* are the twin mechanisms—the "signature response"—identified for compulsive urges to take drugs and for the vulnerability to persistent risk of relapse, even after significant periods of curtailed use or abstinence (Berridge & Robinson, 2016, p. 673). In addition, the usual variety of cofactors (genetics, gender, lifestyle stress, adversity, sensation seeking, social disconnection) are likely to predispose individuals to vulnerability for sensitization and addiction. We are only beginning to understand the differential impact on self-administration of psychoactive drugs that comes when specific drugs are combined with other factors, such as gender, social rank, and hierarchical status, as well as social exclusion or integration (Heilig, Epstein, et al., 2016).

In counseling with struggling addicts and harmful users, it is often helpful to provide this information to them and their families. Knowing about salience and sensitization can help to normalize their experience and offer some explanation for what is happening with them. Even more, the information can lessen the shame of past behavior and become part of future-oriented relapse prevention. Exploring and listing the cues, triggers, and contexts that can lead to relapse—through "functional analysis," for example—can be helpful (Haynes & O'Brien, 1990; Rohsenow et al., 2004).

Knowing how powerful and unconscious these forces are is oddly both comforting and empowering for clients, and can fuel efforts to learn and execute more healthy strategies.

Moving forward in time, how does Joe's dilemma play out?

Once he completed college and began his career, Joe enjoyed neighborhood parties, after-work social gatherings, his involvement in community service activities, and relaxing with the other coaches of his son's baseball league. Work in the financial services industry was rewarding. Joe and his wife, Marsi, were stalwarts of the community. But, over time, his life slowly became more constricted, and he found himself less involved. He worked longer hours but was enjoying it less. This was very gradual, and with the addition of kids and work stresses, it was easy to miss.

If Joe had looked at his life honestly, he would have noticed that previous activities he had enjoyed were becoming more burdensome. He was becoming more isolated. He was increasingly dissatisfied, even with his wife and kids. And his attempts to relax, including his use of alcohol, were less rewarding and more driven. Of course, he did not see these consequences mounting.

He would also have noticed that his engagement with alcohol (cognitively, behaviorally) was increasing. Joe was developing a relationship with alcohol. He talked more often about it, and he kept his bar at home well stocked with his favorite liquors.

Eventually Joe started to register that something was wrong. Perhaps he woke up with one too many hangovers, or he began to worry about his elevated blood pressure and weight gain. Perhaps his wife or doctor commented on his alcohol use or his generally tired appearance. Whatever the trigger, Joe cut down on alcohol consumption or moderated in other ways. He discovered, however, that he always returned to use. He was unable to maintain moderating. This period of alternating use and moderating lasted a long time.

Joe's experience here is not atypical. Many of those who struggle with harmful use of chemicals and addiction do in fact "struggle." Many know at some level that they need help, but contend with both ambivalence and relapse. These feed each other.

Ambivalence *says . . .*

"I don't want the consequences I'm having, but I also don't want to give up the benefits (reward, pain relief, relaxation, diversion)."

"I don't want to admit I have a problem and risk being labeled an 'addict.' I'll look weak and unable to help myself."

"I don't believe (don't want to believe) I have a 'disease' and the stigma that goes with it."

"I cannot talk about problems with a group of strangers."

"My father promised to stop but never could. I felt betrayed."

"I don't know if I can succeed in changing and I don't want to be a failure."

Experiencing relapse *says . . .*

"See, I knew you wouldn't succeed."

"What will you do now, go back to the counselor with your tail between your legs and start over?"

"See, you've tried to change what you use, when you use, how much you use, where you use, with whom you use, and it just doesn't work."

"It is (you are) hopeless."

So, the harmful user or addict struggles with compulsions he doesn't understand and cannot seem to control, with internal and environmental cues she cannot seem to avoid, with pulses of wanting and desire (craving), and with a powerful inner voice—the "anti-self" or "inner critic"[2]—that says "you are a failure; you need this, and change is hopeless." This is a potent brew and, when considering it, the struggling user is impatient, unable to resolve the ambivalence, and hobbled by shame and self-criticism. She or he often walks away from a decision to change without a clear resolution. Even after a decision to quit or moderate use, and the intention to follow through, slips can happen or become full-blown relapses. Ambivalence, often present in the initial process of change, can be accentuated after an experience or two of relapse.

Observations

Some complementary understanding of the neurobiology underneath Joe's chemical use can help the empathic counselor. The neurological reward/motivation and stress systems, as well as their associated neural structures, are critical for adaptation and learning. They drive our response to stressful situations, as well as situations of reward and motivation (Siegel & Hartzell, 2003). They assess the nature of the world around us and help to coordinate appropriate responses. Early adversity set Joe's stress sensitivity so that, even if only at low levels, Joe's systems constantly anticipate danger and work to prepare.

These structures interact with one another and adapt to whatever environment surrounds them; their development is vulnerable to the social environment and early environmental stresses (Schore, 1994). Critical attachment relationships shape these developing circuits (Hart, 2011). From very early on, experiences of attachment and attunement help to prepare our neural and hormonal systems for the environment we learn to anticipate. These are critical structures for survival, no less in our domesticated world than in more primitive and dangerous environments where they first evolved. Raised in challenging homes and toxic environments, children learn to anticipate stress, danger, and the need for protection. They wake up every morning with neural fists raised and ready.

However, these systems are also characterized by ongoing plasticity. Initially formed to be hyperalert to toxicity, they can also learn and adapt to new situations. Counseling can help the client learn new strategies to buffer adversity, moderate stress, and counter pulses of wanting and needing. Managing one's own desires (liking, wanting, needing) can be achieved over time, once the individual acknowledges the urgency of change. But it takes work and courage.

With a look back, one can readily see that Joe's life has taken a turn. First, it is not surprising to find that Joe has developed a more negative and dissatisfied outlook on his life. This is not just the outcome of workaholia or advancing middle-age anxiety, although these should not be discounted. We also know that those subjected to mistreatment and toxic stress in childhood are more susceptible to negative thinking, depression, and anxiety, sometimes decades after the initial episodes. Childhood maltreatment has a graded-dose-response relationship to poor mental health, emotional disorders, and behavioral risks (Chapman et al., 2004; see Chapter 7). The more severe or frequent exposures to adverse child experiences, especially in the absence of buffering social support, the more severe or persistent the dark worldview, depression, and negative thinking (Von Cheong et al., 2017).

Stress, and particularly toxic stress from severe, persistent, or cumulative adversity, interferes with normal development.[3] It wires our neural circuits in unique ways. Toxic stress resets our responsiveness to cues for safety or danger in the environment. Neural and emotional systems that "read" our environment become super-sensitized, overreactive, and preferentially alert to stressors, or blunted because of excess use and the wear and tear on neural circuits. In addition, these miswired systems often operate with an ongoing low level of arousal, always on the lookout for potential threats. Danger detection systems cause individuals to pull back, lessening their social engagement and opportunities for corrective learning, making them less available for calming social interaction, as defenses are deployed for self-protection. Living becomes more precarious and anxious. Low levels of stress hormones, such as cortisol and adrenaline, are continually released, which over time become toxic for brain tissue in crucial areas like cognition, stress detection, and response (Badenoch, 2018). Immune responses are weakened. Emotional weariness and fatigue, as well as vulnerability for depression and anxiety, can flow from neural weathering (McEwen, 2004).

Smart Intervention

Wrestling with ambivalence, struggling with shame from relapse or inability to moderate use, is a challenge. This problem pattern may repeat itself over and over again, and each time it is a missed opportunity. How, then, should the empathic counselor proceed? In attachment-sensitive counseling, the counselor must first establish a welcoming and safe environment. This can open the door to an alliance in therapy. Second, helping the client with concrete strategies for managing the negative voices within provides a way of building trust. Skills can help the client feel cared for and experience a sense of agency.

The *trans-theoretical* or "stages of change" model describes the emotional and cognitive conundrum of ambivalence as the hallmark in a stage of "(pre-)contemplation," in which the client cannot move forward; he either does not believe there is a problem, or recognizes a problem but is perplexed and paralyzed by it in some way (Prochaska, Norcross, & DiClemente, 1994). In the language of *motivational interviewing*, a closely aligned model of therapy, the individual is stuck in ambivalence and unable to find resolution (Miller & Rollnick, 2012). The challenge here is not so much acquiring new insight as finding effective motivation for change. These models present strategies for problem resolution, organized around facilitating "readiness for change" (DiClemente & Velasquez, 2002). *Screening, Brief Intervention, and Referral for Treatment*, or *SBIRT*, a clinical protocol suggested for use in a variety of medical and emergency settings with misusing populations, incorporates this thinking. It combines motivational and readiness approaches with an invitational and non-confrontational style. It has impressive outcomes, particularly for those struggling with harmful use and addiction.[4]

Assisting clients and families in negotiating the initial phase (or, following relapse, re-engaging phase) is essential. Non-confrontational tools are available. *A Relational Intervention Sequence for Engagement* or the *ARISE* model, offers an evidence-based, invitational intervention (versus the shaming or confrontational intervention) that harnesses the power of family for individual and family long-term recovery (Garrett & Landau, 2010; Landau & Garrett, 2008). Rooted in concepts from both addiction and family systems/network theory, ARISE utilizes motivational techniques and invitational protocols designed to establish hope and mobilize group support, while teaching family members to successfully invite struggling addicts and harmful users to begin counseling (Landau & Garrett, 2008).

Each of these clinical approaches is helpful. They all agree that *welcoming* the client and his or her story is the essential place to begin. How does the counselor "stand alongside" (not in opposition to) the client? Welcoming, attentive listening, curiosity, empathy, and positive regard are indispensable in working with persons struggling with addiction and adversity. The field of addiction intervention and treatment, however, has been slow to adopt these insights from person-centered clinical models (Rogers, 1951).

Smart intervention must take advantage of these perspectives. Finding positive ways to approach a person struggling with addiction and a history of adversity, even if that struggle is hidden or denied, takes top priority. Addiction is costly at many levels, and enormous damage can be imposed on individuals and family members while they wait for readiness. One of the myths about addiction is that intervention must wait until the individual has had enough. The truth, however, is different. Approached in a welcoming, invitational, and informative way, those who struggle with harmful use and addiction will eventually enter the recovery process. Understanding the dynamics of change and the varieties of recovery that are available can lead to new methods of intervention and motivation.

A welcoming stance is conveyed by the basic concrete behaviors outlined in person-centered therapy (Bazzano, 2018; Rogers, 1951). Hospitality (welcome) is a behavior and can be learned. Curiosity, attentive listening, accurate empathy, and nonjudgmental positive regard—the basic behaviors and skills that all beginning counselors learn (and sometimes promptly forget, especially when they meet with struggling or challenging addicts!)—establish safety in a relationship and attract openness, honesty, trust, and client engagement. This kind of relating is, by itself, already therapeutic.

It is important for mental health and addiction counselors to understand that welcoming and building trust, and a sense of efficacy and hope, are critical values in *any* counseling relationship. Yes, the individual must have firm and ambitious goals. Yes, there is effort involved in achieving and maintaining lifestyle change. Yes, the individual may prevaricate, deny that a problem exists, try to evade responsibility, or try to avoid compliance with helpful suggestions and treatment plans. This, however, is not peculiar for those who are ambivalent and not ready for change, nor is it unique to struggling addicts. Counselors need to adopt a style of "implacable empathy" to help persuade and attract clients into collaboration. Surely, a counselor can find something to affirm in the client's story, something in the client's history that can be praised. Counselors must be empathic and inviting, while remaining both firm yet flexible about the goals of therapeutic work.

Why is this so? The struggling addict with a history of adversity often comes to us with a wounded and hyperreactive stress response system. They come to us vulnerable, but it does not always seem so. Early miswiring of neural circuits, particularly the circuits that assess safety or danger, creates anomalies that are the fingerprints of life experience and telltale signs of toxicity. Miswiring is woven into neural fabric. Struggling addicts can present to us as compliant, clueless, arrogant, manipulative, or resistant. Underneath, however, they are vulnerable, and they can utilize a variety of defenses.

Drugs or compulsive activities repurpose those safety and danger circuits that help us cope. Learning mechanisms given to us for survival—automatic responses for sensing safe/not safe, stress response, reward circuits, or the ability to utilize experiences of attachment to regulate emotions—may be recalibrated to make people believe that drugs or certain substitute activities are survival-enhancing and hence needed for life. They begin to learn that "substitute regulators," such as drugs or compulsive activities, may better or more immediately/reliably serve their needs. Adversity and trauma damage the individual's ability to access the love and connection that is all around. They find themselves alone in a crowded room of loved ones.

SAFETY FIRST

Consequently, the first step toward initiating a therapeutic relationship must be establishing a felt experience of *safety*. It is difficult to be vulnerable and take the risk for change, if one's fists are up and the self is encased in armor. It is doubly difficult to move forward when that change involves altering what has become the preferred chemical or behavioral means for coping with stress. Learning to risk and rely on another goes hand in hand with the sense that this therapist can be a reliable guide and will value my life experience and agency. Sensing safety helps clients to relax their guard. Without this, no amount of technique or strategy, no matter how evidence-based it is, can help.

Interpersonal neurobiologist Dan Siegel speaks about "feeling felt" or "resonant listening" as empathy augmented with acceptance and personal presence (Carlson, 2008). Clients feel known and valued—there is no pressure or agenda to be rigidly followed. Every counselor knows when those moments arrive. They have been called "moments of meeting" (Hughes, 2007, p. 61). A profound feeling of awe and even a sense of the sacred appears as well. These moments are the heart of healing and psychotherapy (Morgan, 2007). They carry echoes of the original attachment promise from childhood. In counseling, these moments are emotionally and neurologically corrective and healing for wounded clients.

One of the first principles that undergirds attachment theory is that, when the child experiences safety and security, he is free to explore his world. This principle is engraved in our neural systems for safety and social engagement. When we feel safe, we are free to engage the connections around us. Defenses are in place for a reason, and substitute relationships, like addiction, are adaptive safeguards. These will not be relinquished easily. The healthiest ways for individuals to cope are through co-regulation, utilizing safe relationships to address fear, stress, and adversity.

The wise counselor must remember that she is meeting an individual, wrapped in defenses and on the alert. The ability to access and utilize the counseling relationship for healing, safety, and trust must be established. When the individual is in a defensive posture, she or he is transformed from an essentially social being to a solitary one, hyperreactive to drug cues, stressful situations, and toxic environments. Cues, whether they are internal (self-critical, negative or excessive thoughts, feeling states) or external (familiar locations, sights, smells, music), trigger defenses and those "irrationally strong" impulses of motivation or urges to seek and use (Berridge, 2012). They seem to come "out of the blue," since the cues can be hidden and subliminal, and catch the individual off guard. One goal of treatment is to help struggling users/addicts to displace substitutes with real safety, secure relationships, and personal agency. The first anchor for safety can be the therapy relationship. Then, preparation for facing urges to use and pulses of motivation becomes essential.

The Inner Critic

Joe's neural systems for danger became supersensitized to his surroundings and overreactive, especially when his father approached. He was always on alert, but never more so than when he was home, the one place that should have been a safe haven. Even today, with his father gone, these systems scan and check his environment for signs of danger and maintain a neurological and emotional protector or "inner critic" to help keep him prepared and safe. Under the impact of adversity, Joe becomes emotionally reactive and habitually utilizes dysfunctional emotion regulation strategies—such as dissociation, rumination, or drinking—to keep himself safe. Dissociation or cognitive/emotional distancing allows Joe a temporary form of inner escape; he "zones out." (Joe also came to see that overworking was a form of dissociation and distancing for him.) Rumination or scanning/reviewing circumstances for danger becomes a pathway to the "inner critic" and problems with affective overregulation. Drinking allows Joe to dissolve his concerns and, on occasion, open himself to warmer feelings. As he gets older, potential situations of danger proliferate (generalize), and he becomes weary. The "critical inner voice" can become a constant companion (Firestone et al., 2002).

It is not difficult for the protector to morph into an "inner dictator." For those, like Joe, who are struggling with harmful use of chemicals or addiction, managing the "inner critic" is a crucial experience. The critic can become domineering, judgmental, and arrogant, transforming itself into a self-defeating and shaming inner adversary, or it can puff itself up and present a larger-than-life, perfectionist stance toward the world.

A mental health counselor who listens attentively will catch the tone of negativity, pessimistic self-talk, or the "problem-saturated story" that Joe uses. The inner critic dislikes the softer, more vulnerable self; its constant criticism is intended to keep individuals prepared and ready. Its mission is to ensure that no one ever sees vulnerability. The critic operates underneath a number of mental health conditions, like depression or anxiety, but it is often highly active within traumatized and addicted persons (Morgen & Morgan, in press).

The inner critic/protector continually checks the environment for danger while making sure that the addict's softer needs for acceptance and attachment keep under wraps. It magnifies the addict's internal sense of shame and low self-worth, driving a personal style of controlling self and others, while often both judging others and feeling their reflexive negative judgments. This is not a pleasant world to live in. However, this world can be dealt with.

Becoming a "Critic Whisperer"

The critic can be a frequent companion to those who suffered adversity, and when it turns toxic, the critic can catalyze a sense of shame. Joe wrestled with a world-class critic.

It is helpful to search for the functioning of this critic as part of the early therapeutic relationship. The critic may be rooted in the individual's attachment history, and beginning this work can open up that history for exploration. Early trust and the building of a working alliance can be bolstered with a sense of agency, helping the client to understand how he or she functions and sharing tools that can help increase safety or begin virtuous cycles of self-affirmation. Establishing welcome and safety, and working with the inner critic, are essential skills for addiction counselors.

Siegel speaks about this as a "checker," a component of our neural systems that functions to keep us safe from danger. It operates through scanning the environment, alerting us to danger, and motivating us to act. We share it with other mammals (watch how domestic cats react to loud noise or sudden movement). It is a biologically based system, but we experience it as a critical and demanding inner voice. The checker is rooted in neural functioning but takes on characteristics from our social interactions, particularly with caregivers, family members, teachers, and others. In Joe's case, not surprisingly, when his critic was harsh, he heard the voice of his father.

In our high-pressured and performance-focused Western culture, we need reminding about the critical voice that many people contend with. Often this voice is trying to motivate us, but it can be recruited for other purposes. It doesn't take attendance at many 12 Step meetings or group work with struggling addicts to hear the critic behind much of the shame and guilt in people's lives. Many counselors can recognize the critic's voice in their own lives as well.[5]

Siegel, in collaboration with other mental health practitioners,[6] has developed a basic five-point framework for dealing with the inner critic. Helping our clients do this work serves several purposes. First, it helps clients to cope successfully with voices and ruminations that instigate anxiety, depression, and substance relapse. Second, it helps to convey the counselor's respect for clients' concerns and teaches them coping skills that they can employ. Third, it helps the client become more aware of her or his own internal process and feel some sense of agency and self-management.

Here are Siegel's five steps:

One, *awareness.* Many people are not even aware that they operate with an inner critic or how much impact it is having in their lives. When we can help them to discover it, the idea can be liberating. Noticing the inner voice is a crucial first step. Simple questions can get the ball rolling: "When you are quiet, what comes to mind?" or "Can you describe the conversation that goes on in your head?" or "Do you have a voice that tells you about 'shoulds' or 'should nots'?"

Inviting people to identify and discuss their own self-talk opens unexpected avenues. For some, the sheer amount of self-criticism is a revelation and they can experience the oppression of the Critic's judgment. For others, bringing the critic into the open feels risky but empowering. For still others, the recognition that they have had an inner guide or protector all along is a comfort.

Often it helps to have clients assign a *name* to the critic. Identifying and naming something hidden gives one power over it. *Noticing* that it operates and how, allows the client to begin observing it, feeling the tone it brings to life, understanding the triggers and contexts that can bring it forth, and wondering about strategies for coping with it.

Two, *space.* Bestowing or recognizing a name for the critic can lead naturally to curiosity about it and establishes a beginning for making a (potential) new friend. The best initial strategy for coping with the inner critic is to *give it space* to express itself and observe it in many different situations. But, be careful; no judgments, just listen and learn. Clients learn that it is not possible to make the critic go away entirely. Even if they could make it disappear, that would not be positive or helpful—the critic is there for a reason. Constructive criticism can be productive. It's the dictatorial tone and negative, shaming judgments that are unproductive. Noticing the critic's rules of the road and when it is productive/nonproductive both honors its presence as part of life and helps to initiate a plan for change.

Three, *dialog.* This step is an important moment of *joining* with the inner critic and welcoming it as part of the self. Having noticed it and respected its presence, the client often wonders why it is there. Where did it come from? This step allows the client to *discover the story* behind the critic. What life events triggered it into existence, or made it evolve from protector to dictator? What does it want?

In a true dialog, the client can ask the critic/protector what it needs. After all, in some approaches like Internal Family Systems, the critic/protector is only one voice among several and may be loud as a way to get attention. This step is a vital (often initially small) change in the relationship between client and critic/protector—perhaps also with other internal entities (Schwartz, 2017).

Four, *negotiate.* This step allows the client to assume more control and *negotiate change* with the critic. Conversation and curiosity can also lead to relating to it differently. Perhaps the client can thank the critic for trying to protect her or him, even if it was unable to do so gently. Perhaps the client can ask the critic/protector to turn down the volume on its demands, to be less strict and authoritarian, at least at some times or with some issues. Perhaps the client does not need to be so subservient.

Five, *invite.* In this final step, the client invites the critic/protector into a further *redefined role* as inner protector and collaborator for well-being. Perhaps in dialogue the role for an inner nurturer can be developed. With the therapist's help, the client can begin to assume the role of self-healing.

As the reader can see, this is an imaginative, multiple-step process. These steps utilize self-compassion that begins with awareness and leads to acceptance and welcome invitation (Neff, 2015). In attachment-sensitive counseling, welcome, safety, self-efficacy, and self-compassion are important starting points. We take the next steps with Joe in Chapter 2.

2

Attachment-sensitive Counseling

"Connectedness is a biological imperative."

STEPHEN W. PORGES

"...it might not be too much to say that relationship is everything—by our very design."

BONNIE BADENOCH

PICKING UP FROM CHAPTER 1, it is important to see how adversity lays the groundwork for addiction. How did Joe experience the adversity of his child and teen years? How did he interpret the abuse hurled at him? What did it mean to him? Sitting with traumatized persons and hearing their stories convinces the sensitive counselor that the meanings they ascribe to events have powerful and lasting effects.

Joe did not just experience childhood adversity in a generalized form; he was abused and tormented in particular ways and learned how to cope with uniquely matching strategies. His early experience was a potent emotional mix of shame, isolation, longing, rage, and spoiled love, and it compounded the suffering of mistreatment. However, Joe was extremely good at hiding his alienation so that very few people—not teachers, or coaches, or pastors, or peers—saw the escalating torment and disconnection he experienced.

Speaking about his father's abuse, Joe described a constant clash between his father and himself. His now-deceased father was verbally abusive and denigrating toward Joe, beginning in early childhood. His father would roam about the house, ranting about Joe's supposed failures and the deficiencies of other family members. His mother was depressed and unable to defend the children from their father's predations or effectively challenge his abuse. Joe, as the oldest child, often tried to protect the younger children and his mother from their father's verbal abuse. He offered himself as a substitute target.

Joe is not just an alcoholic son of an alcoholic father, but also a survivor of childhood adversity and developmental trauma. Joe told me that he had learned how to "tune out" his father's rantings. Joe functionally moved beyond fight-or-flight, and his systems chose to freeze (dissociate) until the danger passed. Several strategies for "freezing" were available: Joe lost himself in schoolwork, sometimes simply "zoned out" and became numb, and increasingly turned to drinking. In the absence of attuned care, his systems focused on reducing threat and creating safety as his top priorities (Hughes, Golding, & Hudson 2019).

Alone and late at night, trapped in a home environment of toxic stress, Joe would help himself to alcohol from his parents' liquor cabinet. This, he said, "calmed his nerves." Alcohol increasingly became a personal solution for his family difficulties—resorting to this substitute relationship for emotional and stress regulation became second nature. When his father later died of complications from liver cirrhosis, Joe's mother told him to take the cabinet out of the home. He moved it into his own home, and unintentionally set up a powerful drinking cue that continued to trigger his craving.[1] The sight of the familiar liquor cabinet, especially when Joe was under stress, activated the need for a familiar form of comfort. Stress, personal history, and habit narrowed Joe's coping resources and channelized his responses into familiar, well-worn pathways.

Fast-forward to the present day. Joe's drinking has been a problem for a number of years. His wife is fed up with it; his three kids seemingly pay little attention. Joe is now 53 years old and goes to work almost every day. He drinks mostly on weekends. He is irritable during the week and emotionally absent from his family during the weekend. He usually drinks alone. While he has tried to cut down his drinking, once he begins he is unable to moderate.

Joe has a "terrible" ongoing relationship with his aging mother and feels little fondness or attachment toward her. He rarely discusses his father. Yet he often says that he feels "lonely" and "disconnected" from others. Often, the loneliness and anger trigger bouts of drinking, and these feelings come to the fore even more strongly when he is intoxicated.

Joe was raised in a classic alcoholic family and can be seen as the "child of an alcoholic" as well as a "functioning alcoholic" himself, with chronic attachment needs and relationship difficulties due to emotional cutoff and isolation from others. He was insecurely attached in his family of origin, and had difficulty being open with his wife or affirming and warm with his kids. His connections to family and friends now are tenuous at best. Does this background explain Joe's alcohol misuse? Well, yes . . . and no.

A DIFFERENT PERSPECTIVE

First of all, now that he is an adult, Joe (mistakenly) believes that he has left his dysfunctional home life behind him. Those experiences of threat occurred long ago. And yet . . . like many others I have seen in counseling over the years, Joe struggles in adulthood with shame, negative thoughts and attitudes, depression, anxiety, and harmful use of alcohol and other drugs. He is self-critical, and his behavior often appears compulsive and driven. He is an anxious workaholic, and sometimes it is not easy to tell where he resides on the spectrum of substance-related disorders. Joe is not homeless or a failure at living, as some might envision an addict to be. He could be anyone's uncle, father, son, or brother. He functions at work and in the community. Nevertheless, his chemical use is increasingly harmful to himself and others. He represents the majority of those who are in trouble with compulsive use.

Joe also struggles with several other chronic conditions, such as high blood pressure, prediabetes (medical), and anxiety (psychiatric) when under social or job-related pressure. Naturally, he thinks of these conditions—hypertension, prediabetes, ongoing stress—as the results of getting older or overworking. He does not connect them, or his anxieties and alcohol abuse, to adversity in childhood. Who would? The passage of time, denial, and shame prevent Joe from making these connections. However, those experiences are hidden, covert engines of the toxicity and dis-ease underneath all that Joe does.

Joe, like many of us, does not fully appreciate how psychosocial experience, especially when we are young, shapes the development of our neural, hormonal, and immunological systems. Struggling with heart disease or diabetes must be the result of aging, or genetics, or lifestyle choices, we say. Autoimmune disorders like lupus or fibromyalgia must have physiological causes—they cannot be holdover effects from childhood mistreatment (van der Kolk, 2014). Harmful drug use or addiction, like other adult disorders, are likely related to genetic vulnerabilities or poor decisions, aren't they? We simply do not consider the role of early attachment failure, or adversity, or childhood suffering, or family dysfunction in long-term shaping of our physiological and emotional systems.

As a society, however, we are slowly coming to understand that our personal and family history shapes our internal systems, that "biography becomes [our] biology" (Nakazawa, 2015). We must begin to understand more deeply the developmental power of early psychosocial experiences in the present *and* over time. Joe's chemical use, his ongoing stress profile, and the physical and psychiatric complications of his presenting picture (high blood pressure, anxiety, depression) can be traced to the ongoing relational trauma and adversity of his early and teen years. In Joe's case, the trauma he experienced is not related to a single event but to a continuing altercation with his father and the toxic environment of home. He is a classic case of ongoing developmental trauma (Hughes et al., 2019; Weinhold & Weinhold, 2015).

Adversity and its Meanings

Joe's father often called him "useless" and "a waste of space." He internalized his father's denigration and came to believe the slurs he received. Joe experienced increasing alienation and anxiety; this confirmed internal feelings of uselessness. He revisits those feelings easily now in response to events in adult life, such as a poor performance evaluation at work or experiences of estrangement from his wife. He experiences interpersonal difficulties as rejections and often feels belittled.

Dysfunction in his family of origin, directly targeted at Joe, mangled his sense of self, interfered with his ability to regulate his affective life, and recalibrated his anticipation of the kind of world he could expect. The damage, however, was hidden. Joe experienced few other relationships in his life as reliably rewarding. He experienced few buffers against stress, and this increased his ongoing isolation.

For Joe and others like him, the primary social ecology of family and near relationships can twist the sense of self, reset the expectations of their world, and malform the building of critical neurophysiological systems. In later years, he needed to rely on those systems for coping with life, but they failed him. His inner psychological world was misshapen as well.

It is important that we not limit our reflections by focusing only on the individual and her or his near relationships (family, friends). As his adversity and trauma continued, Joe became less able to access emotionally the support and nourishment that was available to him. He became so guarded that he felt "walled off" from others. His wife and family loved him and he was respected at work, but over time these positive sentiments eroded. This is an essential part of the tragedy of early and later adversity, and why it can so easily lead to addiction, or mental illness, or suicide. In a room full of those who care, the individual is unable to experience love and belonging. Defenses get in the way. Families and others often wonder what more they could have done to help. The truth, however, is that the person struggling with active addiction and adversity is often unable to feel the love around him or her. It just does not penetrate.

In addition, the family itself is often fractured, and members become separated for survival into their own isolated silos. As grown-ups, members feel estranged from, and sometimes antagonistic toward, one another. They often experience mutual suspicion and an unwillingness to open old wounds. All these elements present challenges for the counselor. I have worked with many people who, having come to terms with past abuses, want to discuss them and seek validation with other family members. It is common, however, that others do not wish to revisit the past.

A COUNSELING APPROACH

Sitting with Joe, either in individual therapy or in family sessions, was like sitting with an emotional "black hole." All the potential positive energy in the room was sucked out, while resentment and anger, shame and dejection, narcissistic bravado, and resistance took its place. This made his family life difficult and working with him in therapy quite a challenge.

Joe's previous choices, personal history, and sociocultural influences around alcohol had dug a well-worn behavioral and neural path for seeking relief from stress through addiction to work and resorting to alcohol, a potent biochemical coping mechanism and a catalyst for social bonding and self-soothing. When Joe is triggered now by a stressful event, his already strained survival systems go into overdrive and can compromise his thinking and coping. He just doesn't consider alternative ways to deal with the stress, but finds himself isolating and reaching impulsively for alcohol.

Early adversity, abuse, or neglect are capable of impairing the function of reward and stress response systems (Fishbane, 2007). Childhood adversity and trauma have the power to wire neural circuits in ways that make someone's future environments feel unsafe, cutting the individual off from interpersonal nurturing, damaging the immune system and later health, and putting the stress response on a permanent hair trigger. In these ways a potential addict is born, making sure to keep her guard up and his armor on all the time. It can also lead to lifestyles marked by depression, anxiety, or excess.

Early experiences naturally establish baseline levels of operation in neural circuits and affect how people respond in future situations. Children's systems are especially susceptible to these effects of toxic stress because they are developing and malleable (Harris, 2018). Under stress in later life, mis-wired or skewed systems may become overloaded and able to respond only in limited ways, much as an electrical grid can be overloaded in hot weather or climate systems can reach a tipping point and malfunction. Certain situations and cues, particularly those that have sensitized the individual in the past, may throw the regulation of emotional and thinking processes out of balance, inhibit a clear assessment of the current situation, narrow the range of responses that are seen as viable, and consequently interfere with choice and action. The individual becomes emotionally reactive and cognitively impaired simultaneously, less able to evaluate and appropriately respond to the stresses to which she or he is now deeply sensitized. Systems initially shaped by toxic environments may also be continually depleted in later years as the strain of remaining constantly "on alert" takes its toll (Geronimus et al., 2006; Foster et al., 2008).

Now imagine that all these elements—feelings of shame and loneliness, a history of trauma and stress, attachment needs, overactive stress responses, damaged neurobiology, sensitized neural circuits, habit, genetics, family legacies, social cues, internal alienation, and social disconnection—are working in concert with one another as Joe experiences a stressful event such as a fight with his wife or a child's misbehavior. Imagine that Joe is under simultaneous assault from multiple brain systems as well as from emotional needs, psychological dynamics, and overall "ill-being." He has diminished cognitive and emotional capacity to wrestle with these forces, simply because they are working at lightning speed on many fronts and under the radar of consciousness, but also because biochemical changes leave deficits in cognition, self-regulation, and decision making.

Joe does not know that all these levels of influence are bearing down on him. He doesn't even know why he feels stressed and anxious at certain times. All Joe knows is that he feels overwhelmed and, despite promising himself and others that he will stop drinking, he finds himself reaching for the bottle of whiskey.

Does understanding the many layers that are interpenetrating and affecting Joe at any moment help us to comprehend the attraction to intoxication, the difficulty of moderation or abstinence, the snare of addiction, and the enormous effort required for recovery? Does all this help us to be more sympathetic? I believe it does. Does it help us to imagine new kinds of intervention? Yes, if we can be both empathic and creative.

Attachment-sensitive Counseling

A counseling approach that begins with a welcoming relationship and a sense of agency in facing critical inner judgments and shame is clearly an advantage. The process should also begin with tools for soothing the reactivity of stress and safety systems.

I came to understand that, feeling trapped in the house and unable to escape, young Joe dissociated and distanced himself, cognitively and emotionally, as a form of self-protection until his father's rage burned itself out. His response was adaptive, but not necessarily healthy. It helped him to survive, but at what price? He attempted self-regulation and safety by disengaging the connections between his feelings (limbic system) and thinking (cortex). These pathways are critical for affective self-regulation, but with chronic or repeated deactivation, will become impaired over the long term. As a result, Joe's stress response systems became split off and locked in a pattern of chronic activation. Joe needed to find more healthy means of adaptation when stress intruded. Now, as an adult, Joe needed new ways to cope.

Initially, building trust with Joe came easily. He was able to identify with feeling "driven." He would throw himself into projects at work and sometimes turn a blind eye to other competing priorities, like home life and family. It surprised him to see how inner voices drove him like a taskmaster. This insight gave us a chance to learn more about these inner voices. Joe was intrigued as we began to examine his past for echoes of this "inner taskmaster." It also gave us a way to work together without focusing exclusively on alcohol.

P.A.C.E.

Initially, it is important for the counselor to focus on issues of therapeutic stance and approach. When we understand that clients are likely wrestling with ambivalence and at the same time are hypersensitive about safety, we know that they will respond to a safe and welcoming environment. As we saw in Chapter 1, an attitude of welcoming and utilizing the skills of client-centered therapy can help.

Attachment therapist Daniel Hughes (2007; Baylin & Hughes, 2016) recommends that counselors focus on four critical traits or behaviors for facilitating an effective stance: Playfulness, Acceptance, Curiosity, and Empathy (P.A.C.E.). These traits establish a stance of welcome that echoes the (appropriate) attachment dance with caretakers from early in life. It can be the catalyst for "moments of meeting" in counseling (Hughes, 2007, p. 61).

Playfulness is not a flippant joviality. Rather, it is a hope-filled commitment that builds on the counselor's enjoyment of his or her client and resonance (attunement) with positive qualities. Counselors become intentional and skillful diamond miners, searching persistently for qualities to affirm. I chose to underscore the "Joe" who cared about his siblings and mother. I wondered aloud where he found the strength to remain positive with them. I also complimented his discovery of "zoning out" as an adaptive strategy.

Acceptance does not mean condoning every thought or choice of the client. Rather, it allows the counselor to see underneath any particular thought, or choice, or action, and searches for ways to join with the client's intentions and rhythms of living. It is a commitment to the person and welcomes her or him into relationship. Again it echoes the well-functioning, original attachment relationship. We discussed dissociating through overwork or "zoning out" as a clever way to cope with toxic stress back then, but not so productive now.

Curiosity is the "cutting edge" of empathy, drawing the counselor into deeper and deeper understanding of the client's personal experience (Hughes, 2007, pp. 75–76). Curiosity from another caring person allows the client to understand his or her own experience in new ways. The counseling process *in the present* allows the client to re-experience events in collaboration with a caring therapist, whose co-presence facilitates co-regulation of emotions and the co-creation of new meanings in the present. Acceptance of this new experience becomes the catalyst for a new narrative.

With Joe, I wondered out loud about the emotional impact of those confrontations with his father. I brought in my own experience as a father and my attentiveness to the expressions on my children's faces as I interacted with them. I wondered if his father was able to look at Joe and see his pain. We joined in compassion for "young Joe" and what he suffered.

In other words, P.A.C.E. allows *Empathy* to be an "active ingredient" in attachment-sensitive counseling (Hughes, 2007, p. 87). It is a way of being, namely "empathy with . . ." that allows the counselor to "stand alongside" the client and facilitate healing.

These ways of interacting with Joe seemed to soften his presence, and also struck a chord with me. The success of recovery groups reminds us that the emotional connection and communion people find in 12 Step and other groups with those like themselves can echo the attunement of early and later attachment experiences. An accepting and warmly empathic counseling relationship can help to ease entry into recovery from both addiction and adversity. Attending to the dynamics of the counseling alliance will have powerful benefits.

Mindfulness

Once the counselor establishes a caring relationship, several other approaches help to work with those who struggle with addiction and trauma, and other chronic conditions. In working with Joe, mindful strategies presented themselves as one means to explore (Bowen, Chawla & Marlatt, 2011; Siegel, 2010). While mindfulness in conjunction with cognitive-behavioral strategies is recommended for relapse prevention in therapy with addiction and comorbid conditions, it can also be very helpful at the beginning of any therapeutic relationship.[2] All counseling with addiction and trauma is, in essence, relapse prevention; it begins with a caring relationship and moves toward greater awareness of the client's inner states and reactions. It also helps the client feel a sense of agency.

Mindfulness facilitates joining with the client and initiates the kind of present awareness that can soothe emotional and neural reactivity as well as provide a sense of safety. Being mindful ourselves allows us as counselors to be "fully present" in the consulting room (Morgan, 2007). Attunement between client and therapist facilitates both relationship building and the healing process (Siegel, 2010).

Just as counselors can help clients to engage with the "inner critic," so too they can help clients to increase awareness of destructive patterns, habits, triggers, and automatic reactions. Mindful practices help clients to pause, notice, and observe present experience, and then either let the reactions go or choose a different response. Clients learn to pause and observe before acting, which over time can slow impulsivity. In the process, they also learn how to tolerate and manage discomfort and craving, as well as to incorporate a more compassionate, less judgmental relationship with themselves. The goals are (a) to know oneself better; (b) to gain freedom from ingrained patterns and harmful habits; (c) to begin healing damaged neural circuitry and assist in learning new adaptive ways to cope; and (d) to rewrite the client's autobiographical narrative and reshape new internal images of the self. This is essential for recovery, both from trauma and from addiction (Zemestani & Ottaviani, 2016).

Mindfulness can also become a primary means for counteracting shame and learning how to cope with adversity. As clients in our care are able to string together more days of moderate use or abstinence, and begin mindfully to soothe negativity and stress, they will often unwillingly confront memories of misconduct—behaviors of others and of themselves—and trauma from the past. These memories and thoughts arise naturally, and can trigger guilt, anger, regret, shame, or sadness that potentially become catalysts for relapse. This inner struggle around shame and regret has been there all along but dampened by compulsive behaviors. Clients must be taught to mindfully observe these feelings and then release them without self-judgment or reactivity. This is "mindful acceptance," and it can lead to self-compassion.[3]

Often a strategy of informing the client and preparing *in advance* is helpful. Fortifying them with mindful ways to observe negative feelings as they emerge and then letting them go can help clients experience agency and empowerment. Teaching about neural reactivity and impulsiveness can serve to inoculate clients against rash actions. These are essential elements in mindfulness-based relapse prevention (MBRP).[4] Combined with "grounding" strategies (see below), they can accentuate resilience.

Mindful Practice

The regular practice of mindfulness ideally becomes a daily discipline that slows reactivity. It is different from concentration-based approaches (such as transcendental meditation, or progressive relaxation, or focusing). Mindful approaches usually begin with simple observation of the breath and then expand to awareness of bodily sensations, thoughts, or emotional states. They involve "choiceless awareness," suspending judgment of right/wrong, good/ bad, simply observing what emerges within one's own quiet. The roots in Buddhism ground a powerful view of addiction:

> "Engaging in drug use is a 'false refuge' because it is motivated by a strong desire for relief from suffering, despite the fact that continued involvement in the addictive behavior increases pain and suffering in the long run. The mindfulness meditator seeks to develop insight into the impermanent nature of cravings and desires, how they arise, what forms they take, and how they can be managed. This allows him/her to respond with awareness rather than react automatically" (HSU, GROW, & MARLATT, 2008, P. 231).

Mindfulness is a practice; its benefits are often not immediately apparent but mature over time. Devoting a period of time to it each day—10, 15, 30 minutes—helps clients to become more aware and less impulsive. It also furnishes a quiet space that can counteract stress and toxicity (Conyers, 2018). Joe benefited from mindful practice.

Research shows that mindful practice has many benefits that enhance recovery: It reshapes and soothes neural pathways; provides greater self-knowledge and awareness, increases a sense of empowerment; helps to tame anxiety and calm stress pathways. Engaging in mindful practice is an intentional way of reshaping damaged neural connections (Siegel, 2018).[5] Clients can literally "change their minds" and brains.

SEEKING SAFETY

Another approach in counseling that can calm emotional reactivity and become a catalyst for healthy self-regulation is called "Seeking Safety." It was developed specifically for clients who struggle with co-occurring addiction and/or trauma/adversity, and can build on mindful practice.

While it is true that humans are born anticipating care and nurture, it is also undeniably true that there is uncertainty and even peril in living. Some say, "Life is a helluva thing to happen to a person." Just ask Joe. He was a sweet kid, trusting, and willing to go the extra mile for someone in need. Chronic mistreatment, however, turned his gold into lead.

Below, I will briefly review Seeking Safety, formulated by Dr. Lisa Najavits at University of Massachusetts Medical School. SS is an evidence-based, integrated, present-focused, and flexible counseling approach, ideal for work with persons at different levels of health involving both addiction and adversity.[6]

Safety is the top priority. In this program, however, safety has multiple meanings and often requires time in treatment before it is reasonably achieved. Safety includes: abstinence from substances/compulsive behaviors (at least for a time), elimination of self-harm, learning how to manage overwhelming symptoms, securing trustworthy relationships, achieving a modicum of self-care, and removing oneself from dangerous situations, such as domestic abuse or unsafe sex (Najavits, 2007). This is a tall order, but essential as working preconditions. A number of topics in the SS agenda address these issues.

Integrated care, or treating both addiction and adversity simultaneously, is the preferred clinical approach. Back in the day, we said that addiction needed treatment first, since no one was expected to benefit while in an addicted state; afterwards, the person would be ready to face his or her traumatic past, we thought. However, one could wait a long time for clients to get clean, and meanwhile adverse memories and feelings would trigger multiple relapses. We also believed that exploring the traumatic past first would simply trigger the person back into his or her addictive use, and the situation would be worse than before.

We have learned the hard way:

- Treatments helpful for either disorder alone may be problematic for someone with both disorders.
- Tackling harmful use or addiction first may trigger memories or feelings that the person then regulates with chemicals or behaviors.
- Problems with adversity and traumatic memory may escalate with initial moderation or abstinence.
- Past adversities do not cease to be impactful because someone has become sober or clean.

• Tackling harmful use, addiction, *or* adversity without proper safety procedures in place courts disaster.

SS treatment can be offered in group or individual settings and covers
25 different topics. Client and therapist can select which topics to address
in whatever order makes sense for that particular setting. There is flexibility. Each topic lays out a safe coping skill that can help clients deal with
both addiction and adversity. The treatment is specifically tailored to the
initial stage of coping with these problems through achieving safety and
self-care.

Focus on the present, while treating both disorders simultaneously, is
recommended. Both adversity and harmful use/addiction can be addressed
together with a focus on the present. Clinical care proceeds in phases,
beginning with welcoming and establishing safety procedures and exploring options for seeking safety when the client is frightened or overwhelmed.
Over time, the client builds confidence in her or his ability to manage challenging experiences.

Present focus also means that therapist and client eschew extensive discussion of the past history and course of addiction, as well as the details about
the client's traumatic experience(s). Rather, examining the interrelationships
of both disorders *in the present*, investigating their co-occurrence and how
they present themselves in initial recovery, increases understanding and self-
compassion by viewing substance misuse as adaptive, attempting to cope
with the stress and pain of adversity (Najavits, 2007). Common themes for
both disorders will likely arise as time moves on.

Cognitive behavioral therapy (CBT) and client-centered approaches
underlie this treatment, and it is compatible with mindfulness-based work.
It brings a number of important features to the treatment (brief, structured,
includes education and skills training, directive, collaborative) as well as
explicit training in relapse prevention for both substance use and trauma.
Seeking Safety adds dimensions of supportive relationships, as well as case
management (job counseling, housing, medication assistance)—that is,
establishing a firm and secure treatment base for counseling—and attention
to destructive relationships that can hinder progress (Najavits, 2007).

SS Plan of Action

SS treatment, session by session, is straightforward and can be integrated with other approaches. Sessions begin with a *check-in* and end with a *check-out*. These can be utilized to assess the client's internal states, but also as platforms for affirming progress, highlighting successes, and strengthening commitment to change. A *quotation* or striking statement can be used initially to help the client reflect and engage emotionally with the topic of the day. Then the *topic* itself is discussed and related to the client's life in concrete detail. Examples are surfaced from the client's life, specific problems or challenges are discussed, and behavior or attitude changes are rehearsed. Some topics are *honesty, asking for help, coping with triggers,* and *healing from anger.* A wealth of materials for in-session use are provided in the manual (Najavits, 2007).

One topic in particular has been beneficial in my practice over the years, and can serve here as an example of the session format:

Detaching from Emotional Pain (Grounding)

Experiencing post-traumatic stress (or cravings for reward/relief) can overwhelm the individual with feelings or memories from the past (trauma) or the future (craving). The grounding task is intended to "shift attention toward the external world, away from negative [intrusive] feelings" (Najavits, 2007, p. 125). The goal is to move the individual out of his or her head and refocus on the present moment. This is *not* a relaxation exercise, but an active strategy that connects the client to the present moment via focus on the present, where he or she is safe and able to notice what is happening.

Over time, as the client practices this strategy in the office and at home, she or he learns that stress and cravings can be managed. This is a skill that can be learned and is an investment in the client's healthful recovery.

The initial grounding quote comes from Rilke: "No feeling is final" (quoted in Najavits, 2007, p. 132). After discussion of this quote, therapist and client engage in a grounding demonstration (script is provided in manual) that takes up the bulk of the session. The client reminds herself that she is safe, and imagines placing fears and negative thoughts in a separate container. Then the client walks through separate observations and discussion of elements in the room (external world), enumerating and describing colors, furnishings, windows, and so on. Next, observing physical sensations (feet on the floor, touch, sounds) and soothing images (favorite colors, happy spaces, safe environments) may be elicited. At the end there is discussion about the client's reactions and how this exercise could be used in specific situations.

I have used grounding in many situations with clients and with my own children (anxiety, or stress, nightmares, or cravings). It is easy to teach and very helpful. It is a useful tool to practice with clients before exploration of any material that may be anxiety- or fear-producing. It can be helpful to practice with attention to helping clients discover the kinds of grounding they prefer (physical grounding, soothing, grounding, and so forth).

WHAT ABOUT JOE?

Working with Joe was a challenge, and I learned a lot, but it was not easy. I mentioned that sitting with him in individual and family sessions was frustrating. It was difficult to get Joe out of a defensive emotional and behavioral state. Nothing, it seemed, would change until that occurred.

A breakthrough announced itself almost with a whisper. Unable to get him to engage with his current family or address his alcohol use, and in the face of his unwillingness to reconcile with his mother, I felt stymied. I wondered aloud about his current relationships with his siblings. Rachel, Jimmy, and Tommy (the youngest) had had their ups and downs growing up, but all were married (one divorced) and lived within a 100-mile circle of Joe. Joe's mother was disabled and lived with Rachel. After some initial prodding, Joe invited his sister and brothers to come to a session and was surprised when they agreed. Although they had not seen one another for several years, this extended session was like an old home visit. They shared "remember whens" and talked about holidays and favorite meals. I saw a warmth in Joe that I had not seen before.

About halfway through the session, Rachel acknowledged how grateful she was that Joe had "stuck up" for her in earlier years. Jimmy and Tommy quickly got on board and told their older brother that Joe was their hero for standing up to dad on so many occasions. They all acknowledged that Joe had paid a heavy price. Joe was visibly touched and, as we finished the session, thanked his siblings for coming and told them how much he loved them. He promised to stay in touch.

Within several weeks, it was clear that something had shifted. Joe told Marsi, his wife, that he felt a barrier had been lifted between him and his siblings. He wondered whether she would come back to therapy with him and see if they could move forward together. With coaching, she made clear her belief that no real change could occur without getting a handle on the alcohol abuse. Joe was ambivalent, and over several sessions discussed his reluctance about recovery, Alcoholics Anonymous, and other support groups. (Joe's father had attended meetings briefly, raising everyone's hopes, but relapsed shortly thereafter and never went back.) Joe, however, was willing to try an outpatient treatment program in the local area that had a good reputation. He confessed his lack of confidence about succeeding with abstinence, and so we decided to begin with moderation. Pretty quickly, Joe realized that moderate use was unlikely to work for him. He began abstinence.

There were, of course, continued challenges, but by the time I left the practice Joe had attained a number of months of abstinent sobriety, begun attending a 12 Step group on a regular basis, had begun working with a sponsor, and had made progress in couples therapy. I heard later that, though Joe had never reconciled with his mother, he had become a regular caregiver for her during her final illness. He was also happily married.

How do I understand what happened with this case? The reader will find my response to Joe's story throughout this book. However, I do want to highlight a few themes.

- First, Joe had a pretty typical alcoholic résumé. His alcohol use was clearly on the spectrum of "substance-related and addictive disorders." He certainly had a number of the features we identify as "harmful use" or addiction. While he might live in this limbo for quite some time, it was clear that something needed to change. Troublesome and harmful use had become a pathological "substitute relationship" in Joe's life.

- Second, the early adversities and developmental trauma in Joe's life as he grew up were not unique. Joe's early life set him up—emotionally, relationally, neurologically, spiritually, and ecologically—to be troubled later on with chronic conditions. Mental health and addiction counselors bear witness to these stories all the time. Though it would be overstating the case to say that adversity and trauma are underneath every instance of addiction or ill health, far too many people struggling with mental illness or addiction have histories of trauma and adversity. As the ongoing *adverse childhood experiences* (ACE) studies remind us (see Chapter 7), the experience of adversity underlies much of the chronic illness and troubled behaviors that plague our society (Anda et al., 2006; Dubé et al., 2003; Felitti et al., 1998).

- Third, Joe carried a number of predisposing factors that likely contributed to his mental and behavioral health issues. These factors include the likely (epi-)genetic, environmental, and psychological links that are part and parcel of being raised in an alcoholic family. However, other factors must also be considered. His father's perpetual denigration and his mother's inability to intervene created a situation of insecure attachment, disconnection, isolation, and alienation for Joe. He was on his own from early in life. His world had become unsafe and dangerous.

- Fourth, Joe's challenges in areas of self-worth, self-efficacy, self-care, and self-compassion, as well as his increasingly solitary drinking and isolated lifestyle, demonstrate a kind of inner fragmentation and loss of connection with himself and others (Khantzian & Albanese, 2008). He was in a bad way. It was also clear that Joe's early life trauma and toxic stress from his family of origin were playing out in his current family situation. His family system, its dynamics, roles, rules, and scripts were haunted by his intergenerational family past (Byng-Hall, 1995, 2008; James, 2006).

- Fifth, looking back, I believe that Joe needed *an experience of connection that mattered* to him. Restoring connections—or put another way, a corrective emotional and relational experience, or attachment repair—was a trigger for healing and recovery (Castonguay & Hill, 2012). In the simplest of ways, Rachel, Jimmy, and Tommy repaid his protection by acknowledging that it had occurred and expressing their gratitude. In the midst of all that was bad about his early family life, they saw and acknowledged the goodness he showed to them. Restoring these connections allowed Joe to explore other ways to heal. It restored just enough safety that he was liberated to explore connections. The impact was far-reaching. He became entitled to self-worth and self-care (Boszormenyi-Nagy & Spark, 1984). He could now explore healing in other ways.

- Sixth, Joe's journey of healing began in earnest by happenstance. Yes, Joe was in counseling and chose to stay involved. I understand the beginning of change in this case, however, to be a combination of extra-therapeutic and relationship factors. Blocked in moving forward, I turned to Joe's siblings following insights from intergenerational and contextual family therapy. Their presence and openness opened new avenues for healing.

Preview

In our ongoing attempts to understand addiction, several new sciences have emerged that can help us:

1. *Neuroscience* can help to elaborate many of the brain processes and structures that underlie reward, compulsion, and relapse.
2. *Developmental science* can assist us in growing understandings of the role of attachments and adversity in the laying down of neural and psychological wiring that makes us vulnerable to dysfunction and turning to "substitute relationships" in order to compensate.
3. *Interpersonal neurobiology* can aid in our learning about the relationship connections that help to build the neural connections we rely on, while
4. *Ecological studies* help us to look broadly to the human environmental systems and social structures in which we are embedded and function. All four components help us to build a more complete model of addiction and potential avenues for intervention.

The challenge is to foster an interactive and comprehensive model of addiction that can integrate the layers of influence from disparate components. We do not need another single-culprit model; we need a consilient and social ecological way of thinking. The rest of this book will try to examine the components needed for this integration.

3

Addiction:
Facts and Myths

"O God, that men should put an enemy in their mouths to
   steal away their brains!
That we should, with joy, pleasance, revel, and applause,
   transform ourselves into beasts."

WILLIAM SHAKESPEARE

"For most of human history, the addictions were regarded
as everything but medical disorders. They were variously
viewed as evidence of demonic possession, moral/spiri-
tual weakness, or willful misbehavior. The harsh judgments
about addiction etiology are colored both by the extraordinary pain that these disorders inflict and by their seeming
volitional nature: the addicted individual "chooses" to take
drugs or alcohol, despite repeated and painful negative
consequences."

ANNA ROSE CHILDRESS

HOW DO THE THREE TRADITIONAL MODELS of addiction—disease, choice, learning—fare when applied to the case of "Joe" from Chapters 1 and 2? At first blush each model makes a contribution. If we focus on Joe's drinking and its consequences, the introduction of a noxious element into Joe's body and its systems—and the disruption it causes—simulates a disease process. Psychoactive drugs and compulsive behaviors activate reward circuits in the brain and inhibit centers for judgment and decision making, and over time can disturb the functioning and structure of those centers. If we concentrate on the choices Joe makes, then the eventual development of a relationship to chemicals would seem like a logical progression and cause for blame. An adaptation becomes its own problem. If we focus on neuroplasticity and experience-based changes in brain circuits, then chemical use makes sense as a psychobiological learned response and difficult-to-break habit.

Like the proverbial blind men encountering an elephant, each classic addiction model explains important elements of the problem. Each uncovers part of the truth about Joe's situation. Full understanding requires a more comprehensive viewpoint, however. If all three viewpoints offer a rationale, why would only one be considered definitive? If no one model offers the whole truth, why not search for something truly comprehensive?

In this book we will examine the elephant in the room from this more integrated, comprehensive viewpoint.

HOW TO BEGIN

The American public is hooked on addiction in these early decades of the 21st century. In years past we worried about opiates (opium, morphine, heroin), first after the Civil War and again in the 1920s and 1930s, only to see that particular concern eventually replaced by alarm about stimulants (cocaine, crack, amphetamine). Now in the 2000s we are again concerned about opiates and powerful prescription medicines (Szalavitz, 2016). We also worry a great deal about marijuana and alcohol use, even vaping on high school and college campuses, while at the same time many adults are chemically dependent on Zoloft, Paxil, and other antidepressants, or Xanax, an anti-anxiety medicine (deGrandpere, 2006/2010).

We regularly get ourselves tangled up about drugs and compulsive activities. We are aware, for example, of the successes and failures of a War on Drugs that drags on without any real resolution and seemingly without end. We know that the resources of law enforcement and the courts are stretched too thin and that the prison system is filled beyond capacity, mostly with users, street dealers and other bit players unlucky enough to get caught. We also know that many of these drug-incarcerated inmates are members of minorities and subject to harsh sentences, while in some states a major social experiment is being conducted largely on behalf of white majority individuals with a view to medicinal use of drugs, decriminalization, and even legalization of marijuana use. The irony is difficult to miss.

Furthermore, we sense that the very meaning of the term "addiction" is shifting underneath our feet. Knowledgeable people use the term addiction in its formal sense of (a) compulsive use of a drug; (b) impaired control over use; and (c) continued use despite negative consequences. The American Society of Addiction Medicine (ASAM) provides us with the classic definition utilized by treatment providers and addiction researchers today.[1] ASAM goes on to explain that addiction, as a medical concern, is no longer seen as a predictable drug effect like tolerance or dependence; that is, most of those who experiment or even regularly use a drug will *not* become addicted to it— say it again, will *not* become addicted!—although they will likely become dependent, which is a pharmacological term. The main behavioral symptoms that accompany the "neurobiologic" disease of addiction are "behaviors that include one or more of the following: impaired control over drug use, compulsive use, continued use despite harm, and craving" (ASAM, 2001).

By the Numbers . . .

Currently in the United States it is estimated that there are nearly 100 million citizens—that is, one in three—whose drug use (nicotine, alcohol, illegal, and prescription drugs) is "harmful" in some way (See Figure 3.1 below). "Harmful" or troublesome use is assessed here using common-sense criteria—life challenges, illness, and problems in living are complicated by, or understood to be the result of, chemical use or behavioral excess. The individual and/or social relationships are negatively impacted. This gets our attention.

Those struggling with addiction—addicts themselves, their spouses, their children, their friends and coworkers—do make up a significant proportion of our homes, neighborhoods, and workplaces. According to the National Survey on Drug Use and Health, more than 8 million children—over 12 percent of all U.S. children—are estimated to live with at least one parent who is an addict. Many of these children have lower socioeconomic status; increased difficulties in academic, social, and family functioning; and are more likely to have a range of mental and behavioral problems. Many more children live with parents whose use is "harmful," if not addicted. We know that all these "children of addiction" are more than just collateral damage; they are also "in training." They often find it difficult to manage their own drug use once they grow to maturity, or may marry someone (or several

Different Policies for Levels of Severity

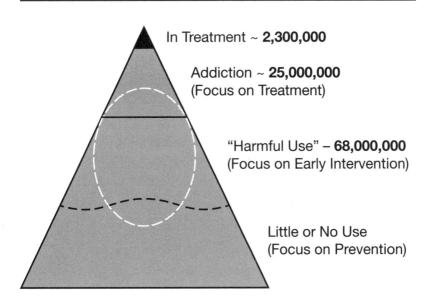

Figure 3.1. "By the numbers": Harmful Use and Addiction. *Source: National Drug Abuse Clinical Trials Network (CTN).*

persons) with an addiction problem, thus perpetuating the problems into another generation.

And we are increasingly aware that addicts do not get into trouble simply from using alcohol or drugs; they also struggle with compulsive activities such as gambling, compulsive Internet use, persistent sexual acting out, and so forth. Discussion continues about which activities or behaviors are appropriately viewed in this way, but the basic premise is now widely and officially accepted. With the advent of the DSM-5, gambling has been added to the range of behaviors considered to be potentially addictive (Clark, Averbeck, et al., 2013), and more such designations may be on the way.

Gambling is a common "leisure activity," seen as an acceptable and harmless form of entertainment (George & Chima, 2014). Lifetime participation is estimated to include 78 percent of American citizens. According to the National Council on Problem Gambling (NCPG), however, approximately 2 million Americans, or about 1 percent of the population, are "pathological gamblers." An additional 2 to 3 percent, or 4 to 6 million people, would be considered "problem gamblers." This reflects research findings that gambling disorder is similar to substance-related disorders in clinical expression, brain origin, comorbidity, physiology, and treatment, as suggested in DSM-5 (Blaszczynski & Nower, 2002; Goudriaan, Yucel, & van Holst, 2014). Now that the door is open for "behavioral addictions" in addition to chemical ones in DSM-5, what other behaviors or activities belong in this category?[2]

Addiction: Let's Picture the Problem

The Office of National Drug Control Policy, or the White House "drug czar's" office, publishes alcohol and other drug use data, along with setting policy for prevention and treatment. The model they work with is instructive (see above; McLellan 2010, 2011).[3]

- The base of the triangle (below the broken wavy line) indicates those individuals whose alcohol and other drug use is of little or no concern. The focus of policy and intervention efforts with this cohort can be population-wide, primary prevention of potential future problems.

- Notice that between the wavy line and the crisp, straight dividing line above, there is a population of people whose "harmful use" is a focus of secondary prevention and early intervention. Estimates are that this population, which fluctuates (notice that the wavy line indicates some variability in the size of the population *and* that we do not know the precise dimensions of this group), is sizeable,[4] and while their substance use does not meet full diagnostic criteria for addiction, their involvement with substances is notable, sometimes problematic, and costly in both human and economic terms.

  Since we do know that unhealthy or harmful use (a) can be the catalyst for acute medical or psychological care; (b) complicates care for a host of medical and psychiatric problems; (c) exacerbates the difficulty of care for many chronic illnesses; and (d) affects far too many persons in the user's family and social world, we need to develop better ways to screen, assess, diagnose, and treat unhealthy or "harmful" as well as clearly addictive use. These efforts will likely include improved strategies for brief intervention (motivating, referring, supporting), reintervening and monitoring eligible persons as needed, and training in self-management for patients/ clients/consumers. It also will include integrating and funding treatment for harmful use and addiction into primary care and a variety of health-care systems, as well as into juvenile and adult corrections systems (Babor et al., 2007).

- Above the solid straight line is the realm of those who meet the criteria for treatment in our standard addiction programs (inpatient, outpatient, extended). This is the territory claimed by the treatment industry, and much of our theorizing and policy development is based on this population. Unfortunately, the small triangle at the very top indicates those who actually receive any kind of formal ("assisted") treatment. It is barely 10 percent of the eligible population. Meanwhile, a sizable portion of those struggling with addiction and harmful use goes without assisted treatment of any kind (White, 2008).

- The broken, egg-shaped circle in the middle of the triangle indicates where more effort is needed to arrive at early detection of emerging harmful use and addiction, as well as effective and affordable treatments. Addiction-related and mental health professions need to invest renewed attention and resources into understanding the issues here.

More than 25 million Americans are estimated to struggle with outright addiction, along with another 68 million whose use falls in the "substance-related and addictive disorders" category, the title of the overall section in DSM-5 that includes significant abuse and full-blown addiction to one or more psychoactive substances (above the wavy line). These are the substance use disorders.[5]

Only about 2.4 million sufferers (about 10 percent) in a given year receive *any* kind of "assisted" or targeted help. This statistic should give pause to those of us working in addiction treatment. The number of those needing help far exceeds those who actually get help *and* far exceeds our current treatment capacity. We work with a tiny sliver of those in need, and often make our recommendations to patients and families based on our experience with this small population (White, 2008). And unfortunately, those we counsel often receive less-than-adequate care. This is a dirty little secret within addiction treatment (Glaser, 2015). We are, for example, far from universal implementation of "best practices," such as use of medication-assisted treatments or truly individualized treatment approaches (Szalavitz, 2016; Volkow, 2014). In addition, we don't really have much in the way of treatment to offer to "harmful" but not addicted users. Often we rely more on ideology or common practice than best science.

What Is My Focus?

This book focuses on both addiction and harmful (problematic) use as a spectrum, a single graded category of destructive involvement with chemicals and behaviors. Think of this focus as residing within the oval (see Figure 3.1). That is, it is simpler and more accurate to approach these behaviors as points along a continuum of devastation rather than as two different disorders—abuse and addiction—as we did previously.

The diagnostic criteria for classifying people with "drug abuse" and "drug dependence" represent arbitrary cut points along a gradual continuum. This means that, as with other conditions, society needs to address a wide array of problem severity, and that interventions appropriate to one region of the continuum may be unhelpful or even coun- terproductive at another level of development. (MILLER & CARROLL, 2006).

This perspective also means that addiction treatment providers and insti- tutions must decide where along the continuum they are willing and able to invest their energies and resources. The field of addiction studies, its treat- ment institutions, and individual providers must come to some understand- ing of how to proceed.

While we are learning that "professionally directed treatment is the dom- inant pathway of entry into recovery from substance *dependence*," natural and nonprofessional approaches to recovery are the "predominant path- way[s] of resolution" for *problematic use* and less severe forms of the disorder (White, 2008, pp. 40–41). Not everyone who struggles with substance- related issues needs the kind of specialized intervention and treatment we offer in traditional treatment centers. "Natural [unassisted] recovery" is a viable and often-used pathway for entry into recovery, particularly for those with later onset, lower severity, relational support, and resources ("recovery capital") for seeking and maintaining a recovery lifestyle. While recovery is still the ultimate goal for those who are ensnared by chemical or behavioral problems, the pathways into recovery, the methods that are most effective for initiating and maintaining recovery, even the very definition of what recovery is, will be the subject of research and ongoing discussion for years to come (White, 2008).

We know that earlier initiation of intervention and treatment improves the prognosis for entering recovery and lessens the burden of harm inflicted on the individual, family, and community. However, we also know that prob- lematic or "harmful" users—those at the less severe end of the continuum— are often reluctant to engage in assisted treatment. The obstacles include (a) the (accurate) perception that there is a mismatch between accepted addic- tion treatment processes and the needs of problem users; (b) delays or lack of urgency in accessing formal treatment for problem and addicted users (involving long waiting lists); (c) a requirement for abstinence in formal treatment; (d) the sense of stigma that is still attached to drug use problems and behaviors; (e) the lack of more diverse, community-based resources for beginning recovery.

A person who is arrested for impaired driving ("under the influence" or "while intoxicated") may or may not be what common parlance describes as an alcoholic or addict. Back in the day, we believed that one DUI was *prima facie* evidence of addiction. Now we must be more discerning. Clearly, his behavior places himself (and potentially others) at risk for injury or even death. It can be troublesome in the extreme. I do not minimize the danger: My own nephew was killed under the wheels of a drunk driver. However, we can no longer treat first-time intoxicated drivers with extended inpatient or outpatient addiction treatment. We cannot treat teens who are experiencing difficulties with early marijuana use in the same way that we deal with long-term alcoholics or those impaired by chronic methamphetamine or opioid use.

Now, with the inclusion of "brief intervention" protocols (such as SBIRT, or Screening, Brief Intervention, and Referral to Treatment) and the extension of substance use screening and assessment into general healthcare practice, we can extend the continuum of care. Effective, evidence-based medications to counter overdose or craving, as well as behavioral and supportive therapies, are helping to address a wider range of substance use disorders. We must now include assessment and judicious referral to a variety of treatment options as the regular way to proceed.

In addition, the development of conceptual tools such as ongoing recovery management, recovery-oriented systems of care, and recovery capital, as well as the methodologies for using and reimbursing them in concrete situations provide a powerful road into the future (see Chapter 8). The recent Surgeon General's first-ever report on *Facing Addiction in America* (U.S. Department of Health & Human Services, 2016) provides some foundation for moving forward.

AMENDED PERSPECTIVE

The newest diagnostic approach (DSM-5) embraces addiction as a *syndrome* with varying levels of severity. It views troublesome behavior with drugs or compulsive behaviors on a spectrum and encourages practitioners to gather varied kinds of information in ongoing assessment. In the current DSM-5 version, clinicians are encouraged to add measures and narratives that describe each patient's difficulties and unique life challenges in some detail. The clinical write-up is envisioned as a "thicker" presentation of the patient's lifeworld and functioning. Practitioners are encouraged to add descriptive information about such things as changes in and frequency of consumption, using the patient's own language in reporting his or her experiences with different substances and activities. Reports are encouraged from knowledgeable others such as family members or coworkers, the clinician's own observations, relevant cultural information, data from psychosocial assessment instruments such as the World Health Organization Disability Assessment Schedule (WHODAS) 2.0, results of biological testing, medical examinations and laboratory findings, and so forth (Bauer, 2014).

Following DSM-5, among 11 overall criteria, an individual must have at least two symptoms or more to be diagnosed with a "mild" form of substance use disorder, four symptoms for "moderate," and six for "severe" disorder.[6] If the clinician can ascertain one more symptom in addition to a "driving under the influence" (DUI) charge, for example—a likely assessment outcome—then the individual's use could be classified as "mild" use disorder. It is the counselor's role then to begin helping that person with her or his "harmful use" (DSM "mild" or "moderate" severity of substance use disorder) and over time judge whether or not that person is struggling with a full-blown addictive disorder.

Using key counseling procedures (establishing welcome, trust, and safety) as well as basic screening, assessment, and follow-up protocols (brief intervention, trans-theoretical, motivational, cognitive-behavioral, and 12 Step facilitation), counseling can assist someone to acknowledge a problem and become "ready" to address it (DiClemente & Velasquez, 2002). The next step then is to assign, in collaboration with the client, a treatment approach that promises success. In attachment-sensitive counseling, this assignment will occur utilizing the client's strengths and resources (capital) as well as challenges. It will also occur in consultation with the family and relational network.

Family and relationship therapy, as a treatment modality for harmful use and addiction, is coming into its own.[7] Family work made its way into addiction treatment originally as family education, sponsored by traditional treatment institutions as part of acknowledging the potentially helpful role of families and addressing relationship side effects. Over time, sensitivity to family issues has evolved into a number of effective intervention approaches that can be used in both inpatient and increasingly outpatient intervention (Morgan & Litzke, 2008). It is important to note that alcohol and other drug dependence is only part of the family therapist's scope of practice. Most drinking and other drug problems, as well as difficulties with compulsive behaviors, are of mild to moderate severity and can seriously affect family members, but are also amenable to informed and brief interventions (Roberts & McCrady, 2003). The ramifications and side effects, particularly for family members, can also range from mild to moderate to severe. Drinking and drug use take their toll. Once the counselor enters the realm of family and relationship therapy, he or she must be prepared to screen, assess, and address issues of adversity and trauma. There is significant overlap between substance using and adversity populations. As we saw with Joe in Chapters 1 and 2, relationship ruptures, family dysfunction, and trauma often co-occur with substance misuse.

Attachment-sensitive counseling, especially for those who wrestle with harmful chemical or behavioral management and a comorbid history of adversity, approaches addictive disorders as the result of adapting to relationship disruption. Attachment-sensitive counseling looks beyond individualized conceptions about alcohol and other drug or compulsive behaviors. Attempting to view the problem user or struggling addict in context, and within a wider frame, the counselor tries to approach his or her practice in an empathic, multidimensional, and systemic way. Understanding harmful use/addiction as an adaptive maneuver gone awry provides a helpful frame. A wider family frame can also assist the counselor to see the conjunction of both problematic use or addiction *and* adversity or trauma. Within families, these often co-occur; they are "brother and sister" maladies (Grant, 1996). Repair and recovery begin with the (re)establishment of attuned attachment. Corrective relationships with family, significant others, and recovery communities of care restore a sense of safety, security, and connection. A healthy and empathic relationship with a counselor or therapist may be the first step and can form a bridge to attachment repair and recovery. These relationships can become the catalyst for healing and forward life movement.

However, in order to hear the narrative of any particular person's suffering in this wider context, counselors may need to clear out some basic misconceptions.

Enduring Myths

Myth #1: Drugs are the problem

Drugs distort and "hijack" the brain in profound and long-lasting ways, we are told. However, if drugs are really the problem, as the dominant narrative says, then why don't they do this to everyone? Some say that addiction is a property that dwells in certain substances. There are "chemical hooks" in these substances (Erickson, 2018; Hari, 2015). Misuse them and they will enslave you. This is an underlying bias in the current, dominant disease model. However, it doesn't quite work that way. It really is true that only a small percentage of those who use a drug, even of those who use over a long period of time, ever become addicted (Volkow, Koob, & McLellan, 2016). Only a small group of determined or vulnerable users become full-blown addicts (Heyman, 2010). It is an enduring myth that drugs cause addiction.

"Capture rates"—a statistical measurement of drug use that addresses how many users will go on to use the substance regularly or become dependent on the drug—remain consistently low. They indicate that a much larger percentage of users do *not* become addicted. Biological, psychological, and social (vulnerability) factors must be taken into account along with the contribution of a specific drug or drugs in order to compute a reliable measure of addiction potential (National Addiction Centre, 2003).

I am old enough to remember the overblown public service announcements—"one puff of crack and you will be hooked!"—and the dire warnings of permanent damage—"This is your brain on drugs." We continue to inflate the power of drugs in drug misuse and addiction, even though the data on this point indicates otherwise. We are also coming to understand that chemicals are not necessary for addiction to occur. Behaviors or activities can trigger the same physiological changes and dysfunction as drugs.

For several years Mike, a semiretired businessman, has been going to the local casino in the middle of the week. He finds the environment diverting and the anonymity welcome. In the beginning he never wagered more than $100 per visit at the slot machines, which was well within his means, and was able to stay all afternoon and into the evening. One day he saw an acquaintance there who invited him to the blackjack table. Mike won $700 and was hooked.

Now Mike finds that he has difficulty sleeping the night before he goes. He is restless and ruminates about the next big win just around the corner. That morning he feels the anticipation building at home and on the drive to the casino. He experiences a kind of "high" and notes that he can sometimes feel his heart racing. His hands shake, and he feels "shaky" inside. He thinks it is odd that he doesn't play the slots anymore but walks directly to the tables. It's like he is on a mission. Once he sits down and orders a beer, however, he is ready to go and quite a bit calmer.

He tells himself that this is harmless entertainment and "just what I need." He knows that if he tallied up his wins and losses, he is probably on the negative side of the ledger. He figures, however, that he is due for a win, which will move him into the positive column. His Wednesdays at the casino make the rest of the week tolerable, and he does not know what he would do without them.

Mike manages the rest of his life around this "diversion." If a missed Wednesday at the casino is unavoidable, he is miserable until he can get there again. He never invites his wife along and jokingly suggests that she find some entertainment that is all her own. When asked whether he won that day, Mike dissembles and won't acknowledge whether he has won or lost. He is uncomfortable not telling the truth, but tells himself that it's "no one else's business."

Mike has begun a relationship with blackjack and with the process of gambling as a mood regulator. The volatile emotional states, alternating from agitation (anticipation) to calm (participation), the ritualization of his behavioral pattern, the isolation and lack of honesty, the characteristic ways of thinking about this activity are all indicators of trouble brewing with his gambling.

I view harmful use and addiction as a commitment to a substitute relationship. This relationship can be to drugs, to compulsive activities, or to other attachments—"-aholias," as in workaholia—that fulfill a purpose, such as wealth, or power, or social influence (Alexander, 2008/2011; James, 2008, 2013). The drug or activity is not primary, however; the relationship is. The drug or activity is simply a tool that has "what it takes," the psychoactive ability to alter someone's consciousness or awareness.

> When people find others to be "unrewarding," they may become more likely to seek out alternative rewards. Money, status, objects, cats and dogs, or even the exquisite suffering involved in self-harm can be reconditioned to activate pleasure centers. The problem, when you depend on a substitute for love, is you can never get enough" (COZOLINO, 2014, P. 126).

It is important to remember that throughout much of his working life, Mike did not struggle with gambling. He and his wife went to the casino as an every-once-in-a-while fling, and after retirement, he began going by himself on a more regular schedule. However, when it turned, he went all in.

Myth #2: Intervention and treatment

We hear that an addict cannot stop on his or her own, that no one stops unless she or he "hits bottom" or has a life-altering experience, that no one stops without treatment, and that the only way to stop is abstinence (each of these assertions is inaccurate). In effect, the models we are given seem inadequate, or at least explain only some of the addiction problem.

For example, we now know that the older version of an "intervention," as seen on television in a show that bears that name on the A&E Channel, is ineffective and can even be counterproductive. It's called the "confrontational intervention," and research suggests that it is successful only a small percentage of the time. Other more "invitational interventions," such as the A Relational Intervention Sequence for Engagement (ARISE) intervention, are much more powerful, assisting addicted persons to enter treatment more than 70 to 80 percent of the time (Landau & Garrett, 2008; Landau et al., 2000). Many studies point in this direction, and no studies suggest that direct confrontation is a helpful procedure (Szalavitz, 2016).

If addiction really hijacks the brain and renders the addict unable to resist the temptation of drugs, why is it that so many people can say enough is enough? Why is it that in laboratory settings, in many instances, addicts will choose alternative rewards over drugs (Hart, 2014)? Few people seem to be willing to explore the implications of this information and connect it to what we hear from addicts themselves and to what the researchers tell us (Alexander, 2008/2011; Hart, 2014).

It is critically important that we come to terms with this. We need early intervention and treatment protocols that work, not just for confirmed addicts but also for the many more people struggling with harmful use. We need ways of thinking about healthy, safe, and enriched environments—that is, a social ecology of addiction and recovery—that can complement drug-focused and psychological strategies to neurobiological, behavioral, and psychological strategies (Alexander, 2016).

Myth #3: We will find the cause of addiction and harmful use

Despite the promises made by single-culprit approaches—disease, choice, learning—the societal challenges of addiction and harmful use continue unabated (Alexander, 2008/2011). Single culprits cannot provide comprehensive treatments. Yes, we have new medications that can surely help, but we seem no closer to solutions than we were years ago. We need to look elsewhere while holding on to the gains we are making in scientific exploration.

One risk in paying too much attention to the ongoing debate among the *disease, choice, or learning* models of addictive behaviors is that it limits our vision and our vocabulary. Our natural inclination is to consider the problem of addiction from the point of view of the individual, and the traditional perspectives reinforce this natural predisposition. Adams (2008) calls this an atomistic or "particle" (versus a "social" or "system") orientation; it reinforces an extreme individualistic view. The disease model focuses our attention on brains and neural structures, on the promise of therapies and medications. The choice model concentrates on the individual's responsibilities and the amount of free will involved in each person's choices, while learning models focus on neuroplastic characteristics of individual brains. All three paradigms suggest that their way is the best way to view the problem, but each one narrows our frame of reference to the isolated individual and his or her predicament.

These perspectives can only take us so far in understanding addiction (Satel & Lilienfeld, 2013a & b). They provide insights, yes, but they also leave a lot of territory untouched. A more comprehensive perspective is needed—a social ecology perspective that is more adequate to the full nature of human persons—in order to explain what is happening in addiction.

A DEVELOPMENTAL ARC:
HOW DO "SUBSTITUTE RELATIONSHIPS" FORM?

An attachment-sensitive counseling approach moves our focus to relationships, social context, and culture as areas to examine. Yet, an adaptive relationship to addiction as a substitute for secure attachment and true connection does not spring fully formed into life; it requires development, and to an increasing extent, commitment. No one becomes addicted overnight. No one continues using until he or she discovers that it serves a purpose. This is a process.

Much chemical use and compulsive behavior begins in adolescence and young adulthood, a time of change and accelerated development as well as vulnerability for risky and impulsive action. That's where our story begins. These are times of vigorous neural change and emotional enhancement. Physiological changes underlie developments in emotions, cognitions, and motivation, and in assessment of risk, impulse control, and the potential of poor judgment to affect decision-making. These changes also facilitate the formation of new attachments and the broadening of other connections into wider social circles.

One of the fundamental rules of neuroscience is that brains change and adapt. The tree-like branching of neurons and synaptic connections, fittingly called arborization, is enhanced and a large amount of synaptic pruning and rewiring helps to increase the efficiency of the adolescent brain. This is a "sensitive period" of change during which the brain undergoes both disorganization and reorganization (See Cozolino, 2014, pp. 33–35). Neural networks are enhanced and greater integration of cortical and subcortical areas, that is, the cognitive, motivational, regulatory, and emotional circuits, occurs. Thinking and planning gradually supplement emotions for guiding behavior.

Psychological changes cannot happen without these neural structural changes, while neural and psychological change is enhanced or damaged by social interactions. It is a three-way process—neural, psychological, relational—and relationships are key. Changes in the brain are an essential feature of adolescence. However, we are only just learning about how those changes interact with the multiple impacts of adversity and trauma. Even more, we are coming to learn that the adolescent and young adult brain, while coping with normal system-wide changes and the effects of adversities, is also integrating the effects of alcohol and other drugs as substitutes for deficits in relationship. This is a tall order, and it does not happen all at once.

Daily (2012) points out that there is a natural or typical progression to people's engagement with psychoactive chemicals and compulsive activities. This is not to say that everyone follows the same linear course, but that there is an oft-used pathway into potential trouble that follows a roughly predictable, if varying, pattern. I am indebted to Daily for the way in which he lays this out. I have adapted his thinking for my own purposes.[8]

It is important to note as we begin that those with a history of adversity, developmental wounds, and neurological dysregulation are likely more susceptible to progressing along this pathway into deeper trouble. As we are learning with conditions like post-traumatic stress disorder (PTSD), developmental trauma disorder (DTD), or major emotional illness, early adversity seems to predispose individuals for later challenges (van der Kolk, 2014). Moving farther along the path to trouble is facilitated in those who are wounded along the way. For them, the path can become a slippery slope.

Progression from Use to Abuse

Many people begin their engagement with chemicals or compulsive activities with a phase of *contemplation* during which they are either consciously or unconsciously preparing for use. Typically this might occur in high school or college, or early military life. This is a phase of observation, in which they watch others using or participating in activities, and assess vicariously the experiences those others are having. They watch people's reactions to the experience of high or relief. They notice social bonds being built, as people connect with one another in new ways. Said differently, they are observing the "drug culture" that surrounds them, which may become a major social and environmental hook for their own choices and behavior, and they are engaged in a lively internal conversation: Should I? Shouldn't I? Questioning of friends and relatives may also be part of this phase: What was it like? What happens? Do you think it's okay?

The next phase is *experimentation*, in which people go through initial experiences with chemicals or potentially compulsive activities ("meet and greet"). Even this early, some persons begin to develop relationship and fantasy bonds with those substances or activities, and the effects they generate. Use or engagement changes mood and shifts thinking in ways that provide reward and/or relief; they experience that use can meet a need or serve a purpose. This information is noted and tucked away for later consideration.

Experimentation sooner or later leads to a first experience of "*intoxication*." At that point experimentation is over and there are choices to make. Several paths lead from this experience, which may extend over a period of time. Some people discontinue use or choose to use moderately. They find that a little is enough and too much is uncomfortable. They examine the consequences and choose to moderate or discontinue. They become social or infrequent users and put chemical use or diverting activities "in their place."

Others, however, find that the experience of intoxication is to their liking or is useful in a variety of ways, and they continue to use; something has clicked for them and we see the beginnings of a relationship to the intoxication forming. For some period, intoxication may be an infrequent event ("flirting") and may occur in response to emotional or stressful situations. This can be a potentially effective time for intervention (commonly seen as secondary prevention). Using tools such as empathic listening, eliciting motivation, decisional balancing, expressing concern, can tip the scales toward healthier choices (Miller & Rollnick, 2012).

If use progresses, it will likely be in hidden or covert fashion; the person will not realize that amounts or frequency are escalating. The person may not see a relationship pattern forming. Tool (drug, activity) and process (relief, intoxication) become associated with one another and are fused with the process of seeking reward or relief from stress, or discomfort, or boredom. Use or participation is found to have a function and the relationship takes deeper root.

This is a time when individuals may begin to use more impulsively (Koob, 2009a & b). The person seeks reward without consideration of consequences. It is a kind of automatic action, a major element in difficulties with self-control and self-regulation, which are critical executive functions. Early stress or adversity can predispose individuals to this path; current stresses may trigger impulse. In response to emotional or environmental cues, the individual reaches for a drink, a joint, or a needle, or places another wager. Impulse triggers thoughtless action.

As people continue to use in ways that meet a need or serve a purpose, they may begin the phase of *misuse*. They personally experience that use or participation is pleasurable, addresses stress, or provides relief from anxiety or boredom. Use at this stage may be infrequent or episodic. The transition from infrequent intoxication to a pattern of *likely* misuse over time may be short-lived, or seamless and difficult to discern. They may use impulsively when it is socially inappropriate or risky, for example when driving. They may initiate use in reaction to strong emotions such as elation or anger. They begin a phase of harmful or troublesome use.

They may begin to experience unwanted consequences, either mild or severe. These consequences may or may not get their attention. The person, however, and the people around her or him sense that a relationship has begun—an emotional connection with reward or stress relief has been made—but it is not yet a settled issue. Individuals can decide to pursue other means of coping or relaxing, and may choose alternative ways to find relief besides intoxication.

Consequences can be helpful at this point. Several counseling approaches suggest that allowing users to experience their consequences without buffering (contingency management and motivational incentive approaches) can assist users in coming to terms with misuse and promoting change (Prendergast et al., 2006).

Others may take care to preserve the relationship to intoxication, however. They may find themselves anticipating the next time they will use or engage. They are developing a fantasy bond with their preferred drug or activity, and with the process of intoxication. Often without the individual becoming fully aware, a variety of stimuli—that will eventually become "triggers"— are folded into these experiences as reminders of good times or examples of relieving unpleasant states. What is remarkable is that this is also how most important relationships become salient, that is slowly, bit by bit, with feelings, memories, images, desires, events, all rolled into a package of memory and feeling, and becoming part of our lives.

This is a natural result of the brain's ability to learn. Cues and memories become part of our salient relationships. These cues by themselves can signal that the real thing may be approaching, even before it arrives, and will trigger a hormonal and neural event of anticipation that is much like the real thing. This is how learning and memory teach us and motivate us to seek what is good and life-giving. Life provides "learning signals" (Satel & Lilienfeld, 2013, p. 52). Slow, step-by-step movement toward relationship evolves into a narrative. This normal process of relationship formation can be subverted, distorted, and usurped by compulsion, however, and intoxication rises in the individual's list of priorities.

Notice that along the way there are ample opportunities for healthy or less-risky choices. There is no doubt that choices to stop or moderate use are available. Such choices continue to be available. However, no one knows the exact amount of freedom to choose that any particular individual has at hand in any particular situation. Many factors, including neurobiology or painful social dislocation, may impinge on freedom of choice.

Misuse to Abuse

The move from impulse to compulsion is seen as one key indicator of the onset of addiction, a definitive move to the more severe forms of substance use (Koob & Le Moal, 2005). The precise mechanisms of this development are still mysterious.

As things progress (and let me stress that things do *not* always progress beyond here), the individual enters a deeper phase of harmful use. The person is establishing a pathological, emotional relationship and a likely neurochemical connection both to the experience of intoxication and to the drug or activity of choice. Stress, life challenges, emotional pain, alienation, loneliness are now *preferably* relieved through external chemical or behavioral comforting. Over-reliance on external or substitute coping deters users from developing their own internal skills to identify, express, and cope with emotions, or distress, or life's challenges. "Substitute relationships" shove healthier relationships and ways of coping to the side. Coping through intoxication becomes a likely strategy and is adopted as a "crutch," weakening other styles and alternatives for coping. Attachment to a drug or activity, and to the process of coping-by-intoxication, has become the preferred route for managing bumps in one's life. Resorting to this strategy for stress relief accelerates. Self-regulation (and the normal developmental process of co-regulation through relationship with another person) now becomes more difficult as cognitive skills are blunted, and is sidetracked as external regulation of emotional states through false substitutes becomes the norm.

Many of those who arrive at this place don't yet realize that their chemical or behavioral engagement is affecting their daily lives and their other relationships. Their use is beginning to negatively affect quality of life, as other activities and relationships are gradually crowded out and replaced while intoxication takes a priority (Adams, 2007), and yet they may not fully meet the diagnostic criteria for full-blown addictive disorder. Families find this a very difficult time for dealing with their loved ones who seem clearly impaired, yet family members do not know what to do. Demanding or sending someone to addiction treatment seems like overkill; many treatment providers are not willing to diagnose a condition that does not fully meet the criteria.

This is where early intervention, including motivational enhancement, contingency management, family training, and skills-based intervention can be helpful.[9]

Abuse to Addiction

In the final phase of compulsive use the individual becomes deeply attached (addicted) to intoxication and to the drug or process that meets her or his needs. She or he becomes "dependent," physically and emotionally on false fixes.[10] An emotional and neural relationship has been forged, and the person's internal systems (attachment systems, reward and motivation systems, stress response systems, self-regulation systems, pain response) have been reorganized to function within and through an environment dominated by chemical or behavioral excess. One might say that coping-by-intoxication has reached a "critical transition" (Scheffer, 2009) or a "tipping point" (Gladwell, 2006) and a variety of internal psychological and biological systems have begun to "run away" with a momentum all their own. Vital systems have become catastrophically unbalanced. The bonds with a process and objects of compulsion have been solidified. The individual slides, or runs head-long, into addiction.

Runaway Systems

The metaphor of "runaway systems"—a seismic shift in system behavior once a "tipping point" or "critical transition" has been reached, as a way to imagine the mechanics of addiction—has been adapted here from the functioning of natural ecological systems (McNeill, 2009; Scheffer, 2009). Addiction as a runaway system may be able to serve as a complementary—perhaps even more adequate—metaphor for addiction, serving alongside the "chronic relapsing (hijacked) brain disease" model as well as the varieties of choice and learning models. The rhetorical device of runaway systems may be more apt today than medical (disease), criminal justice (hijacked), educational (learning), or moralistic (faulty choice) language. Individualistic language gives way to systemic.

Nested biological and psycho-emotional systems that interpenetrate one another and mutually interact within a personal and social ecology of relationships can be vulnerable to runaway conditions. Nested systems make for efficient learning and can be valuable in many ways. However, their very interactive features can become a liability. Think of a loving family that is trying to cope with a grandparent's cancer. Nana is the emotional heart of her family. She has cared for generations of children and couples, and always with a smile. She is beloved. However, with the diagnosis of a terminal cancer, her presence is now time-limited. Her three children, now in their forties and fifties, are understandably anxious and experiencing some difficulties in managing her care. They are bickering among themselves, preoccupied, and largely unavailable at home to their spouses and children. Each of the children have their own children, and the grandkids are sad about Nana's imminent passing. One grandchild is finding it difficult to concentrate at school; another is becoming somewhat reclusive and isolated from others, refusing to talk about what is happening; yet another gets into trouble with the police because of several recent bar fights and intoxication.

In systemic terms, the invasion of this family by cancer seems to have caused the family to reach a "critical transition." Previously calm and well-regulated relationships are becoming unbalanced. Levels of anxiety and sadness have reached a "tipping point" with reverberations throughout the multigenerational family system. At this moment of crisis, what was once a well-functioning family system has devolved into a "runaway system" that requires regrouping and work before it moves into full dysfunction.

I am suggesting that we consider the move into addiction as the individual's nested systems reaching such a tipping point or "critical transition" in one or more essential biopsychosocial systems. Addicted behaviors and choices ensue, and become a runaway natural system.

One more example may help to clarify. My assessment of Joe (Chapters 1 and 2) is that he had reached several tipping points. Throughout his early life and young adulthood, he had struggled with an underlying sense of shame and feelings of humiliation that he kept tightly under wraps. Experiencing ongoing adversity at home, Joe developed "blocked trust" in reaction to relational mistreatment and withdrew part of himself from social engagement. He became adept at "living defensively" (Baylin & Hughes, 2016).

As he became a father himself and lived a hectic, engaged life with Marsi and the kids, these feelings were tapped and rose to the surface. Every parent and spouse knows that it is impossible to fully measure up every minute and in every situation; there are inevitable disappointments, relationship breaks, and attachment wounds in any family. The same is often true in the work setting. These times are when self-regulation helps a person to reach a balance of affect, to move forward and repair the problem. Joe, however, did not experience these as normal occurrences. In his life, not "measuring up" was too close for comfort to feeling "useless" and being a "waster of space." And so, he experienced them as failures and shameful embarrassments.

Without the skills for self-regulation, Joe's internal life became increasingly unbalanced. He reached a major emotional tipping point and turned to a familiar substitute, namely a relationship with alcohol. This met the need and quickly became an escalating "substitute relationship" for Joe's self-regulation dilemma. Rather than turning to Marsi for comfort or support, he increasingly sought "chemical comfort" and each subsequent life-problem tipped the scales further.

Entry into Recovery

Is addiction the end of the developmental process? If this progression, or something like it, is a common pathway into addiction, what do we know about the ways out? Interestingly, not a lot from a scientific point of view.

No one knows for sure the exact size of the entire population that seeks and finds recovery. A. Thomas McLellan reminds us that we do not yet have a "science of recovery" to match our knowledge base about addiction (Feliz, 2012). Understanding the size and make-up of the recovering population and how it functions is a first step in developing this "recovery science." The documentary film, *The Anonymous People*, quotes a figure of 23 million adult Americans currently in recovery (Williams, 2013). This echoes national survey data.

There is now sufficient information to suggest (a) that a significant number of drug users and addicts move into a kind of "natural recovery" in their late 20s, 30s, and 40s, and (b) do so without formal intervention or treatment of any kind (Granfield & Cloud, 2001; Sobell, Cunningham & Sobell, 1996). Alcoholics and harmful drinkers do seem to eventually enter recovery in large numbers (Humphreys, Moos, & Finney, 1995). Severe and problem drinkers often recover without formal intervention, and appear to remain in recovery for significant periods of five years or more (Granfield & Cloud, 2001, 1996). That is, there is a case to be made that addiction may be a self-limiting, even self-correcting condition for many, and not necessarily the chronic disorder we have believed it to be in every case (White, 2016). Unassisted recovery is more common than we acknowledge.

A recovery focus is exposing the uncomfortable fact that, while the best science in addiction studies may be closing in on effective treatment methods, the addiction treatment industry is woefully behind the curve and unprepared for the transformation that is needed (Glaser, 2015).[11] The critical need for this transformation has been highlighted in a number of studies by the Institute of Medicine (2001, 2004, 2005). And that's not all. As we have reached greater clarity about the extent of harmful versus addicted use, it is also becoming clearer that many persons seem to find their way into recovery with brief, minimal, and even no formal intervention (Spinelli & Thayer, 2017; Klingemann & Sobell, 2007). Intriguing data about the many people who seek recovery by various routes has been available for years.[12]

It is now accepted that there are many pathways into recovery (White & Kurtz, 2006a). However, there is significant risk in repeating this mantra, as it may desensitize us to the numbers of people who remain addicted and do not get into recovery at all, a small and stubborn minority we must not forget. The risk is a kind of complacency to the plight of that group of people who are unable to find or achieve a healthy outcome. They are the most wounded and may have come to addiction with wounds already in place from childhood adversity and developmental trauma. Mostly we know about these persons through the work of compassionate providers who accompany them at the margins of society, such as physician Gabor Maté.

Maté describes his own experience working with such "hopeless" cases of addiction in his riveting book, *In the Realm of Hungry Ghosts* (2010). He tells the stories of his patients and along the way tries to describe his understanding of the addiction process. The group of "hungry ghosts" he describes are society's "shadow side," Maté believes. We are reluctant to know much about them.

Many people know someone—or know about someone—who was unable to quit her or his addiction. Many of us have such persons in our families or in our caseloads. Nevertheless, we do not have good information about this population. We do know that they exist, despite the good news about those who seek and find recovery through a myriad of pathways. We also suspect that this grouping of people has experienced more than their share of adversity and suffering, which likely predisposes them for addiction at its worst.

Maté says that his patients are . . .

> ". . . without exception, people who have had extraordinarily difficult lives. And the commonality is childhood abuse. In other words, these people all enter life under extremely adverse circumstances. Not only did they not get what they need for healthy development, they actually got negative circumstances of neglect. . . . That's what sets up the brain biology of addiction" (QUOTED IN KARR-MORSE, 2012, P. 212).

Diverse Paths and Outcomes

While there is emerging data suggesting that a majority of people who at some point met the criteria used to define addiction and harmful use no longer do so later in life, and that many have recovered without attending meetings or treatment, we also need to learn more about those who are not counted or surveyed anywhere. These stories are also part of the tale of addiction.

The numbers of those who are unable or unwilling to quit are a challenge to procure. How might we estimate them? Dying from a drug overdose or DUI is one thing. Do we also include dying from lung cancer when it involves someone who cannot quit smoking? It may well be that those who are unable to quit their addiction—let's say those who are familiar to treatment providers and who use the "revolving door" into treatment over and over again—and those who die prematurely through illness or accident, actually lived their addictive careers in response to traumatic events in their lives.[13] The ACE Study and developmental trauma studies would certainly suggest that. Much anecdotal evidence would suggest that revolving door patients in addiction treatment are victims of multiple and unresolved trauma. In those cases, is it more accurate to say that they died from addiction or from trauma?

It may well be that those who seek recovery through intensive treatment will need to engage in a lengthy period or lifetime given to abstinence, while those who do not engage in formal treatment may enter recovery through moderation of use. A substantial number of those who enter recovery do so by reducing their consumption "to levels that would not be considered a health risk and did not incur consequences" (Sobell et al. 1996, p. 970). A number of factors may contribute to this, including severity of illness, socioeconomic resources, and even education. Those who initiate recovery through formal treatment may have more serious alcohol- and drug-related problems and consequences.

A case can be made that, while there is a robust literature on self-change/natural recovery experience and processes (Klingemann & Sobell, 2007), this research continues to be over-looked, even repressed, by a wider field dominated by the biomedical models. "Self-change," the possibility of recovery without formal intervention—even the possible recovery pathway of return to moderate use from addiction—is seen as a challenge to both the biomedical and treatment industry perspectives. This is an instance of subjugated or marginalized perspectives in addiction studies.

Thus, there appear to be different paths into recovery for those on the more severe end of the addiction spectrum as opposed to those at the mild to moderate end. More research and deeper understanding is needed here. Those who examine the pathways out from addiction and into recovery certainly understand the traditional roads into recovery: formal treatment, use of mutual support groups and programs, even "brief intervention" (White & Kurtz, 2006b). Others, however, use a variety of terms to describe alternate entryways into a healthier life-course: spontaneous remission or spontaneous recovery, "natural recovery," or self-change (Klingemann & Sobell, 2007).

Finally, what might a counseling approach informed by natural recovery look like? Most likely, it will be outpatient work with sensitive practitioners who incorporate principles and methods of attachment-sensitive counseling, as laid out here.

SUMMARY

We have reviewed the numbers of those who struggle with addiction and harmful use of chemicals and behaviors. The overall population is in the tens of millions. We also inspected diagnostic issues as well as myths that still surround the experience of addiction. DSM-5 adds new scaffolding for a more modern, nuanced look at addiction that highlights a spectrum of troublesome disorders and helps to dispel several myths. We considered the progression of addictive behavior from fascination and contemplation through intoxication to full-blown addiction. These way stations along the road to addiction can give us a foothold on times and ways to intervene.

Next, we look at current knowledge about the neurobiology of addiction.

4

Neurobiology Basics

"Addiction reflects the control of behavior by drug actions on brain circuitry that has long served more biologically primitive and species-typical needs."

ROY WISE

". . . the human brain is an anachronistic menagerie, which confronts the psychotherapist with the challenge of treating a human, a horse, and a crocodile, all attempting to inhabit the same body."

LOUIS COZOLINO

A COMPLETE PICTURE OF ADDICTION requires some basic understanding of the neural structures and processes that undergird our experience. How the brain is built and how it works are both essential. Understanding the naturally functioning brain, we can begin to explore neural structures and functions under the impact of non-natural rewards, such as drugs or compulsive activities. The process of addiction will then stand out as a way to understand a natural system strained and over-extended, a dynamically balanced and balancing system pushed to a tipping point. Addiction can be seen as a runaway system process.

The construction of basic brain architecture, especially the networks and circuits devoted to motivation and reward, memory, stress and pain response, attachment/affiliation, and self-regulation, may leave individuals with vulnerabilities for coping with life. Mechanisms given to us for survival, such as responses to distress, or utilizing attachment to regulate emotions or stress, may be recalibrated so that drugs or compulsive activities become substitutes. This contributes to an individual's vulnerability to misuse and addiction.

In recent years there have been criticisms regarding a neurobiological perspective on addiction. The main complaint has been that neuroscience cannot be the whole story, and of course that's true (Kalant, 2009; Satel & Lilienfeld, 2013). The criticisms do not change the fact, however, that neurobiology is an essential element in the experience of addiction. Nor does criticism call into question the accuracy of neuroscience findings. No serious commentator suggests that neurobiology is irrelevant to the process of substance use and addiction. Rather, discussion abounds regarding the exact mechanisms and extent of neural involvement and its relative power as an explanation for addictive experience. Neurobiology is one level of explanation for what is a multilevel human puzzle (Satel & Lilienfeld, 2013).

A neurobiological perspective provides vital pieces of information that can tie together the facts of infant and adult attachment, the vagaries of human development, the wounds and potential strengths that accompany traumatic experience and toxic stress, into a robust conceptualization for guiding treatment and recovery. My approach incorporates the principles of interpersonal neurobiology and places these principles within the wider context of social ecology. Why is this important? Because interventions and treatments that work depend on accurate and complete information. A consilient, interconnected view of the problem is needed.

What follows will be a simplification of complex structures and processes, but should be sufficient to serve as scaffolding for what is to come. Our bodies and brains are complex and not static, but rather are developing and changing all the time.

THE HUMAN BRAIN

Neuroscience is the study of the brain and nervous systems. Neurons, neural circuits, and systems extend throughout the body and manage a variety of functions. The brain and central nervous system is the overall command center, if you will, while the peripheral systems in the extremities and connecting to organs, muscles, glands, and other systems, translate, execute, and send and receive messages. These peripheral systems also communicate the state of the organism back to the brain.

All our experience as human beings is processed through the brain. It is composed mainly of billions of neurons, organized into circuits and systems, with layers and complex branches between neurons and circuits reaching into the trillions of connections (Gazzaniga, 2008). Neurons, it seems—just like people—thrive in community. We are learning that the construction of this network, a marvel of gene-environment interaction (epigenetics), is our greatest strength as a species, but is also highly vulnerable to adversity. Experiences such as neglectful or abusive relationships, insecure attachments, toxic stress, malignant environments, can disrupt the developmental course.

Over millions of years our brains and our psycho-emotional systems have evolved in tandem beyond the tasks of survival, self-protection, and reproduction—the biological imperatives of all animals—to include a set of complementary tasks. Attaching to a tribe or clan, caring for our young, the development of language and abstract thinking, as well as the refined emotional expressions of music and poetry, the fashioning of cultures, and the development of empathy and altruism are all evolutionary achievements. The basic neural architecture that services all these varied domains resides in the brain. Evolution has built and "wired" our brains to meet complex environmental challenges and has thrust us toward more social abilities and adaptive functions (Liebermann, 2013). Neural development is the result of an intricate dance between nature and nurture, between inherited processes and structures *and* experiences, largely interpersonal experiences. Relationships and experience build brains; social interactions "wire" brain circuits. In this neural alchemy, experience is literally written into our brain architecture (Siegel, 2001a & b).

The human brain sits at the intersection of two complementary psycho-biological actions, a kind of double alchemy (Wilkinson, 2010). On the one hand, psychosocial experience builds brain networks: Biography becomes biology (Nakazawa, 2015). Experiences leave their footprints in neural wiring. On the other hand, this flesh and blood neuronal organ gives rise to a sense of self and identity: Brains give birth to psyche and mind. The product of brain activity is not just moving limbs or processing vision, it is a feeling and thinking *self*, coherent over time, aware of its purpose, and able to choose a path for living (Schore, 1994). This is an extraordinary gift and science is only beginning to comprehend how it works.

Most of our genes and brain structures are similar to what can be found in other animals, particularly in the primates, our close cousins. We share some older circuits that come into play when we are under stress or when frightened and distressed (Gazzaniga, 2008). The amygdaloid complex, for example, a more primitive part of the brain, tells us when threats are near or imminent; this helps our bodies prepare to fight, flee, or freeze. The vagal nerve complex serves a similar and complementary function (Porges, 2011, 2017). Alternatively, compassion and loving—advanced attachment behavior *par excellence*—emerged over time as part of newer circuits. The extended limbic system and its connections to orbitofrontal cortex (OFC) and other cortical structures are involved here. These circuits employ different strategies for survival. They prepare us to "tend and befriend," to band together for safety and nurturing (Taylor, 2006). These neural circuits require a calmer state in order to come into play. They are incompatible with the older, more defensive circuits that enjoy a certain priority when activated. In other words, when I am frightened or enraged, it requires much more focus to remain open and compassionate, since the more primitive circuits are telling me to fight or flee.

CHANGE IS THE RULE

Professor Allan Schore (1994, 1996, 2018) reminds us that the period from the last three prenatal months through age two or three years is a period of remarkable neural development. During this time, many neural circuits take root and expand as experience nourishes brain development. In particular, the formation of connections within the limbic (emotional) system, particularly on the right side, as well as between the limbic system and both higher cortical systems and more primitive (reward/motivational) systems, occurs at a rapid pace. These are essential systems for affect regulation and developing a sense of self.

Brains change and reform all the time; they add and prune connections in response to experience. Synaptic pathways that are regularly used are reinforced. Pathways that are used minimally or not at all are pruned. This is the basis of learning. It can also form the basis of healing in counseling and psychotherapy. Reinforcement and repetition lead to well-formed neurological pathways. Brain development continues up to at least the age of 25 years, and there is a significant period of brain remodeling in adolescence, particularly in the frontal lobes and connections between these and the limbic system.

While there may not be continued physical expansion, we now know that there is ongoing and rich interconnection, conservation, reorganization, and specialization. The brain continues to build new neural pathways, alter old ones, and recruit systems for needed tasks. Neuroscientists call this "plasticity," the brain's ability to respond and alter itself in the face of new experiences and requirements. This insures that postnatal and ongoing neural development occur under the significant influence of kinship systems, environment, culture, and social ecology. Contrary to what we believed previously, our brains are—*we* are—ongoing open systems (Caccioppo et al., 2010).

Brains are connected and open, developmentally and functionally. There is no such thing as an isolated brain. From its simplest structures to its most complex functions, the human brain is social and interpersonal (Cozolino, 2014). "Brains are embedded in bodies, and bodies in turn in families, and families are nested in communities and in particular niches in the wider social structure" (Reinarman & Granfield, 2015, p. 7).

A Basic Rule Book

I want to lay out a few basic principles of brain functioning before we move to consider specific structures and functions in addiction.

1. In primitive life forms, the brain serves life-sustaining functions (nour-ishment, survival, reproduction). In more advanced animal life forms the brain mediates both life-sustaining and life-enhancing functions, such as maternal care and social bonding, collaboration, and communication; in humans this extends to thinking, language, and culture. All these emerge from the brain.

2. Drug use and addiction/dependence have a biological basis throughout the animal kingdom (Siegel, 1989, 2005). Both humans and animals will self-administer and work for drugs; they even demonstrate with-drawal symptoms, that is, they share an innate vulnerability or "hunger" for these substances (Samorini, 2002; Siegel, 2005). Presumably animals do not bring moral failings or defects of character to the drug experience.

3. We often speak simplistically about the brain as though it were a three-pound mass of jelly that produces a kind of chemical soup (for example, depression or anxiety come from a "chemical imbalance"). Neuroscien-tists are learning that the brain actually functions more like a living system of electro-chemical patterns or "neural net profiles," constantly changing and adapting.

4. There is ongoing debate about this. One side of the debate (*modular*) tends to focus on the role of different brain areas. In this view, the brain is broken down into various modules—structures or sets of intercon-nected structures—that specialize in certain activities and these areas are defined by their functions (the cortex does thinking; the amygdala does stress or fear). The other side views the brain's activity as more interactive (*distributive processing*). The focus is not on specialization, but intercon-nection. For now, it seems that there is persuasive data on both sides and that a more *collaborationist* stance is warranted. Clearly, some neural areas seem to specialize in certain kinds of processing, but it is probably too simplistic to say "this area does this, that does that." Rather, most areas are deeply interconnected and the patterns of activity seem most important. This is certainly true in those areas implicated in addiction, such as the reward and motivation centers.

5. The brain contains neural circuitry that is essential for survival. This is both reward and motivation circuitry, as well as stress response circuitry,

developed through evolution to insure that whatever activates the circuits tends to be repeated.

6. Useful behaviors for survival activate the reward and motivational circuitry naturally (eating, drinking, reproduction). This is a basic design feature. Psychoactive drugs also activate these circuits reliably, and more powerfully and persistently, than natural reinforcers. Addictive drugs, for example, selectively activate dopamine levels—directly or indirectly—in the nucleus accumbens (NAc), a critical part of the limbic system.

7. One of the brain's main functions is to mark objects/experiences as rewarding, activating circuits that signal reward or relief ("liking"). From an evolutionary and survival perspective, however, it is not enough to know from moment to moment what one "likes." Therefore, the brain has complementary circuits that mark these objects/experiences as survival-enhancing and infuses them with motivation (energy) and desire ("wanting"). This enables the organism to pursue and repeat survival-enhancing interactions. These objects/experiences are also marked with *salience*; they become higher-order values and preferred options. The more rewarding the experience, the more it is invested with salience and likely to be repeated. To motivate goal-seeking, liking and wanting have to collaborate. Feeling good leads to wanting more. In the brain "liking" is mediated by natural opioids (e.g. endorphins); "wanting" (craving) is facilitated by dopamine.

8. Addiction has been described as "motivated repetition that gives rise to deep learning" (Lewis, 2015, p. 173). Genes and experience, but particularly experience that carries emotional weight (salience), change the brain. This occurs over time with addiction, and deep entrenching of learned behaviors into synaptic pathways, principally within the brain's "motivational core" (the striatum, OFC, and amygdala) occurs as well. Liking, wanting, seeking, craving, getting—these all become unified within addiction.

9. Learning changes the brain, not in one or two systems but in many. So does addiction. So does falling in love. Learning what feels good and how to get more is a fundamental basis of learning, so is learning how to escape what hurts (Lewis, 2015). Learning's constant companion and

collaborator is emotion (fear, anxiety, desire). Addiction takes emotion and desire to an extreme; it is a runaway process.

10. The drive to repeat, while built into the brain's dynamic processing, can also be a form of learning gone rogue. If pushed too far, this normal and natural process can tip over into excess. The experience of intense wanting and behavioral seeking carves deep neural ruts (entrenched synaptic patterns) within the brain (Lewis, 2015). Dopamine drives this process.

11. The major classes of drugs related to addiction are psychostimulants, opiates, ethanol, nicotine, marijuana, and phencyclidine-like drugs (PCP, "angel dust"). The major addictive behavioral manifestations include gambling, internet gaming, sexual addictions, and eating disorders. While each has specific actions within a variety of structures in the brain, there is also a common set of interconnected pathways, several of which utilize neural structures in more than one way.

12. Research into these neural systems provides working models of brain function that can lead to both chemical and behavioral interventions (Baylin & Hughes, 2016; Hughes, 2007). Focus on attachment, attunement, and the elaboration of neural structures and functions can provide clues about medication-assisted, behavioral, and other forms of treatment. Attachment-sensitive counseling must incorporate these modalities.

ADDICTION-RELATED NEURAL SYSTEMS

As addiction neuroscience comes into its own, it appears that a number of addictive disorders (substance-related disorders, behavioral disorders such as gambling or sexual addiction, or eating disorders like bulimia), share a *common underlying pathological process*. This process is set in motion by developmental (attachment) failures that leave their imprint on psychobiological structures (van der Kolk, 2014) and operate through neurobiological pathways. The interplay of genetic, experiential (attachment), and environmental (social ecology) factors results in miswiring of neural circuits as well as psychosocial deficits. What psychiatrist Aviel Goodman calls the common "addictive process" is a shared, psychobiological dynamic that we see at work across a range of addictive behaviors (1995, 2008, 2009).[1]

The conceptualization of a shared common process underlying addictive behaviors helps us to understand a number of different manifestations. Persons diagnosed with one condition, for example alcoholism, have a higher than average likelihood of being diagnosed with another addictive condition (multiple or "comorbid" addictions), concurrently or at some point in their lives. Biological relatives of these persons have a higher than average likelihood of also being diagnosed, and likewise the possibility of responding to similar treatments. In addition, these disorders share a number of clinical features across persons, such as similar course of illness, tendency to relapse, behavioral substitution (one addictive manifestation comes under control and a different one arises), common relationship themes (for example, low self-esteem, self-centeredness), comorbidity, and/or co-occurring affective or stress-related disorders, such as depression or PTSD.

Goodman has also laid out a convincing argument that the shared addictive process underneath specific manifestations is the result of interpenetrating impairments in several neurobiological systems: reward/motivation, affect regulation, and behavioral regulation (Goodman, 2008, 2009). Impairment in one system adversely affects functioning in connected systems. In addition, he sees these impairments as the outcomes of interaction between genetic factors and adverse psychosocial and behavioral experiences, such as trauma, maternal gestational stress, and exposure to adverse and stressful environments (2009).

From a psychobiological view, Goodman's thesis represents an integration that is highly persuasive. It helps to explain a number of phenomena in addiction while tying together neurobiological architecture and function with compulsive behaviors. What it misses, of course, is the full social ecology of relationships and environmental systems that surround addicted individuals.

Systems One by One

To understand the inner workings and experience of addiction requires some neural topography in the form of five interrelated systems/functions. These intertwine and connect neural and hormonal systems that communicate reciprocally:

- Reward and motivation (memory) systems;
- Stress response systems;
- Self-regulation circuits and processes;
- Attachment and affiliation systems;
- Pain response systems

1. REWARD/MOTIVATION (MEMORY) SYSTEMS

The *mesocorticolimbic dopamine system* (MDS) is a neurobiological hub for reward and motivation. It is located deep within the brain, behind the eyes, and in the center of the skull. Essentially, it is the site of the rewarding effects of psychoactive drugs and compulsive behaviors, even though specific drugs act in other systems as well and have varying effects. The MDS utilizes structures in the (emotional/motivational) limbic system, but also has communication pathways reaching into both the more primitive and the more advanced (cortical) brain structures. It is richly interconnected.

While other systems throughout the body and a complex array of neurotransmitters and hormones are implicated in, and affected by, addictive compulsions and behaviors, the MDS "lights up" on brain scans while the person is engaged in substance use. This is the normal, expected action of any naturally rewarding behavior, such as eating food or having sex, and of using a psychoactive substance, like having a beer, smoking a cigarette, or snorting cocaine. We can also see this system "light up" on brain scans *in anticipation of* chemical use or intoxicating/rewarding behavior, even before the stimulus or drug ever gets to the brain or the behavior begins. Apparently, when the brain expects something good to happen, it sets the table in advance. Desire (craving) for the experience leads the way.[2]

The MDS is the brain's central reward system and dopamine (DA) is its main messenger chemical. Other neurochemicals are engaged as well, including endogenous or naturally occurring opioids and cannabinoids. Activity in this area of the brain designates our experiences as "survival enhancing"; these activities are marked with pleasure (reward) and salient memory, as well as heightened motivation for seeking them out and repeating the experience with them. We remember these experiences with fondness and anticipation. This is the primary reward/motivation circuit in the brain and it is believed that because critical portions of this circuit function below consciousness and preverbally, alcohol and other drug dependence is able to develop without conscious recognition and is resistant to conscious control (Erickson, 2007, p. 53).

The MDS is ancient and functions like a dopamine pump for the rest of the brain. Neural projections innervate primitive brain structures essential for arousal, reward, motivation to seek rewards, and preferences of one reward over another, as well as the nucleus accumbens (NAc), part of the striatum which is responsible for coordinating reward, motivation, and planned movement (Fisher, 2004). Activation of these areas signals reward or pleasure either in the normal range or in response to the hyperstimulation of drugs of abuse. This interconnected bundle of circuits helps the organism prioritize those things that are useful for survival and triggers repetitious seeking.

Finally, the prefrontal (PFC) and orbitofrontal (OFC) cortices, the neural areas for planning, decision-making, inhibiting, and moderating behavior, interact—in ways that are not yet fully understood—to help the individual make choices to seek rewards, or not. These pathways are integrated with other brain regions that color the experience emotionally and direct the individual's choices and actions. The amygdala assesses whether the experience is pleasurable (or as pleasing as expected), and ties the experience to a variety of cues, both internal (emotions) and external (environment). The hippocampus records memories of where, when, and with whom the experience occurs. Then, of course, the PFC and OFC coordinate and process the information and determine subsequent behavior. It is important to note that with addiction the sensitivity of neural systems for reward, incentive motivation, and memory (called "Go" systems) is heightened, while cognitive control and inhibition ("Stop" systems) are gradually lessened (Volkow, Fowler, & Wang, 2003; Goldstein & Volkow, 2011).

All these areas communicate back and forth in feedback loops, part of a neural net, often via the neurotransmitter glutamate. They also change and adapt with experience. The activation of reward, motivational, and memory circuitry by addictive drugs facilitates repetitive alcohol and other drug use, helping to create the "habit" of drug use (Lewis, 2015). This initiates mechanisms that produce the behavioral and physiological characteristics—the "signature response"—of addiction.

MDS Neurochemistry: A More Detailed Look

While dopamine has been "consistently associated" with reinforcement from drugs of abuse, we now know that several other neurochemicals are also involved. Natural opioids, gamma-aminobutyric acid (GABA), glutamate, and serotonin, to name a few, are also implicated. Use of drugs increases the magnitude and duration of chemical release as much as five- to ten-fold over the natural process, and in addition strengthens the motivational salience of the experience, leading to greater drug seeking (Volkow & Li, 2004). "Drug-induced increases in dopamine will inherently motivate further procurement of more drug . . . [it] will also facilitate conditioned learning, so previously neutral stimuli [sights, smells, acquaintances] that are associated with the drug become salient" (Volkow & Li, 2004, p. 964). This "associative learning" guarantees that previously neutral stimuli will now increase reward expectancy *by themselves*, stimulating both craving and renewed drug-seeking (Koob & Le Moal, 2005, 2008).

We know that some drugs, such as cocaine or amphetamine, stimulate production and release of dopamine quickly and in much greater than normal amounts. This creates a tsunami of dopamine that, because of the drug's ability to degrade normal mechanisms for deleting dopamine in the synapses (reuptake), lasts far longer than required. This short-term effect can be extended with continued chemical use as the brain adapts to repeated exposure to the drug and periodic flooding with dopamine. The MDS becomes sensitized or super-reactive to this process, while over time becoming depleted of natural dopamine.

Finally, these processes of adaptation and sensitization lead to "lighting up" of the exact same neural areas *in anticipation of taking the drug*. The MDS has come to expect the flood—indeed because of dopamine depletion may "need" the flood—and ensures that all is ready and the likelihood of drug use is increased. That is, in response to cues in the environment or internally (through stress, or pain, or associational cues), the experience of craving (runaway "wanting"!) is triggered and assists in motivating the individual to seek and use.

Psychoactive drugs corrupt neural processing in ways that heighten desire and promote reward-seeking while depressing brain processes for judgment, risk assessment, clear thinking, and decision-making. Thresholds for reward are reset so that there is (a) decreased sensitivity for natural reinforcers, (b) disruption of inhibitory mechanisms and salience, and (c) decreased interest in everyday, natural rewards (Volkow, Fowler, & Wang, 2003). When this is combined with conditioned (associative) learning, euphoric memory, and lack of competition from other rewards, acquiring the drug becomes the main motivational drive and life's top priority.

Neuroscientists now believe that disruption of neurotransmitter systems throughout the MDS is a hallmark of addiction. Altered function of these circuits may occur because of (a) genetic heritability, (b) long-term exposure and adaptation to alcohol and other drugs, or more likely (c) a combination of genetic vulnerability, drug exposure, experience, and environmental influence, such as attachment and/or trauma via developmental miswiring (Erickson, 2007, p. 51). Dysregulation of MDS circuits, in combination with drug exposure and environmental influence, is a neurological adaptive response, and causes individuals to "connect" with alcohol and other drugs in a highly personal way. The addict feels that this or that drug brings him into "balance" or helps her to feel "normal."

Craving and Relapse

Childress (2006) and others are mapping a more refined analysis of limbic structures involved in desire for drug use and in return to drug use following moderation or abstinence (relapse). It is in the interconnections between highly sensitized brain reward systems and the cortical areas responsible for inhibiting behavior and judging the advisability of drug use that an important area of neural dysfunction has been identified (Goodman, 2008). This is where the term "hijacking" came into play.

Continued use of drugs increases the limbic craving for use while at the same time decreasing the functions of cortical control structures. In facing a choice to use again, the individual is literally amped-up with desire (craving) and disabled in thinking and choosing wisely. Struggling addicts are also likely to begin experiencing physical symptoms of use (racing heart rate, hand tremors) and psychological symptoms (anxious anticipation, pleasurable memories of previous use) as well. This is the experience of craving and it can help us to grasp more fully the experience of relapse.

The effects of drugs on projections to the frontal lobes are what eventually lead to the impaired control over drug use, through a reduction of cortical decision-making functions. However, users continue to have a significant element of choice in their compulsive use (Hart, 2014). Those who are pharmacologically dependent approach chemical use or addictive activities from a different starting point, namely a compromised brain. Their ability to make choices is impaired. The neurobiological experience is now one of "needing."

This is where thoughtful intervention can be helpful. Often it is the contingencies or results from one's choices that can provide a way forward. Whether it is legal consequences (DUI, or arrest for intoxicated/criminal behavior, or involvement in drug court), medical consequences (ER visits, injury, infections, or disease management), school or work complications (poor performance), or relational consequences (breakups, divorce), encountering misusers or struggling addicts when they must confront the aftermath of intoxicated choices is an opportunity for change. Screening, intervention, and referral, amplified with motivational enhancement, can move clients along in their readiness for change.

In addition, as Katehakis (2016) and others point out, addicts who have begun the change process often relapse, and not always to the chemicals or behaviors they used before (called "behavioral substitution"). For example, alcoholics commonly replace the sugar in alcohol with sugary (ice cream, anyone?) or fatty foods (Kenny, 2011); gambling addicts may turn to cocaine or methamphetamine. And, rather than following balanced and life-sustaining connections, they turn to another obsessive and single-minded focus on new pursuits (such as workaholism) that once again bring shame and chaos. In a new way, then, they find themselves caught up in addiction's "dark side" (Koob 2009a & b; Koob & Le Moal, 2005). For Katehakis (2016), Goodman (2008), and others, this cycle of compulsion/substitution/relapse argues for a common underlying psychobiological and pathological process of addiction, and a psychosocial process of substituting false relationships for reality.

Attachment-sensitive counseling with addiction has to attend to this process. In combination with counseling, psychoeducation, psychosocial and behavioral interventions, utilizing a number of potential new anti-craving medications (such as naltrexone for alcoholism[3] and buprenorphine or methadone for opioid addiction[4]), is becoming the accepted standard in current evidence-based practice.[5] In addition, working closely with Marlatt's cognitive-behavioral model of relapse prevention (see below) provides the counselor with many areas of potential intervention.

Relapse Prevention

In the following graphic, readers will notice a basic chain of events running through the middle of the diagram, moving from left to right. *Lifestyle imbalance* on the left begins the chain that leads to *high-risk situations* in the center. If the individual *lapses*, the model envisions the chain ending at the *"abstinence violation effect"* and a decrease in personal agency, which will likely begin a full relapse episode. However, above and below this central chain are many potential points and tactics of intervention that can prevent the slide toward relapse. For example, at the very beginning of the chart, "lifestyle imbalance" can be counteracted with lifestyle interventions, such as exercise, meditation, recreation, and the like.

The counselor continuously monitors the recovering client's lifestyle, making her or him aware of self-regulation and balance in living. This also establishes a place for building "recovery capital" as a means of restoring balance (White & Cloud, 2008). Awareness and effort counteract rationalizing and denial. Understanding past relapses and warning signs, strengthening mindfulness, self-monitoring, and behavioral assessment can help to prevent high-risk situations from getting out of hand. Preparing clients for potential relapse and discussing responses (for example, urge and lapse management) are essential in early recovery. I have found these tactics and tools invaluable in helping those in recovery maintain health and sobriety.

Two catchphrases in this model need brief explanation. *AIDs* or "appar-

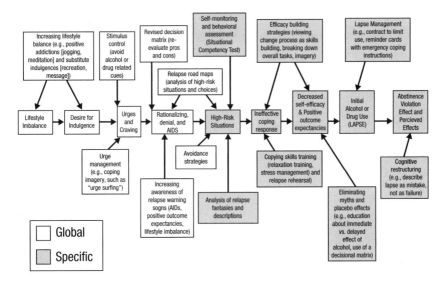

Figure 4.1. Cognitive-behavioral Model of Relapse Prevention. *Source: Larimer, Palmer & Marlatt (1999), Public domain.*

ently irrelevant decisions" can lead to situations with high-risk. Walking into a bar, ostensibly "just to buy cigarettes," could place a recovering alcoholic in peril. The choice may seem irrelevant to relapse but is fraught with danger. Joe's relocation of his father's home-bar into his own home (Chapter 1) is one such decision. *AVE*, or "abstinence violation effect," refers to thoughts and feelings that arise from a lapse or "slip." A decision to abstain from marijuana, for example, may be followed by a slip. Guilt or shame accompanied by negative self-criticism can follow; discomfort left unattended can lead to renewed use. This chart can furnish the attentive counselor with a useful toolkit.

2. STRESS RESPONSE SYSTEMS

As the extended MDS is to reward and motivation, so the *hypothalamic-pituitary-adrenal axis*, or HPA, is to stress response.[6] The wiring and function of this important neural and hormonal system are critical for understanding normal response to stress as well as the excessive or panicked reactions to toxic stress, threat, and trauma. A dysfunctional stress system can predispose individuals to seeking relief in "substitute relationships"; it is a significant factor in vulnerability to addiction (Herman, 2015).

An alert and sensitive sentinel system is essential for survival in the wild and in the jungle of human relationships. Linking of memory and situational awareness with stress-responsive systems provides real survival value through rapid behavioral and psychological responses. Experiences of stress or threat trigger a cascade of biological responses, flooding our bodily systems with hormones and chemical messengers (Danese & McEwen, 2012; Everly & Lating, 2013). Chemicals, like cortisol or adrenaline, initiate physical actions and reactions, as well as functional and even structural changes that help to meet the dangers brought by stress and adversity. This is the way our systems are designed (Sinha, 2008). When the danger passes, our bodies self-regulate and return to balance. However, adversity also engraves the experience into learning and memory so that the occurrence of similar situations triggers the stress response more quickly. Again, this is how the process is supposed to work.

The neurological stress systems (amygdala, HPA and SAM axes, vagal complex) and their associated structures drive our response to stressful situations. The orbitofrontal cortex, or OFC, is critical for adaptive responses and is richly connected. It assesses the nature of the world around us and helps to coordinate appropriate responses. It reacts slowly, however, in comparison to more primitive danger systems (amygdala, vagus). These systems interact with one another and their development is vulnerable to the social situation and to early environmental stresses (Schore, 1994; Hart, 2008).

The healthy operation of stress systems keeps us safe and ensures survival. Shaped under the right conditions, the individual's nervous and hormonal systems are prepared to function normally. Shaped under conditions of toxic stress, however, these systems can become hyper-sensitized, miswired, and uniquely vulnerable to present-day stressful conditions (Herman, 2015; Sapolsky, 1994). These influences set the organism's systems to expect a dangerous world. Childhood neglect and trauma wires neural circuits in ways that make someone's future environments feel suspect and unsafe, and put the stress response on a permanent hair-trigger (Fishbane, 2007). These early adverse conditions can also increase the allostatic burden that over time leads to premature age-related disorders and "weathering," such as cardiovascular disease, metabolic and inflammatory disorders, and cognitive decline (Danese & McEwen, 2012).

Connection and attachment are the lifeblood of development. However, when development does not progress well—when attachment is thwarted, or undermined, or betrayed—cracks open up and the individual feels the need for substitutes. Stress enters the picture when expected attachment relationships do not materialize or are distorted (Harris, 2018). Affect, stress, and neural dysregulation as well as inability to turn to others for co-regulation (emotional soothing and comfort) contribute to the onset, continued use, and relapse into drug use and addictive behaviors (Daily, 2012).

When these systems are miswired, malfunction, or are on constant yellow or red alert, the results can be disastrous. The continuing or excess operation of stress-related chemicals can lead to runaway neurotoxicity or inflammation, which can in turn generate a number of neurocognitive or immunological illnesses. They affect physical and mental health. Behavioral health can also be affected, as dysfunction of stress response systems leads to taxed and over-extended coping mechanisms, deficits in self-regulation, and resort to substitutes for chemical comforting (alcohol, drugs, food) and behavioral self-soothing (gambling, internet gaming, shopping, sex).

Cortisol is the primary neurochemical of the HPA system in humans. Elevated cortisol levels appear to be part of the biological cost of environmental adversity and adaptive functioning (Gunnar, 1992). Research over several decades points to stress and release of cortisol as a major cause of childhood illness and is associated with degradation of stress-related neurocircuits, immunosuppression, and long-term inflammatory and immunological illnesses in adulthood (Gunnar, 1992; Felitti et al., 1998). Toxic stress is also associated with substance misuse and addiction (Dubé et al., 2003; Dubé et al., 2001).

We know that early trauma sensitizes the HPA so that it hyper-responds to later stresses with excess production of cortisol and other neurochemicals. These in turn heighten the stress reaction, which can trigger relapse to alcohol and other drug use. Cortisol also works in the reward systems to heighten the effects of alcohol and drugs, making them more potent. This is a neurobiological expressway to the experience of relapse (Stephens, McCaul, & Wand, 2014).

Catch-22

Early, even prenatal, experiences naturally establish baseline levels of operation and affect how neural structures respond in future situations. Early stress and trauma have negative effects on the formation of reward *and* stress response systems (van der Kolk, 2014; van der Kolk, McFarlane, & Weisaeth, 1996/2007). Facing adversity in later life, the overall system, stressed by wear-and-tear, can overload or reach a tipping point, making the individual emotionally reactive and cognitively impaired, less able to evaluate and appropriately respond to the stresses to which she or he has become deeply sensitized (Danese & McEwen, 2012). In addition, systems that were initially shaped by toxic environments may also be continually depleted in later years as the strain of remaining constantly "on alert" takes its toll. Emotional reactivity and relief-seeking through substitutes may become an embedded lifestyle.

With the advent of psychobiological studies, we are learning that what began as a social and interpersonal process (trauma and adversity) is transformed over time into a physiological process as well, and becomes more deeply inscribed into the brain (McFarlane, 2016; van der Kolk & McFarlane, 2006). Environmental elements are folded into the traumatic memories as triggers, and augmented in memory, that can become catalysts for increasing reactivity. Certain situations and cues, particularly those that have sensitized the individual in the past, may inhibit a clear assessment of the current situation, narrow the range of responses that are seen as viable, throw the regulation of emotional and thinking processes out of balance, and consequently interfere with choice and action. In addition, humans, as opposed to animals in the wild, can become "worriers," revisiting or anticipating situations of distress. This increases the emotional and neurochemical burdens on stress systems.

Early Treatment

The impact on motivation and stress response recounted above is daunting. Any counselor who tries to intervene in active addiction must take these facts into account. However, if the client is motivated to seek solutions and has a trusted advisor/counselor for the journey, then the next steps can commence.

1. The question of recovery group support and participation should be raised. The testimony of many group members (12 Step, Rational Recovery, Women for Sobriety) suggests that this is a helpful step in early treatment/recovery. But, it is not for everyone and timing is important. The counselor should explore what group participation means to the client and let him or her know that our best science recommends it (Kaskutas, 2009; Moos & Moos, 2006). However, alternatives for enlisting group support, such as therapy groups, church support and service groups, local informal affiliations of recovering persons,[7] and committed family members can help as well. It may be that formal recovery group participation (for example Alcoholics Anonymous) may be more effective later in the recovery process. Stanford's Keith Humphreys (quoted in White, 2011) suggests that counselors recommend searching out group affiliation like a dating process. If you like what you see, stay; if not, move on.

2. The counselor needs a working relationship with a physician who can prescribe and monitor collaborative medication-assisted treatment. Using appropriate medication approaches, combined with psychosocial treatments, is recommended, despite hesitations from some scientific circles and the general public (Connery, 2015; Roman et al., 2011). Use of medication-assisted approaches is an evidence-based, best practice.

3. Standard psychosocial counseling approaches, especially behaviorally oriented therapies, enhanced with mindfulness and stress-reduction tools may also be used. In addition, the therapist should keep in mind the importance of body-oriented approaches to healing (physical exercise, yoga, dance, qigong, karate), especially in the treatment of co-occurring addiction and trauma work (Ogden et al., 2006; Zschucke, Heinz, & Ströhle, 2012).

4. Finally, ongoing recovery management, client monitoring, and reintervention when needed, and ongoing recovery support services are essential components in fostering long-term recovery (See Chapter 8).

Neurobiological research is proceeding in an attempt to develop medications that can quiet the HPA response cycle (Sinha, 2007), while psychosocial research works to help buffer individuals against stress with a range of interventions, including mindfulness and the building of recovery capital (Best & Laudet, 2010). It is also worth noting that enhanced and enriched environments, including proactive caregiving, family support, and communal and social support, may lead to neural buffering (Lupien et al., 2009).

3. SELF-REGULATION CIRCUITS AND PROCESSES

If survival is evolution's prime directive, then for human beings regulation is our master plan. Self- and affect regulation allow us to be part of a functioning group, to be taken care of, and to make a contribution to the group's well-being. Self-regulation is geared to individual and species survival, and it is essential for a coherent sense of self. Regulation keeps emotional or stressful states within tolerable ranges of intensity and stability, and allows us to function within balanced parameters (Goodman, 2008). Attunement and attachment are the twin grounding experiences out of which self-regulation flows.

Schore returns again and again to the earliest phases of the infant's life, from the last trimester of pregnancy through the first two years. Here he focuses on the development of affect regulation as a critical achievement. Right-brain limbic and cortical areas, crucial for regulation and mature affect, wire up in this attachment dance. This dual-purpose project—regulating affect and wiring the relevant neural structures—occurs through sensitively attuned and relationally reliable caregiving. Attachment experience during this critical developmental period holds so much promise and equally important risk, and also vulnerability.

Schore speaks of the caregiver's pleasure and interest in the baby and developing child as a powerful affective experience. "Feeling felt" becomes the catalyst for emotional stability and a positive sense of self. Focused early onto the caregiver's face, the exciting experiences of pleasure and interest are communicated through the caregiver's "gaze," expression, eye contact, quality of presence, tone of voice, and reliability. Delight is contagious. When attachment fails, as it inevitably does from time to time, the responsive and engaged caregiver quickly repairs the injury. This dance of attunement, response, injury, and repair strengthens the attachment bond and instructs the child in the earliest nuances of mutual comforting and co-regulation (Schore, 2002, 2005).

Adverse environments and less-than-responsive caregiving in infancy and childhood may create the conditions for "over-reactive stress response systems and subsequent impairments in affect regulation, motivation-reward and behavioral inhibition" (Goodman, 2009, p. 4). Both prenatal and infant caregiving affect the developing stress systems. In addition, disruption of development in oxytocin and vasopressin systems, designed to facilitate nurturing and affiliation, may also occur, interrupting affect regulation and social relationships. Goodman states that this creates a psychobiological vulnerability, not only to addiction, but also to affective and anxiety disorders (2009; see also, Huizink, Mulder, & Buitelaar., 2004).

Bradshaw and Schore reinforce the point:

> Early attachment trauma is "affectively burnt in" the hierarchical apex of the limbic system and the HPA axis, the right frontal lobe. . . . Altered sociality therefore translates to altered patterns in core survival functions that govern coping behavior and stress regulation abilities (BRADSHAW & SCHORE, 2007).

For our purposes, it is important to remember that the developmental processes are psychobiological and at their heart are reliant on psychosocial exchange and respond to experience. The social, relational, and familial environment surrounding the child have a crucial role to play.

Brain development occurs through the encouraging and inhibiting actions of an attuned caregiver; the attuned attachment relationship is the safest environment for learning self-regulation. Caregivers modulate both hyper- and hypoenergetic states of the child through enjoyment, wise and loving guidance, or supportive discipline. The caregiver sets guardrails for behavior and emotions, lovingly supports the child, tolerates the child's negative reactions when necessary, and maintains the relationship as a safe haven and secure base. In these ways, the child learns constancy and patience, establishes positive feelings of self-worth, and internalizes self-regulation protocols that serve for a lifetime. As Winnicott (2012) had indicated, "good enough" mothering was needed to support and regulate the child, through reward or disciplinary reactions followed with relational repair. This process, painstakingly carried forward day-in and day-out, fosters the development of a self, building the hardware of functioning neural circuits, and writing the software of memories and internal images that are devoted to regulating affect, responding to stress, and living fully. Sensitively executed counseling and psychotherapy echoes this "good enough" caregiving template. The caregiver's behavior reflects the mores and needs of the larger social environment; so does the counselor's. A welcoming and safe counseling relationship slowly restores trust and connection, and can provide a correcting dynamic for relationship and neural repair (Baylin & Hughes, 2016). High-quality clinical relationships of this kind also intentionally build bridges to wider social networks, such as family and kinship, where these positive dynamics can be replicated.

4. ATTACHMENT/AFFILIATION SYSTEMS

Attachment has roots in our mammalian origins and is part of the equipment we need for bonding with others and for self-regulation. Together with its companions, attunement and affiliation, attachment has its origins in mother-child dialogue, through face-to-face, body-to-body, and right-brain to right-brain communication (Schore, 2001).

The limbic system is intricately connected and maintains what Katehakis calls the "dynamic geography" of human affect, affiliation, and abilities (2016, p. 50). These connections can be nurtured and enriched by appropriate care and attuned attachment behavior. However, they are also fragile and vulnerable to attachment damage, environmental distress, and familial dysfunction. "Poverty" of attachment experience—through abuse, neglect, interactive and unrepaired ruptures, misattunements large and small, and developmental trauma—can impede the building and enhancement of neural architecture and the full social and psychological development that depends on it.

We know that love and active, attuned caregiving are critical in the overall development of neural pathways (Fisher, 2004). Dopamine, oxytocin, endogenous opioids, and other neurochemicals play a decisive role in this development, facilitating the construction of pathways and systems that richly intercommunicate. Oxytocin is a pillar of the bonding process between mother and infant. It is also implicated in adult female-male attachment, as is vasopressin, a chemical that underlies the paternal instinct. These "cuddle chemicals" are essential to pair bonding in mammals (Insel et al., 1998) as well as in attachment behaviors (Nelson & Panksepp, 1998), and caring activities more generally throughout the lifespan.

However, without attuned early caregiving and later ongoing attachment relationships, these pathways are left fallow or miswired and become dysfunctional. We also know that attachment and the wider caregiving setting extends into interactions with other members of the caregiving environment (fathers, siblings, extended family). These relationships continue the process of neural wiring and help to form the social brain. Bridging out from the foundational maternal care relationship, these allocaregivers help to create expectations of safety and security, not only in the family but in the world beyond.

Reward and motivation, as well as a balanced approach to stress, assist in "belonging," making our lives tolerable and enjoyable. When life experiences—often working in tandem with genetics and adversity—conspire to build a flawed machine or to press it beyond the ability to cope, then the person reaches out for assistance to whatever or whomever is available. Substitute relationships ensue when relationship ruptures continue unrepaired.

5. PAIN

Investigators and clinicians can sometimes forget about the relief, even pleasure, which can accompany amelioration of pain. Many people begin drug use, particularly prescription opioids, to cope with acute or chronic bodily pain, or try to "drown their sorrows" and emotional distress (negative reinforcement). Drugs or some behaviors can also assist in coping with physical and emotional discomfort, social isolation, rejection, or disconnection. Additionally, pain relief is an important element in craving and relapse to drug use, as the pain of acute and post-acute withdrawal becomes salient in one's life, and leads to using once again (Koob, 2009b).

Today, with the daunting challenge of the opioid and prescription drug crisis across the country, and rising use of alcohol in the U.S. as well, it is a bit easier to point to acute and chronic physical pain as a reason for resorting to self-medication and pain relief. Modern pharmacology and medicine excels at the development and prescription of a variety of medications for pain relief. These developments accompany advances in treatment and relief for many conditions that went unaddressed in years past (Kolodny et al., 2015).

Pain medications work and are effective at what they do. They may not always eliminate pain—which is what some patients clearly desire—but they can lessen the pain experience. What these medications also do, however, is generate pharmacological dependence and in some patients a desire to continue use. This experience is not yet addiction, but it can lead one down a dangerous path. The large percentage of people who have experienced "adverse childhood experiences" and who may come to the opioid experience with a history of toxic stress, may be the most vulnerable.

There is little doubt that once a patient experiences significant pain relief, she or he will continue to want the drug that helps *as long as the pain itself continues.* In other words, as long as the painful condition perdures, the medication that addresses it will be sought. Despite development of alternative and non-medicinal treatments for pain, the experience of pharmaceutical relief can lead patients into alternate paths of drug seeking, resorting even to street drugs if legitimate drugs become withheld or are difficult or too expensive to procure.

Physical and Social Pain

Physical pain is one thing. It is less clear, however, how stress and emotional pain can lead down the same road. Intriguingly, there exists a slippery connection between physical and emotional pain that may have neural foundations. Those seeking relief from pain often discover that medications that lessen physical pain can also address elements of emotional pain, and vice-versa. Science may be catching up to this discovery (DeWall et al., 2010). And when we open the discussion to distressing experiences of social pain, such as isolation, rejection, and marginalization, cultural disconnection, or social dislocation, the discussion becomes even more challenging. It can be difficult to convince the general population, as well as many researchers and general practitioners, about the notion of substance use and addictive disorders as adaptive strategies that emerge from trying to address social and cultural forces. However, drug-seeking in order to address emotional or social pain is more common than we know.

Affective and social neuroscience, and neurobiological research into the brain's pain systems, may be able to help. What is becoming clear from the work of Naomi Eisenberger (2015; 2012a & b; 2011), Jaak Panksepp (Panksepp, 2003; Stein et al., 2007), and others is that the neurological systems for physical pain may supply a bridge to understand important phenomena around pain more generally.

Perhaps the first thing to note is that several neurological systems that register physical pain and motivate us to seek its resolution are shared between experiences of physical and emotional/social pain. There are indications that the neural systems for experiencing and responding to pain (insula, cingulate cortex, somatosensory cortex) are wired in such a way that processing physical and social pain, especially the pain of marginalization, social rejection/exclusion, or grief, overlap. Several neuroscientists suggest that the social attachment system may have "piggybacked" onto the physical pain system as a result of evolution (Eisenberger, 2011; Panksepp, 2003). Isolation, after all, is a threat to survival. When social relationships are threatened, the brain's pain signal is recruited to call attention, just as distress vocalizations are (Heilig et al., 2016).

Researchers are not in complete agreement about this—physical and social pain are clearly distinguishable and the brain seems able to tell them apart—suggesting that, even though there is overlap in similar brain areas (Kross et al., 2011), these experiences are not interchangeable (Woo et al., 2014). Nevertheless, social rejection and grief "hurt."

"Physical and social pain [that is, feelings associated with social rejection, exclusion, loss of connection] rely on shared neurobiological and neural substrates" with physical pain centers. It is as though "the social-attachment system—which ensures social bonding and connection—may have piggy-backed onto the physical-pain system, borrowing the pain signal to highlight social disconnection and motivate social re-connection" (EISENBERGER, P. 42).

Shared Pain Circuits Rooted in Attachment

Let's dwell on this for a moment. Reward and relief from pain, or loneliness, or rejection, can come through attuned caregiving presence. Naturally occurring opiates are present in the brain for both analgesia (lessening of pain) and to signal reward (euphoria). Oxytocin, for example, appears to have analgesic as well as affiliative properties. These positive, rewarding effects may help to alleviate isolation distress as well as encourage attachment behaviors. Manipulation of natural opioid levels can encourage social contact (Nelson & Panksepp, 1998, p. 441).

Rooted in attachment, experiences of touch, holding, and warmth trigger endogenous μ-opioids for relief of physical pain; opioids within our brain circuits soothe the pain of emotional distress as well, and form the chemical glue that binds infants and caregivers together. When I am hurt or frightened on the playground, for instance, I cry, and mama comes running. Her soothing brings relief through attunement, care, and neural chemistry (Stein et al., 2007, p. 513). These attachment experiences are woven into the strategies we learn for social attachment, emotional connection, and analgesia. The neural circuits that signal safety, relief, and connection are also involved in experiences of pain (Eisenberger et al., 2011b). Connection can make pain tolerable.[8]

Research on humans and animals supports the notion that physical and social pain "rely on shared neurobiological and neural substrates" (Eisenberger, 2012a, p. 42; Hsu et al., 2013; Kross et al., 2011), through chemical endogenous opioid-related (μ-opioid) and cannabinoid processes as well as areas of shared neural activity (cingulate, insular, and somatosensory cortices). These areas are activated with sensations of physical pain and with experiences of social rejection, loss of connection, and affective distress.

An understanding of vulnerability to addiction as a substitute relationship relies on these mechanisms (Stein et al., 2007). These also lead us to the exploration of self-medication as a coping strategy. When someone learns that the drugs or behavior that can lessen bodily pain can also address emotional distress (Eisenberger, 2011, 2012a & b), then the process of self-medication can begin. Taking opioids, drinking alcohol, or other chemicals (and behaviors that have what it takes) can be a resort to self-comfort and coping with life stresses.[9]

For many people in contemporary society, larger feelings of dis-ease, of loss, of estrangement from others, of interpersonal rejection, of societal fragmentation can be acutely painful or can lurk in the background as an ever-present stressor. As we will see in Chapter 9, this experience of ecological dis-ease, societal fragmentation, and cultural dislocation may function as a hidden engine underneath addictive behaviors.

SUMMARY

This chapter helps us to understand that there are multiple dynamic systems, experiences, and environmental factors—all of them interacting to create the unique matrix that is *this* person's set of challenges and potential solutions—involved in the development of our human brains. Addiction is a complex phenomenon with physiological, genetic, psychological, environmental and even spiritual elements intermixing and mutually influencing one another. Understanding the neurological elements involved can help us to take a step toward comprehension.

The next chapter will take us into the world of attachment and attunement, helping us to comprehend the formation (and deformation) of valuable neurological circuits and inner experiences.

5

❖❖❖

Wired to Connect: Addiction as an Attachment Disorder

"... we are born into relationships and come to our own individual identity
while resting upon social connectivity."

LOUIS COZOLINO

"A person is a person because of other people."

ZULU FOLK SAYING

I TELL MY YOUNGEST SON, Rusty, that I first met him on "the toaster." Having heard the story many times before, he smiles and pats my hand patronizingly (he's 14 years old), then he moves on to his next project. For me, however, that moment of meeting is indelibly etched in my memory.

After 23 hours of labor, my wife was exhausted, and we were worried. Nothing was happening. The doctors finally decided on a caesarean procedure and rushed us through the preparations. Within a short time our Rusty was born. He had to be unraveled from the umbilical cord that kept him trapped and immobile. His head never engaged the birth canal. Now, however, we were finally able to relax. The nurses cleaned him up and placed him in a small bed under a heat lamp ("the toaster") to keep him warm. It was quiet.

When invited, I approached the bed and the space between newborn Rusty and me seemed filled with keen anticipation and even a sense of magic. Unprepared for what might happen, I gently said, "Hello, Rusty Oliver." Immediately, his head snapped around to the direction of my voice and his whole body seemed to reach for me. Minutes old, his eyes still glued shut with medication, his body seemed eager for connection.

For me, this first encounter with Rusty is a metaphor for the reality of attachment. I can still feel its power. It doesn't lessen the wonder or sacredness I experience to know that critical chemical and biological processes helped to mediate this moment. In fact, I stand in awe of the complexity—multifaceted, multilayered processes between us and inside each of us—that was involved in that first meeting. I tasted the truth that nature prepares newborns for social engagement and connection. Nature also provides caregivers with inborn capacities to respond.

Susan Hart, in her book *The Impact of Attachment* (2011), explains the dynamics of these early moments with Rusty and the critical importance of attachment in the early months of life. As she describes, an "innate readiness" motivates the infant from the beginning to be available for connection and to engage in a synchronized dance with the caregiver. Caregivers also are available for this dance which is mediated by "tend and befriend" neurochemicals (vasopressin and oxytocin) in the caregivers' brains as well as reward chemicals (such as dopamine and natural opiates) in a variety of neural structures in the brains of both infants and caregivers. Attachment choreography shapes the architecture of our developing brains and psycho-emotional systems. Personal transactions build neural and social connections and are essential for healthy human development. Our neural machinery anticipates, indeed expects, these interactions; without them, there is over time an experience of pain and loss. The absence of attuned connection betrays an existential promise woven into our human fabric. As we have seen, without these interactions—or with abusive, traumatic, or neglectful interactions—a troubled future becomes more likely.

Hart goes on to say:

> One purpose of the child's innate signals is to facilitate attachments with adults and trigger caregiving behavior. All the infant's communication systems are open to beings that resemble humans and to events that resemble human behavior. Immediately after birth, babies explore their environment and attempt to make sense of what they are seeing, hearing, and feeling. The ability to reach out, respond to, and organize in relation to the environment is strong from the first moments of life (2011, P. 9).

ATTACHMENT

Closeness and connection with others is essential for living. Humans do not depend on survival of the fittest, but "survival of the nurtured" (quoted in Nakazawa, 2015, p. 145). The old debates about nature versus nurture have given way to appreciation of the critical importance of nurturing environments and social ecology. Nature and nurture dance together. This means that "the modern human brain's primary environment is our matrix of social relationships" (Cozolino, 2014, p. 1).

Our mutual connectivity within this matrix is perhaps our greatest strength as a species. Mothers and newborns nuzzle and feed, but so much more is happening. We now know that a double-sided matrix is put into operation. On the one hand, powerful chemicals are released in the brains of both caretaker and child—natural opiates, cannabinoids, dopamine, oxytocin, GABA—and provide both reward and calm. The actions of these chemicals strengthen the natural bonds of relationship and connection, acting like a kind of "chemical glue" and preparing the ground for the wiring of connections between neurons and the forming of new and more elaborate neural structures.

On the other hand, in tandem with this neural construction, a psycho-emotional relationship is built. This relationship (a) maintains survival, safety, and security, (b) assists in learning how to calm and self-soothe—what is called self-regulation—and (c) fosters lasting impressions of my caregiver, our relationship, and the world of relationships it represents. These mental representations or internal working models are stored in early implicit, and increasingly explicit, memories and help to generate a sense of self. Brain development and the construction of an inner world go hand in hand. In this psychobiological alchemy, "biography becomes biology" (Nakazawa, 2015) and biology becomes the foundation for the emergence of a self (Schore 1994, 2016; Siegel, 2001a & b).

The security and strength of the attachment bond fuels the formation of identity. As the infant learns trust in relationship to caregivers, she also learns step by step how to regulate her inner states and behaviors. Back-and-forth (or "serve and return") interactions trigger neural and chemical changes that help the partners to modulate and balance their emotions.[1] This capacity for self-regulation—in effect a kind of co-regulation—defines the core self, its developing autobiographical narrative, and its stance vis-à-vis the environment. Attachment, then, is the ground out of which our self emerges and it is our best defense against adversity, stress, and psychopathology. These activities become the neural and psychological foundations of our identity, and the dynamic roots of our humanity.

It is important here to remind ourselves that these neural, psychological, and social changes are happening concurrently. Each level of change and development interpenetrates the others. We study these changes separately from within separate disciplines and this gives the impression that they are distinct processes when in fact they are facets of one complex, multi-layered process. Allan Schore, the developmental neuropsychologist, says that the entire process is "psychobiological" (2001b, p. 302).

Attachment Transaction

Let's slow down here; we've quickly covered a lot of territory and need to appreciate what's happening. While our different disciplines can tease apart this or that aspect of human development, the weaving together is truly awe-inspiring.

Take, for example, Katie (18 months old) and her mother, Laura (35 years), playing on the parents' bed. They are in harmony, attuned. Laura feels a surge of love for her daughter and pulls her into a warm snuggle. Laura's brain reward centers and associated structures are flooded with pleasure and motivational chemicals (natural opiates, dopamine) as well as bonding chemicals (oxytocin). She sighs with delight as her mind flutters from memories of Katie's birth, to the feeling of safety in her bed with Brad, her husband. She experiences herself as "Mom" and loves it.

Katie has a similar "psychobiological experience." Dopamine, GABA, and opiates are released in her brain, particularly in the connected systems of her right brain, which are developing at this time as she registers this moment in her mind's eye with a feeling and memory of safety. Under the influence of these chemicals, connections are built between neurons in her brain that mediate reward, memory, and calm. At the same time mental representations of warm safety in her mother's arms are fused with this picture of them together through activity in the cortex and hippocampus, part of the brain's extended limbic system. This is a collection of neural circuits whose primary functions include emotion and memory. Katie feels valued in this moment and hears her mother's soothing voice. Right now, she is loved and the world is safe. She is ready for anything.

Understanding our abilities for attachment and social functioning, and their roots in neural structures, will help us to appreciate the delicacy and profound fragility of brain organization. The dance of attachment, working in tandem with the environment, with here and now relationships, as well as genetic and biological capabilities, wires and enhances the brain. Various relational experiences, however, particularly if they are traumatic or highly stressful, may alter the attachment equation and create faulty wiring and system vulnerabilities that can lead to problems in living. Psychological elements that emerge alongside neural functions can also be disrupted by faulty attachment experiences.

THE ATTACHMENT PARADIGM

Events that occur during infancy, especially transactions with the social environment, are indelibly imprinted into the structures that are maturing the first years of life. ALLAN SCHORE, 2014

John Bowlby, originator of attachment theory, was committed to anchoring his nascent perspective in the findings of biological science. He believed that psychoanalytic thinking would be enhanced through detailed empirical observation of infant-caretaker relationships and comparison with findings from ethology about those very same relationships across the animal kingdom. Connecting attachment with the biological sciences, he believed, provided a firm footing for psychological study. Ethology became Bowlby's touchstone.

Today there is a blossoming of interest in the connection of attachment theory with another biological science. An explosion of discoveries and information in the field of neurobiology, aided by technological advances, has captured the imaginations of scientists and moved us toward a joining of perspectives in collaborative exploration. Attachment can now be studied with a new partner: neuroscience.

Attachment is a process of interpersonal exchange that is built step-by-step by the interactions between children and their caregivers, primarily the person who provides mothering and responsive care.[2] The interactions are an intricate dance in which each partner is active, although initially the engagement is asymmetrical (Hart, 2011). In the early stages the more active partner is the mother, who responds to her infant with warmth and timely responses; increasingly, however, her baby becomes a more active partner, learning to engage with her, anticipating and adapting to her responses, drawing her attention, and maintaining contact. Over time, attachment dynamics generalize to other family members and caregivers, creating a social arena of protection, safety, and care. Author Daniel Goleman (2006) calls human infants "tiny masters at managing their caretakers" (p. 163).

As we have seen, babies come to us capable of, indeed expecting, such interactions. Even in the womb, babies are adapting and responding to the environment around them, to mother of course, but to the wider surround as well (Scaer, 2005). Attachment needs and drives are hardwired into us from birth, like Rusty's reaching toward the sound of a human voice, and they remain active throughout our lives. As the brain's neural wiring matures through interactions with caregivers, the developing circuits evolve the capabilities for further growth. Mutual attachment behaviors form the links in a chain that shape us as individuals and bind us together.

Attachment is the life-blood of human development, and presents the background against which addiction stands out in sharp relief. One reason for the choice to examine attachment as the mainspring for development is due to the mutual explosion of contemporary knowledge between attachment and neuroscience. Alternatively, understanding the intersection of attachment and neuroscience opens a door into deeper comprehension of the phenomenon of addiction. In line with the goals of this book, knowledge of attachment psychology and neural development is essential for understanding the origins, nature, and consequences of addiction.

Substance-related and addictive disorders may be seen as potential outcomes when attachment processes go awry or attachment needs remain unmet (Fishbane, 2007; Flores, 2004). In other words, while human connection is essential for development and buffers us from life's travails, disconnection creates fertile ground for the emergence of addiction and other troubles later in life. I view addiction in large measure as *a disorder of attachment and human connection*. Unfulfilled interpersonal needs can be shifted toward bonding and relationship-building with a drug, an activity, or a behavior that partially fulfills the role of a substitute. All that is required is for the drug or activity to "have what it takes" in order to fill the role of substitute. What does this mean? The drug or activity must be able to facilitate comfort or relief, reward or analgesia, or diversion. It brings something of value to the relationship. Some have called this kind of substitution an "unholy attraction" (Lewis, 2015). Unmet attachment needs can be addressed, even if only partially, by a relationship to addiction.

Attachment and Attunement

In my office, along with numerous photos of my wife, Ellen, and our children, I have three pictures, one of each child, that always bring a smile to my face. The kids are about 9 to 10 months old. Ellen is holding our daughter, Sierra, with obvious expressions of joy on both their faces. In the other two Danny, our middle child, is seated on my lap and focused on a toy, while Rusty is in a backpack on my back at the beach in February, with coat, gloves, and an adorable hat. Again, all smiles.

These pictures speak to me of the bond between children and parents. We know that for a long period of time young children require closeness and care. Proximity to caregivers is essential for survival and evolution equips children to attract and hold the attention of adults. However, for healthy human development, presence is necessary but not sufficient. Physical nearness must be paired with emotional closeness and interaction. This is attachment *and* attunement. All three pictures with the kids portray a sense of joy, of security, of sharing a history in which love, safety, and care are paramount. In other words, these pictures capture something of the caregiving attachment relationships and attunement between us and them.

Someone seeks proximity, care, and attention; someone responds and meets the needs of the other. Seeking and responding over and over again creates a relationship. In the best cases, this relationship is a selective and enduring bond in which I learn that someone is "concerned about me, someone has me in mind" (Byng-Hall, 1995). This is the "feeling felt" that Siegel (2007) so eloquently discusses. If we are honest, any of us will admit that this kind of attachment and belonging is essential all the way through the lifespan, even if one particular figure is not currently available. Attuned "feeling felt" is the basis for all mature dialogue and for the possibility of authentic encounter. It also forms the sturdy ground of all good therapy and echoes the original attachment relationship. It is a foundational human yearning that transcends individual and even cultural differences. These relationships are the ecology in which we become human.

Not all partners or caregivers, however, can provide optimal care. Life stresses, mental illness, preoccupation with one's own past and unresolved issues, lack of support, struggles of poverty, racism, and oppression, and other factors can impair a caregiver's ability to be present and responsive. When the attachment process breaks down, the consequences can be bitter. One of the saddest things ever said to me in 30-plus years of counseling practice came not long ago. I was working with someone in his seventies who was struggling with depression as well as terminal cancer. He described growing up in a family in which his father was both physically abusive and a "yeller"; his mother was somewhat passive and emotionally absent. He had five brothers and sisters, three older and two younger. Beginning around the age of 9 years old, he realized that he could leave the house early in the morning and didn't have to return until the evening. He was not missed. He could escape. The adults at home were otherwise occupied. He would spend the day on the streets of his small city, working odd jobs for pocket change, and would take the money home to his mother to help with the family. Over time, he began staying out all night and was brought home several times by the police before eventually being put into an orphanage.

He told me that many nights he would hide in an alley, trying to stay warm and unnoticed by the police, wondering out loud "why nobody was coming to find me." He knew even then that no one—not his parents, nor his siblings—had him in mind. When he told me this, the counseling office briefly reverberated with the ache of his sadness. It wasn't until much later that, after a stint in the military, he married someone from a big family. They "took him in," he said, with a wistful look on his face. She and her family became his "secure base." However, the attachment injury from those early years hung around him like a cloud; his anxiety and depression were symptoms of the lingering pain, and reasserted themselves after his wife died. He ignored symptoms of his own growing cancer and, when referred to me, simply longed to move his residence out West to be with his only daughter and her family, pursuing treatment in a state where he could procure both medical and recreational marijuana. His relationship with his daughter and grandchildren would be his "safe haven." His stated goal was to "mellow out," using marijuana and the relationship with his daughter as substitutes, for whatever time was left to him.

In 2013 a group of attachment scholars and clinicians gathered in London to discuss their thoughts at the Twentieth John Bowlby Memorial Conference titled, *Addictions from an Attachment Perspective*. Their proceedings were collected into a monograph, edited by Richard Gill (2014), and their answer to the question they set for themselves was a resounding "yes," addiction does indeed result from broken attachment bonds. Early adversity, trauma, and toxic stress set the conditions for requiring chemical and behavioral self-soothing, for defective affect regulation that must be fortified by external means, for exertion of control in the face of relational suffering and despair. Their collected papers offer a "fundamental understanding of addiction as a response to early attachment breakdown" (Gill, 2014, p. xvii). Their hope was to offer a more comprehensive and compassionate perspective on the suffering of persons struggling with addiction and to challenge society with the critical importance of early relationships, parenting, family life, and the formation of a society in which human connections are prized, a human ecology in which no one is left behind, a circle of compassion and inclusion.

Louis Cozolino and the Social Brain

It is often difficult for scientists to grasp the idea that individual brains do not exist in nature. As much as one may adhere to the notion of the isolated self, humans have evolved as social creatures and are constantly regulating one another's biology. Without mutually stimulating interactions, people (and neurons for that matter) wither and die. LOUIS COZOLINO, IN *THE SOCIAL NEUROSCIENCE OF EDUCATION* (2013)

As I approached "the toaster," a space opened between newborn Rusty and me, and what neuroscientist Louis Cozolino calls a "social synapse" was created (2010, p. 179f). Synapses are open spaces between objects. We are familiar with them in regard to neurons, the basic building blocks of the nervous system. Neither neurons nor their branches (dendrites) are physically connected to one another. Neurons live in close proximity with neighbors, but they do not touch. There is a gap—a synapse—between them that links the neurons functionally, if not physically. We know that each neuron has the capacity to form thousands of synaptic connections with neighboring neurons. There are many billions of neurons—billions with a B—in the brain alone. Connections are estimated in the trillions.

Learning to (re)connect across a relational and intersubjective field, a kind of social and ecological synapse, is essential for shaping a social brain. We are by design social animals with social brains. When the process malfunctions, however, disruption and pathology are not far behind. How this may be so and the implications of attachment breakdown are the tasks for this section.

Looking at living neurons under the microscope, one can see how active they are, reaching toward others, exploring their environment, and building connections. Each synapse is filled with a variety of chemical messengers and proteins, and communication between neurons happens as various chemicals interact within the synaptic space and connect or release in relation to receptors, or docking stations, in the next neuron. This happens with lightning speed and triggers the electrochemical interactions that are the bread and butter of neural communication. A parallel process occurs between people in the "social synapse."

Imagine yourself standing and talking with a colleague. There is a space between you, and yet it is filled with all sorts of communications—facial expressions, posture and nonverbal displays, muscle movements, hand gestures, words, looks, even odors. A lot is happening in this small space between you that conveys a wealth of information, but even more importantly, connects and perhaps even nourishes the two of you. There is a consciousness of the other, a "feeling felt," that says, "I see you. I'm listening. What you have to say is valuable to me. And I see you looking at me in the same way." Of course, this kind of communication across the social synapse doesn't always go so well. Perhaps the interaction is matter of fact or businesslike. Perhaps it's distracted and less than personal. In some cases, it might be manipulative or abusive. Nevertheless, the social synapse is a space for connection and communication between persons. It is across this space that much of human development occurs, and here is where attachment, sensitive attunement, and neurobiology join hands.

Interaction across the "social synapse" builds, shapes, and enhances the social brain. Experiences and relationships are embedded into our brain architecture and biology, both at the beginning of infancy and throughout our lives. Experience leaves footprints in neural architecture. "Human connections create neuronal connections," Siegel tells us. (1999, p. 85). The mechanism of this neural alchemy is attachment.

This is a core idea. From an evolutionary perspective, an inborn attachment system is highly efficient and serves many different and vital purposes. Through proximity and care from adult caregivers, infants are protected from danger, fed, and nurtured. Emotional stability and regulation come through this proximity as well. An unhappy or uncomfortable infant learns that warm cuddling (proximity) actually soothes. The closeness calms. This is a process of "co-regulation" (Siegel, 1999, p. 70). Hart (2011, p. 3) tells us that "the most important evolutionary function of the human attachment system is to generate a self-regulating control system within the child."

The social synapse is a fundamental building block of attachment and self-regulation. Cozolino (2006) describes the social synapse as a kind of "high-speed information linkup." It facilitates "ongoing physiological and emotional synchrony" (p. 447). Without it, the goals of attachment would be unachievable—safety and survival, social connection, building the social brain, self-regulation, modulating the response to stress. The quality and consistency of attachment experience in childhood affects emotional and physical health later in life as well. Over time, young children learn to "borrow" their caregiver's emotional state, their regulation strategies, and use them for emotional stability and personal balance in the face of stress, until they can function on their own.

Even very young children—indeed, even as yet unborn fetuses—can experience internal and external stressors (Scaer, 2005; Schore, 2003a, 2005). Being raised in a "war zone," for example—whether that conflict is between nations or competing social groups, or among members of a family—brings stress to far too many children in our world. Struggling with feelings of sadness or grief, experiences of loneliness or oppression, adversity or discrimination, or financial hardship can also burden individuals, families, and groups. Stress response systems are built into the brains and neural/hormonal systems of persons through experiences in the social synapse. Responses to stress, the capacity for self-regulation, the foundations for a sense of self all depend on attachment.

ADDICTION AS AN ATTACHMENT DISORDER

Attachment is a fundamental mainspring driving human development. When all goes well, the individual becomes securely attached and capable of moving out into the world on his or her own. But things don't always go so well. When a child, primed and ready for connection, encounters indifference, neglect, preoccupied caregivers, a lack of adequate care—or worse, hostility, manipulation, relationship challenges, or outright victimization—then she or he becomes burdened with deficits and imperatives to cope in any way possible, or to crumble.

As counselors and mental health professionals witness every day, the human spirit is incredibly resilient, but it can be overwhelmed or distorted. Let us look at the case of Joe from Chapters 1 and 2 one more time. When I began seeing Joe in counseling, he had several difficulties: marital estrangement, depression, and substance-related disorder. As I got to know him better, it was clear that he also suffered ill effects from deficient self-regulation and lack of connection.

Although in his youth he had tried to protect his mother and siblings, his memories of childhood and adolescence were dominated by fear and loathing for his father. Whenever he thought about his relationship with his father—the social synapse between them—he could only imagine his father's red face and bloodshot eyes in close proximity, the smell of alcohol, and the sound of his voice yelling, "You are useless." Rage and grief were the dominating emotions toward his father; shame was the primary feeling about himself.

After a confrontation, Joe would leave the house, then go off by himself or sometimes with friends. I wondered many times about the neural and emotional footprints that remained in Joe's brain, psyche, and spirit. I have a better appreciation now of the near-constant activation cycle of Joe's primitive fear, shame, and panic circuits and the transformation of his emergency systems (for example, in the HPA axis or vagal complex) into a permanent defensive status. Key systems became twisted into chronic activity and colored with emotions such as shame and desolation (Katehakis, 2016). Stress response systems became hypersensitized and overly quick to react. Needs for defense and self-soothing became paramount.

I realized then, and even more, now, that the difficulty of sitting with him in therapy was an echo of the emotional mangling he had endured. Far from being the wellspring of connection and compassion, for Joe, the social synapse had become a quagmire.

Attachment Regulation and the Mechanics of Addiction

There is a rhythm between responsive caregivers and their infants. They knit together their emotions with each other's behavior, like ballroom dancers in time with each other and with the music. Unresponsive caregivers cannot manage the reciprocity, the open-ended give-and-take involved. But if a dancer is ignored by his partner, no lasting harm is done; the same is not true of an unresponsive caregiver and an infant. OLIVER JAMES, 2006, P. 171

Ethology gave John Bowlby a set of tools that he brought to bear on the observation and assessment of behaviors centered on maternal/infant bonding. Bowlby began to see the process of attachment between human mother/child as a *primary* drive and motivator. For him, providing closeness, nearness, and warmth in caring connections was essential for survival and response to the environment (Bowlby, 1958).

"A Secure Base"

The notion of a "secure base" was a metaphor that guided attachment theory and its applications. Mary Ainsworth (1913–1999) fleshed out this image and helped to elaborate a typology of secure and insecure attachment styles.

Ainsworth and her colleagues (2015) described distinct patterns of children's behaviors when together with, or separated and then reunited with, their mothers. She also formulated a classification system.

Secure attachment develops when a caretaker responds promptly and reliably, addressing the child's needs. These needs include play, distress relief, proximity. Child and caregiver are attuned to each other, behaviorally and emotionally. It is believed that this occurs between 57 to 73 percent of the time in a normal population (Byng-Hall, 1995). Child and parents have fun together and there is mutual warmth. Communication is sensitive and respects the child's growing autonomy. The relationship is adaptive and flexible, as well as mutually responsive. The child experiences belonging that is secure enough to support exploration outside the dyad.

Insecure attachment styles come in several forms. Children with *anxious-ambivalent* attachment show high levels of distress when the caretaker is absent or unresponsive, and anger or anxiety at the caregiver's return. The child's emotional needs or distress are not met appropriately or consistently. Caregiving responses are experienced as intermittent or neglectful. Caregivers may be emotionally unavailable and may be seen as preoccupied and not ultimately attuned with the child. Their preoccupations lie elsewhere. Consequently, the child may remain close and demanding, forcing the parent to notice and be attentive. This occurs in 4 to 22 percent of a normal population.

Children with an *anxious-avoidant* style show a distinct lack of attachment, demonstrating little distress when the caregiver leaves or is absent, and avoiding contact when the caregiver returns. Parents and children can appear to be detached or disengaged from one another. There is a lack of sensitive care for the child when it is needed, and the child remains at a loss for exploring feelings and intimacy. This occurs in 15 to 32 percent of the population.

There also appears to be a third group of insecurely attached children, described later by Mary Main and labeled as *disorganized/unresolved*. This group may be 15 to 25 percent of the normal population, but 80 percent of a maltreated group. They seem likely to become part of the clinical population.

Ainsworth's work affirmed that childhood experiences shape later attachment styles. Children who responded to their mothers with ambivalent or avoidant styles had "a less than optimal relationship with her at home," compared to those children who sought contact and interaction with her (Bretherton, 1991a, p. 24). The experience of a safe and secure base, a relationship in which I experience that there is someone who is concerned about me and "has me in mind," is essential for human relationship and ongoing development. This is not simply a psychosocial process. Attachment experiences also leave their footprints on our physiology as well as our psyche. Psychosocial attachment experiences, secure and insecure, are translated into neurobiological strengths and vulnerabilities.

Not surprisingly, psychological and emotional symptoms emerge more frequently from insecure versus secure attachment styles. Insecure attachments can be fertile ground for current and later developmental problems, such as psychiatric, behavioral, and even physical illness, including problematic substance use and addiction. Insecure attachment may not cause psychopathology directly, but early child attachment, family context, and other social experiences may shape a person in such a way that certain developmental pathways are more likely to be followed than others (Weinhold & Weinhold, 2015). People struggling with adversities are a huge presence in the mentally ill population, for instance; post-traumatic symptoms abound in our clinical mental health community.

In psychosocial care, and social services more generally, diagnostic chaos is rooted in a developmental matrix of insecure attachment, childhood adversity, dysfunctional family systems, and skewed neurobiological wiring. Understanding this background is crucial for applying the correct diagnoses, treatment, and recovery regimens (Schore & Schore, 2008). Trauma and toxic stress interfere with the capacity to regulate internal states and behavioral responses, which often becomes the catalyst for "substitute relationships" as a replacement for attachment.

The Adult Attachment Interview (AAI)

What mechanisms might account for the transition from childhood attachment to adult behavior, from childhood insecurity to adult psychological and behavioral troubles? Mary Main, a student of Ainsworth's, studied the key notion of internal working models.

In her Adult Attachment Interview (AAI), parents described their own attachments in childhood through responses to a series of open-ended questions (Main & Goldwyn, 1988). They described their attachment experiences with *their* parents and the impact of those experiences on their own overall development and current functioning as adults as well as with their own children. Parents' responses as well as the quality and coherence of the narrative they gave were collected.

Granted that secure or insecure relational styles emerge through caregiving experiences in childhood, Bowlby and others believed that *later adult relationships were at least a partial reflection of those early experiences with caregivers.* Constructing a coherent narrative—a detailed and meaningful story—of one's origins is part of the task of development. There are far-reaching implications for the quality and coherence of these narratives regarding early and significant attachments and adult relationships later in life.

There is compelling research evidence that the coherence of a primary caregiver's autobiographical, relational story is a key component in parenting. There is good reason to believe that the quality of children's relational lives, as well as their sense of security in the world, will be affected by how their parents have come to understand and narrate their own relational history.[3]

Main's work confirms the conclusions of attachment theory more broadly:

- The quality of parenting a child receives will affect the security or insecurity of that child's attachments and the relative security of her or his world. Security leads to exploration in one's world; insecurity results in more constricted or defensive styles of engagement.
- Attachment style affects the person's health and future relationships, and allows her or him to relate to others flexibly and reliably, or in a more rigid and unresponsive form.
- The security or insecurity of the child's attachments has repercussions on the quality of presence and relationship she or he can provide to later offspring or a spouse.
- In this manner, intergenerational transmission of secure or insecure attachment may become more likely and patterns from the past may repeat or echo themselves.

Internal Working Models (IWM)

Interactions with parents and other early caregivers shape adult relationship style (James, 2006). The mechanism for stability of a person's relational style is the formation of internal working models or mental representations. Fraley & Shaver (2000) suggest, for example, that the attachment system, originally adapted for the ecology of infancy, continues to influence behavior, thought, and feeling in adulthood. This is an important element in the intergenerational transmission of attachment patterns (James, 2006). Much of intergenerational family therapy is based on similar assumptions (Boszormenyi-Nagy & Spark, 1984; Framo, 1992).

Repeated interactions with attachment figures, as well as their responses to needs for closeness and support-seeking, forge mental representations, something like interactive movies or holograms, that carry expectations of care and predictions of how interactions will turn out. These "cognitive/affective schemas or representations" of self and others crystallize experience with caregivers into narrative form (Bartholomew & Shaver, 1998, p. 25), and become the "foundation of a person's individual attachment style" (Dallos, 2004). They are the psychological mechanisms by which attachments become ingrained—the psychological and relational reflections of neural patterns carved into the brain's electrochemical processes—and direct how one interacts with others (Bretherton, 1990, 1991a & b).

Think of your smartphone. The attachment paradigm, especially when described through psychodynamic theory, suggests that our repeated interactions with significant others produce an internal gallery of "representations," something like snapshots or video clips, which include images of caregiving others, of ourselves ("selfies"), of being cared for (multi-person snapshots), and even of the relationships between caregivers (mom-and-dad or mom-and-grandma). This is, of course, an oversimplification, but can help us to imagine what is happening.

This gallery of representations supports several psychological and social functions. It helps to *ground* a sense of (social) self. Our "galleries" define our selves in action and interaction, providing consistency. If the interactions between infant and caregiver are positive, the self is experienced as worthy, valuable, lovable; this instills an expectation that the world, represented by caregivers, will be responsive and reliable. The gallery also *guides* how we will act toward others later on, even in adulthood. We adapt our behavior to conform to the world we expect to meet. We interpret the words and actions of others, filtered through these mental models. Perhaps we respond positively to a coworker because he or she reminds us of someone we loved, or we react negatively to a child who displays traits similar to those of an abusive sibling. The internalized working models guide our own attachment style, with profound implications for emotional appraisals and automatic assessments of safety versus danger in potential relationships. Finally, the gallery can also operate as a *gyroscope*, steering us into the kinds of relationships with which we are familiar and comfortable, whether or not those relationship patterns are healthy. Think of the spouse who leaves an abusive, alcoholic partner, only to begin a relationship with another one (or two, or three) just like him. Her gyroscope, compiled from a skewed gallery, can lead her astray.

No one actually walks around with a set of pictures in her or his head, of course. As neuropsychologist Daniel Siegel says, "there is no 'storage closet' in the brain" (2001b, pp. 999–1000). Rather, neurons fire in particular patterns (what are sometimes called a "neural net profile"), reacting to the environment; these patterns are then encoded through synaptic changes and each similar configuration increases the probability of firing together again. "Neurons that fire together, wire together" (2001b, p. 999). Now this is not really so different from what happens in our smartphones. Light and sounds pass through lenses and interact with sensors in the phone, and are transformed into electrical impulses. These are translated by the phone's CPU into the formats we recognize, such as JPEG. These impulses (pixels) are then stored in miniature transistors for later retrieval. Again, no smartphone literally carries miniature pictures and videos inside it.

It is important to note here that the internal working models are both conscious and unconscious; they are built on explicit and implicit memories. They operate above *and below the radar*. However, the earliest experiences we have of attachment—and perhaps the ones with longest and deepest impact—occur before we have words to name them. Elements of the brain's limbic system are active from very early on in life and respond to events that are colored with powerful emotion. Attachment neuroscientists call these "implicit" memories and working models. They appear to be stored differently than explicit memory and often do their work outside of our awareness to influence our thinking and behavior. Inside, we carry unconscious memories and models from interactions with caregivers, families, and significant others.

Mental health, addiction, and trauma-focused counselors encounter implicit memory phenomena in their work with persons having a history of trauma. Clients may not be able to describe actual remembered events of abuse or calamity, perhaps because they occurred before explicit memory processes were intact or because of defensive dissociation during the event, but they do describe "body memories" or sensations of panic, sadness, or grief when an event or experience of *déjà vu* occurs. Dr. Bessel van der Kolk poignantly calls this process, "the body keeps the score," in his book of the same title (2014). One patient of mine, who knew that her three sisters had all been sexually abused in childhood by their grandfather, had no explicit memory of abuse herself but would freeze and be unable to participate romantically when her husband, whom she loved, approached her sexually. All she felt was a "nameless dread" and a sense of panic that began following her grandfather's death.

Attachment-based Alchemy

The biologically driven need for connection and mutual affect regulation relies on attachment and attunement. Sensitive and responsive caregivers establish an emotional force field within which the two participants—caregiver and receiver—can share a kind of "resonance" or attunement, each person influencing the other. This is the ideal condition of the social synapse and serves as the foundation for secure attachment, for loving relationships throughout life, and interestingly enough for the power of the relationship as a healing factor in psychotherapy. Initially with primary caregivers, and then as we mature, with ever-wider circles of connection, we utilize being-in-tune with others for our own self-development.

> Secure attachment is built on the attunement of the parent with the infant. . . . With parental empathy, the child 'feels felt'. . . and develops a confidence in his or her experience.

> Self-esteem and self-confidence are built on this interper-
> sonal dance of attunement and empathy (FISHBANE, 2007,
> P. 402).

Care-seeking and caregiving behaviors are reciprocal psychobiological events that can be observed, described, and measured. These behaviors are the links in a chain that form the bonds of psychological and relational attachment. Concurrently, however, so much more is happening at so many levels. Attachment behaviors are also triggering new internal images, working models, and memories that become the foundation of a sense of self, of others, of the world. Underneath, these same behaviors are instigating the formation and wiring of neural connections, structures, and neural net patterns that "hold" these memories and are ready for retrieval. These are the deep footprints of attachment, and the basis for ongoing neuroplasticity.

When Attachment Fails

Adult problems in living and the presence of debilitating illness likely have their roots in our earliest days. Insecure attachments are the hidden engine of much later suffering. We now know that formation of attachment bonds and neural structures, particularly in the right hemisphere of the brain, is proceeding at a rapid pace during the first 18 to 24 months and is particularly sensitive to the social and interpersonal environment. The infant's right brain structures, especially the limbic system, amygdala, and orbitofrontal cortex—the brain's executive systems—are developing at a remarkable rate. This maturation depends upon secure attachment. Perturbations in the social environment lead to insecure attachments of various kinds (anxious, avoidant, disorganized) with troublesome outcomes in the short and long term, and malformation of neural executive systems.

Given the challenges in human relationships and the biologically driven need for emotional management through relationship, it is understandable that in the face of deficiency, struggling persons might turn to "something else" for emotional management. Due to unmet developmental needs and neural impairment, insecurely attached persons lack the ability to manage emotions through mutual regulation. They turn to external sources and anxiously latch on to them. These lesser, second-best, or substitute relationships serve as counterfeits for real human connection.

> Attachment theory recognizes that human beings are interactional and constantly impacted by our relationships and the environment around us. When the fundamental ability to connect with others is damaged, it is not surprising that some seek external emotional support and regulation from a substance. As the use of substances increases, the individual's ability to interact with others is further impaired, and the cycle of addiction is set in motion (FLETCHER, NUTTON, & BREND, 2015).

Naturally, this substitution only works with external sources that have "what it takes" to provide comfort and emotional management. These external crutches must be able to "shift" a person's conscious and affective experience and address emotional needs. Psychoactive drugs, other substances such as food, and certain behavioral activities possess "what it takes." Their actions within the brains and psyches of addicted individuals address their attachment needs.

It is important to note that the external crutches that "have what it takes" to shift someone's emotional experience do not all come in bottles and pills. Chemical comforters are only one form of mood modifiers. Available for recruitment as substitute connections, these can be behaviors, such as gambling or internet gaming, or process attachments—what I call "-aholias" (as in work-aholia)—such as attachment to power, influence, wealth, or possessions (James, 2008, 2013). The lust for power or wealth can be every bit as addicting as heroin, and just as deadly. And while it is tempting to limit our thinking to psychoactive chemicals and compulsive activities, human beings have the capability of utilizing many other elements of living into counterfeit substitutes for true relationships. This dynamic is not something that traditional psychology has investigated. However, sources within traditional moral and ascetical spiritual traditions, as well as generations of literature and art, have documented the dangers of obsessive attachments to wealth, power, influence, or reputation (Alexander, 2008/2011).

"Earned Secure" Attachment

We now know that attachment experiences are woven into the patterns of neural development, during sensitive periods of child development, and throughout our lifetime. This may help to explain what many of us see in clinical practice. Attachment-based deficits help us to understand the prevalence of a number of contemporary social and clinical dysfunctions from divorce to child maltreatment, from physical illness to addictions. Based on the work of Main and other attachment-oriented researchers, it is estimated that as many as 45 percent to 50 percent of the U.S. adult population may be insecurely attached (Benoit, 2004). As author Kathy Brous reminds us, "this huge 'insecure' figure is a predictor of broken homes and broken hearts for half the nation" (Brous, 2018).

While there is stability in intergenerational transmission of attachment style, does this mean that people are stuck with the insecure or secure style they absorbed early on? Main's later work into something called "earned secure" attachment and "attachment repair" provides some hope (Main & Goldwyn, 1988). Attachment-oriented clinicians have taken this insight and developed it further (Roisman et al., 2002).

Mary Main and Daniel Siegel (2010) have stated: "What's even more important than the specifics of what happened to us is how we've made sense of our own childhood experiences. When we come to make sense of our memories and how the past has influenced us in the present, we become free to construct a new future for ourselves and for how we parent our children. Research is clear: If we make sense of our lives, we free ourselves from the prison of the past . . ." Narrative understanding is key.

Daniel Siegel speaks about this eloquently:

> The brain appears to have a narrative function that can detect themes of our life story and draw heavily on prefrontal functions as they integrate neural maps that form

the underlying architecture of our episodic and autobiographical memory systems. With narrative reflection, one can choose, with consciousness, to detect and then possibly change maladaptive patterns (2010)

"THE EFFECT OF RELATIONSHIPS ON RELATIONSHIPS"

From the 1960s onward, the time was ripe for augmenting attachment theory beyond individuals and child/caregiver dyads to exploration of the social, familial, and systemic relationships that surround them. Systems theory, the initial ground for family therapy, suggested what common experience confirmed, namely that "every relationship affects every other relationship" in families and kinship networks (Byng-Hall, 1991, p. 238). A number of persons who were influential in the development of attachment theory began exploring the connections with systems theory, but none was more active than John Byng-Hall (1991, 1998). He took his cue from John Bowlby himself who interviewed families clinically as a complement to individual therapy and who published one of the earliest articles in the emerging family therapy literature (Bowlby, 1949).

Byng-Hall's starting point was the notion of the secure base. Rooted in the interaction of care-seeking and caregiving, *family systems are composed of a number of interlocking, mutually influential attachment relationships.* The goal of family life—and of family therapy when needed—is for these relationships to exist in harmony and for the family as a whole to become a secure base in which members' needs are met and the capacity to explore other relationships within and outside the family flourishes. Relationships among brothers, sisters, moms and dads, even intergenerational relationships with grandparents, aunts, and uncles interrelate and intersect; they can be mutually supportive and satisfying. Family members will facilitate the meeting of attachment needs by others in the family or at the very least will not obstruct the meeting of those needs. Clearly, some secure and insecure relationships may coexist in a given family (for example, one child may have a secure relationship with father and an insecure one with mom) and these relationships may be in competition, vying for care. Some relational balance needs to be struck.

Family Scripts

When attachment writers spoke of "internal working models," Byng-Hall and others saw shared, multi-person working models of these behaviors among family members. Byng-Hall called these *family attachment scripts* (1985; 1990; 2008).

Family patterns and relationships may not repeat themselves, but they often rhyme. That is, there is a kind of predictability to family relations based on the patterned ways in which people relate to one another. Family scripts are part of this picture.

> Transgenerational parenting scripts are those models of parent/child behavior learned in childhood and currently drawn up as working models for parenting the next generation. These transgenerational parenting scripts can be divided into two areas: (1) replicative scripts that replicate what happened then and (2) corrective scripts that attempt to avoid repeating past painful experiences. Marital partners may be partly chosen on the basis of their ability to enact roles in these conflicting scripts. (BYNG-HALL, 1990, P. 233).

Family scripts are multi-person constructs. They help to stabilize family relational patterns and convey a sense of each person's role in the family dance (James, 2006). Participants then "know their place," know how they belong, know how to act. Like scripts for a drama or musical play, they function as the internal working models for relationships in the family dance.

These scripts can be evoked and become active in many contexts, but are most powerfully enacted under the influence of stress. In the case of a major illness like childhood cancer or a situation of major life-threatening injury, for example, the stressor evokes a patterned set of reactions from family members and the assumption of a variety of *roles* in family relating. Mother may become the primary caregiver to the ill member while Dad steps into the background and becomes the strong, silent supporter. Johnny, the eldest brother and family star (high achiever), becomes even more visibly active and pressures himself to perform over and above expectations, while Jenny, the youngest sister, becomes the worrywart and expresses the family's anxiety. Bobby, the middle child and "identified patient" with cancer, puts on a brave face and talks to no one about his fears. It is as though each person knows his or her role in the face of this danger to the family, and enacts an interlocking family script. In these ways the family stress is managed and a precarious balance is maintained.

These scripts can go so far as to include *words to be said* (one person may express himself as the "Pollyanna"—"it will all turn out okay"—while another is the voice of doom and gloom—"we should prepare for the worst"), *rules* about how and when attachment needs are met (Bobby gets a lot of "I love you" comments; Johnny's achievements are taken for granted; Jenny is "just like that"), *whose needs have priority* (Bobby's needs are primary and can be accommodated; Johnny should be "self-sufficient"), and so forth. Byng-Hall explains it this way: "It is the overlapping reciprocal nature of each person's script that enables family members to coordinate their behavior. A shared script provides a mutually held working model of how all the various attachments operate . . ." (1991b, p. 201).

British psychologist Oliver James (2006) describes a developmental model of these narrative scripts and roles. Many readers will be familiar with the now-classic roles of Chief Enabler, Hero, Lost Child, and Mascot in alcoholic family systems. Much of that literature draws on similar notions about inter-locking family scripts (Dayton, 2012). Psychiatrist Peter Steinglass (Steinglass et al., 1987) adopted this thinking into a family-based focus on substance abuse. When chemical or process addictions become the main stressor, the predictable sorting out of relationships into scripted roles and the emergence of patterns such as over- and under-functioning family members (Bepko & Krestan, 1985) are prime examples of script theory.

Assessing and working clinically with individual and relational scripts is an important part of attachment-sensitive counseling.

ALLAN N. SCHORE: "THE AMERICAN BOWLBY"

The development of a self-regulatory capacity requires an early experience with a regulating primary caregiver. . . . As a result of an interactive history of psychobiological attunement, the motive force of the attachment process, the child forms a secure attachment with the caregiver (SCHORE, 1994, P. 373).

Like John Bowlby before him, Allan N. Schore is passionate about integrating a variety of scientific disciplines into a coherent perspective on human development. One particular focus of his investigations is the process and development of *emotional regulation* as essential for the emergence of a conscious, psychological self.

Emphasizing the interconnectedness of the psychosocial, the environmental, and the biological, Schore links together psychological realities with biology and demonstrates how emotions, thoughts, and a sense of self emerge from neural structures and processes (2014). Schore returns again and again to the earliest phases of the infant's life, from the last trimester of pregnancy through the first two years. This is the period of most rapid brain growth. Here he focuses on the development of "affect regulation" as an essential achievement of this critical period. *Regulation* is the capacity to tolerate stress and modify intense emotions; it includes healthy strategies used to manage emotions and their expression in pursuit of goals. *Affect* is more than (and deeper than) a feeling (Fishbane, 2007). It is a psychological and embodied response to a stimulus; its regulation often requires tools and strategies for tolerating strong reactions and keeping an individual on an even keel. *Affect regulation* helps the individual respond in healthful ways as opposed to overreaction (hair-trigger sensitivity or bigger-than–life emotionality) or underreaction (emotional cut-off), substance abuse, or dissociation.

Schore focuses on a dual-purpose project—regulating affect and wiring the relevant neural structures—as the outcome of sensitively attuned and relationally responsive caregiving. The dance of attachment during this critical time of development holds so much promise and equally important risk, vulnerability, and the possibilities of mental and physical ill health. Joe from Chapters 1 and 2, for example, did not tolerate stress well and lived unbalanced; he often employed alcohol as a substitute relationship and strategy for regulation.

Think of Katie from earlier. Early experiences influence the development of interpenetrating, multiple layers of living. Schore points out that the cortical areas of the brain are just forming and coming online around 10 to 14 months of life. The most important neural areas to wire-up during this time (limbic system) are already functioning but being greatly enhanced. They are involved with emotional and relational development. They are also core areas for the development of the brain's reward, motivational, and regulatory systems, central areas for addiction. Many addicts may be already vulnerable by the time they are only a few years old. While genes make contributions to this process, the attachment relationship directly influences the genetic programming at work here. Which genes come into play, the timing, strength and sequencing of their involvement unfolds in dialogue with real-life experience. The entire process is epigenetic.

Emotional Regulation and Addiction

Attachment and self-regulation are dynamic processes, susceptible to a variety of alterations (genetic anomalies, relationship insults, preoccupation, neglect, trauma). They are part of an open system, built for plasticity and change in order to allow for ongoing development and learning. The downside of this openness is vulnerability to miswiring, to forming connection patterns that can be led astray or overloaded, what neuroscientists call "maladaptive regulatory processes" (Schore, 2000, p. 23). When regulation is needed, it can fall short. This leads to defective regulation and a variety of faulty outcomes, pathological symptoms and disorders, as well as the effects and changes that can accompany them, such as depression, anxiety, substance abuse, and so forth.

This notion of defective regulation is a primary way to understand the mechanics of addiction. But plasticity also carries the seeds of hope. Psychosocial attachment experiences give us new ways of understanding addiction;

they can also show a way forward in counseling. They provide opportunities for repair.

While survival is the central purpose of the brain and human organism—its "prime directive," if you will—regulation is its core function. Keeping everything in balance and pursuing one's goals are essential skills for survival and overall health, critical for being connected and functioning as part of a tribe. Learning to employ these skills independently is a necessary long-term outcome.

Neuroscience tells us that these processes—survival and regulation—are built into the structures of the brain and enhanced by experience. The neural apparatus essential for regulation is the orbitofrontal cortex or OFC, located between structures for reasoning and emotion, and widely interconnected. It enfolds the amygdala, our "emotional guardian," and is the key point of convergence between lower (limbic, reward) and higher (cortical, reasoning) neural areas. These structures are also connected with the hippocampus, our memory recorder. Sensations and experiences that are colored by strong emotions are deeply embedded in these circuits.

Because of its unique location in the brain, the OFC receives sensory and relational information from the environment as well as information about deep internal bodily states, so that interpersonal experiences can be associated with emotion and motivation (Karr-Morse & Wiley, 2013). Siegel & Hartzell (2003) see the OFC and its associated structures as the "brain's emotional regulation system" and "chief executive officer." Schore calls these interconnected circuits the "senior executive of the emotional brain" (2000, p. 23).

In addition, tasks that involve experiences and reflection involving the self are associated with the medial prefrontal cortex (mPFC). Self-regulation may be coordinated here (Heatherton, 2011). It depends on top-down control by cortical regions of subcortical regions involved with reward and emotion. Regulation fails when the balance is tipped toward emotion or reward (Heatherton & Wagner, 2012). Drug addiction models suggest that neural reward systems become hypersensitized to drug cues and detached from higher level cortical control. Drug consumption shifts activity from PFC to subcortical areas; excessive use causes degradation in cortical control. These structures are also vulnerable to impairment by excessive stress through early adversity, neglect, or trauma (Fishbane, 2007). These systems develop and enhance in early infancy.

The neurons of the OFC, particularly the neural right side of the OFC, are "directly influenced by the nature of the attachment relationship," and particularly sensitive to emotional expressions on the human face, a primary source of information about the social environment (Karr-Morse & Wiley, 2013, p. 42). Relationship with an emotionally attuned caregiver provides a growth-enhancing environment and a primary pathway for regulating and coping with stress. Relating with an unresponsive or abusive caregiver, however, can negatively affect the child's ongoing development. And since the rudiments of these systems are active very early in life, and are responsive to strong, emotionally laden experiences, the deep body memories of experiences can be carried with us for a lifetime. Adversity can be encoded into such memories as "deep feelings" that act as templates for interactions far into adulthood (Karr-Morse & Wiley, 2013, p. 49).

Substance-related and addictive disorders are disorders of regulation and conscious control. The dynamic involved in clinical psychotherapy is a blending of personal narrative, sound science, and the art of empathy and relationship. This process can lead to insight and healing. Employing repair strategies that strengthen regulation and mindful reflection while also providing safety and connection are paramount.

In early development, a period of stress followed by the return of synchrony with mom provides the infant with a period of recovery or "interactive repair" (Schore, 2000, p. 35). This enhances development when it occurs within tolerable limits. Therefore, the model is maternal interactive co-regulation that maintains positive states while also coping with negative, stressful states. The outcome is homeostatic repair and regulation as a two-person or dyadic dance.

In all these attachment scenarios mom brings that experience of "feeling felt," of being known and understood from the inside out (Cozolino, 2006). She attunes to the baby's state and the two of them can engage in mutual synchrony. This is the foundation for balanced self-regulation and empathy. We need these dynamic relations for neural and emotional development when young *and* for ongoing development as we mature. It is also the basis for deep friendship, romance, and intimacy. Attachment-sensitive counseling builds on this experience.

COUNSELING FOR CONNECTION

The ongoing development of attachment theory into its modern forms has pushed toward core conceptualizations of affect regulation and emotional integration. These have led to deep re-conceptualizations of counseling and psychotherapy. Early emotional and psychobiological transactions initiate, nourish, and establish brain *and* psychic structures. The choreography of attunement, misattunement, repair, and reattunement shapes the psychological birth of a human person (Schore & Schore, 2008).

These are the foundations for a self and for the impact of later psychotherapeutic treatment, if needed; attachment-sensitive counseling depends on it. As the sensitive counselor builds the welcoming environment and relates empathically with the client, a healing force field of intersubjectivity is constructed and internal working models are revised and repaired. Echoes of the original attachments, verbal and nonverbal, resonate in the current therapy transactions; the affective "music" of early relationships can be stirred up. Connection with another self becomes healing and "growth-facilitating" (Schore & Schore, 2008, p. 13; Siegel, 1999).

Within this person-person healing field, what can also be stirred up are the past insecure or wounded attachments that helped to create current difficulties. Thus, the sensitive counselor is aware of the need for empathic and nonjudgmental relating. An important goal for counseling, then, is the co-creation of a new, safe, and more secure interaction. Over time, this may supply a corrective (reparative) relational experience. The same kind of attunement, misattunement (rupture), and reattunement (repair) process that can cultivate synchrony in a new healing dance brings healing and openness to learning from experience once again. Social enagement, as opposed to defensiveness, takes over the process (Baylin & Hughes, 2016).

These dynamics highlight the critical nature of therapist development and excellence (Hughes, 2007):

An attachment-based clinical approach highlights the unconscious nonverbal affective more than the conscious verbal cognitive factors as the essential change process of psychotherapy. Thus, at the most fundamental level, the intersubjective work of psychotherapy is not defined by what the therapist does for the patient, or says to the patient . . . Rather, the key mechanism is how to be with the patient, especially during affectively stressful moments (SCHORE & SCHORE, 2008, P. 17; EMPHASIS MINE).

"How to be with the patient" emphasizes again the stance of the attachment-sensitive counselor. We know that the therapeutic alliance/relationship and the therapist's capacity for compassion and acceptance are critically important elements in the counseling process. This argues for attending to counselor variables (openness, empathy) in order to foster healing change while learning to monitor the therapy and measuring needs and improvements.

Attachment Focus

Several more recent attempts to work clinically from an attachment point of view emphasize the notions of plasticity and change toward "earned security" in people's worldviews. The counseling focus I advocate, called attachment-sensitive counseling, is an integration of (a) Daniel Hughes's "dyadic developmental psychotherapy" (Hughes, 2007; Baylin & Hughes, 2016), (b) the model of *attachment-based family therapy* (Diamond, Diamond, & Levy, 2014), and (c) the field of interpersonal neurobiology. This integrative theoretical focus offers counselors a way to see and understand the dynamics of addiction and trauma that can lead directly to methods of attachment repair and healing.

Whether it is used directly with children and families or adapted to work with attachment wounded and substance-using adults, attachment-sensitive counseling uses the counseling relationship (and later family and kinship relationships) to communicate "consistent messages of safety and approachability" that allow damaged neural and relational circuits to reboot, come on line, and support new learning (Baylin & Hughes, 2016, pp. 94–95). It is a process of "enriched caregiving" (p. 99).

The new learning incorporates processes of reversal learning, reconsolidation, reflection, and reappraisal (Baylin & Hughes, 2016). Clients learn to slow down the old, defensive ways of reacting to perceived dangers/risks. They begin to notice the differences between old and new situations (old and new support people), and integrate this new learning by "turning toward" the new caregiver/support person/counselor and trusting the new interactions. This means inhibiting the defensive brain systems and allowing higher functions from the orbitofrontal, prefrontal, and anterior cingulate cortices, as well as the hippocampus, to incorporate new experiences. This demands patience at first with slow learning—on the part of the client, kin, colleagues, and counselor—as the individual shifts back and forth between old and new, and experiences errors as well as successes. Over time, this *reversal learning* can become more routine and habitual.

For this to occur, it is often necessary for the client's memories of poor care or adversity to be revisited, but only when she or he: (a) has learned and become adept at practicing safety with an adequate sense of self-agency,[4] and (b) feels ready to begin. It is important that this next step continue to be a process of co-regulation of affect and memory. Monitoring the client's experience is essential within the therapeutic relationship and in conjunction with other members of the client's social relationships. Recalling and revisiting painful memories can offer an opportunity to re-experience, face and confront that memory in the context of effective buffering and co-regulation. It can now be experienced as a safe memory that becomes available for integration (*reconsolidation*). Without careful attention to adequate support, however, increased stress, interpersonal conflict, turning to substitute means of regulation (such as drug use), or flight into dissociative processes can occur.

With careful attention to new experiences, fresh learning, and interpersonal support, clients can *reflect* and begin to change their thinking about self and relationships, about trust and safety. In this process, previous internal working models can be reshaped; fear-based memories and defensive postures can be detoxified and new ways of interacting can take their place.

Healing narratives about self and others can emerge within therapeutic inter-actions and be validated.

Reappraisal, then, can help clients revise their sense of self-worth and update outmoded beliefs. The individual's defensive systems can be calmed. The overall process of neuroception can shift from self-defense toward social engagement. Ongoing development can than proceed through less defensive and more engaged living under the guidance of balanced neuroceptive learn-ing (Baylin & Hughes, 2016).

Attachment-sensitive counseling, then, is a therapeutic process of extended attachment repair and psychobiological reintegration. It is ideally suited for work with individuals and families struggling with substance use and trauma-related stress disorders. However, it demands close attention and patience with slow processes of integration. But, there is hope.

6

Adversity, Trauma, and Toxic Stress: The Royal Road to Addiction

"The current concept of addiction is ill founded. Our study of the relationship of adverse childhood experiences to adult health status . . . shows addiction to be a readily understandable although largely unconscious attempt to gain relief from well-concealed prior life traumas by using psychoactive materials."

VINCENT FELITTI

"How might viewing us humans as adaptive rather than disordered change our way of relating?"

BONNIE BADENOCH

SUBSTANCE-RELATED AND ADDICTIVE DISORDERS are not always what they seem. Hidden drivers, influences, and motivations are often at work. In this chapter and the next, I hope to provide some insight into a key mechanism—internal to the individual and in the surrounding environment—underneath these behaviors, and provide insight into an effective approach we can take as counselors.

Individuals with a history of adversity do not approach involvement with psychoactive substances and compulsive behaviors from a neutral position. Those who have lived with significant stress while growing up bring that history, and the needs it generates, with them. Those who have experienced later adversities can use addictive relationships for coping and comfort. If traumatic encounters have engraved emotional wounds or psychic scars on battered hearts, those experiences will interact with chemicals and behaviors that "have what it takes" to provide comfort, or relief, or distraction. It is easier to develop coping relationships with objects that meet emotional needs. Those relationships can be difficult to renounce.

Whether we are talking about outright addiction to substances or harmful use and involvement with dangerous drugs and behaviors, the numbers are telling: Close to 100 million people in the U.S. are involved with substances at different levels of harm and severity. In addition, approximately six to eight million people are involved with some level of problem or pathological gambling. Entanglements with other destructive behaviors, such as online gaming, promiscuous sexual behavior, or extreme shopping, ensnare many others; excessive attachments ("-aholias") to wealth, or power, or celebrity can be debilitating as well. When we add the numbers of children, family members, and friends who are concurrently affected, the range of those touched by their own or others' excess is appalling. This is a critical public health challenge (U.S. Dept. of Health and Human Services, 2016).

We know, for example, that one in four children and adolescents experiences at least one traumatic event before the age of 16 years old, and in some geographic locations (ZIP codes) the numbers are even higher (Harris, 2018). More than thirteen percent of 17-year-olds, or one in eight, have experienced full-blown post-traumatic stress disorder (PTSD) at some point in their young lives. Forty percent of low-income kids live with significant adversity. One in five adolescents in the U.S. between the ages of 12 and 17 years old engages in problematic use of alcohol and other drugs, while 59 percent of those with PTSD eventually develop substance use problems (National Child Traumatic Stress Network, 2008).

One major social issue lurks in the background of any discussion of addiction and may help to explain the prevalence of substance use and addictive concerns as well as many of the mental and physical health struggles of today. Stress, adversity, and trauma, as well as failures or deficits of effective coping and resilience, are covert engines underneath many of the social, medical, and psychiatric crises we face (Harris, 2018).

CURRENT STATE OF AFFAIRS

In my classroom, I often state that the two most frequently underdiagnosed and misdiagnosed conditions we see as mental health clinicians are trauma and the addictive disorders. Many clinicians still shy away from asking about sexual or emotional abuse and have difficulty inquiring about problematic use of chemicals. Powerful barriers prevent seeing and labeling each disorder clearly (Bonn-Miller, Bucossi, & Tafton, 2012; Grinage, 2003; NIAAA, 2006).

Both disorders involve life experiences and consequences that polite people often do not discuss. It can be challenging to inquire about someone's experience with adversity, or seek information about excessive drinking, drug use, or out-of-control behavior. Our patients and we ourselves avert our eyes and ears, or resist, consciously and unconsciously, acknowledging each condition. Perhaps the most powerful barrier confronting counselors and those struggling with trauma and addiction is the experience of shame and discomfort, of blame and societal judgment that surrounds both conditions. Safety to speak and inquire must precede honest truth-telling, and clinicians need to adopt making safety a priority (Najavits, 2007; Najavits et al., 1998). Openness to hearing stories of shame and victimization is also required.

Both trauma and addictive disorders have been, and continue to be, controversial in their attribution of causes and assignment of resources. As a society, we are ambivalent about ultimate responsibility. Are those affected responsible for their own fate or is there a shared responsibility between them and wider society (McFarlane & van der Kolk, 1996)? Complicating matters, neither side of the professional schism separating trauma and substance use treatment and social policy communicates well with the other. Authorities conduct research and disseminate findings in different journals and conferences. They utilize separate certifications and licenses; there is little cross-training or sharing of ideas. Each condition is also considered the "turf" of a specialized field of study and practice, and is publicly administered through separate silos and personnel, as well as funded with different revenue streams (Ouimette & Brown, 2003; NIDA, 2010).

All this occurs, despite several facts: (a) there are symptoms of stress and high rates of post-traumatic stress disorder among those seeking help for addictive disorders, and (b) the patients with PTSD/SUD comorbidity also have higher rates of other comorbid psychiatric disorders such as anxiety or depression, poor treatment outcomes, and very high rates of addiction relapse (Jacobsen, Southwick, & Kosten, 2001; Najavits, 2017; Ouimette, Brown, & Najavits, 1998). To top it off, the sheer volume and confusion of resources as well as requirements for participation in care can be daunting for patients and families in need of help as well as practitioners. Unfortunately, only a few treatment settings offer providers and staff dually trained in mental health *and* addictions. As a society, we are woefully unprepared to offer trauma-sensitive addiction care or addiction-sensitive trauma care.

A Troubling Reality

Traumatic events and their relationship to other health and psychiatric conditions are currently at the forefront of clinical and public interest. Even by conservative estimates, most people in the United States experience some form of trauma or adversity with lifetime prevalence approaching 60 percent for men and 50 percent for women (Najavits, 2007). A 1998 study using the DSM-IV criteria found the actual exposure to a qualifying trauma event to be closer to 89 percent overall (Ouimette & Brown, 2003). Let that sink in.

Notably, it can be difficult to obtain accurate and agreed-upon statistics. However, some things are beyond dispute. A large number of those with substance-related and addictive disorders also struggle with greater than average stress, adversity, and trauma-related symptoms. Of those seeking treatment for substance use disorders, 30 to 50 percent meet the criteria for lifetime PTSD (Brady, McCauley, & Back, 2014). Estimates are that the odds of drug and alcohol use disorders in those with PTSD are three times greater than with the general population (Ouimette & Brown, 2003, p. 15). The majority of psychiatric inpatients have comorbid histories of trauma (van der Kolk, 2014; van der Kolk et al., 1996/2007). Approximately 25 million U.S. women, and about half that number of men, report being sexually assaulted *in childhood*. PTSD, the diagnostic entity at the extreme end of stress experience, is 10 times more prevalent than cancer (Bremner, 2002)!

STRESS, STRESS RESPONSE, AND
STRESS-RELATED DISORDERS

I want to acknowledge at the outset that *both* traumatic stress and substance-related disorders exist on a spectrum. We saw earlier that the newest version of psychiatry's *Diagnostic and Statistical Manual of Mental Disorders* (DSM-5) views substance-related and addictive disorders on a continuum or spectrum of severity from mild to moderate to severe. There are advantages to this. It allows us to preserve the notion of a common pathology—the "addictive process" (Goodman, 1995)—and common symptoms underneath a recognizable, but diverse diagnostic entity that reveals itself through multiple versions (alcoholism, cocaine addiction, gambling; chemically harmful behavior or addiction).

Researchers are learning that there is also real benefit to viewing trauma and toxic stress along a similar kind of spectrum (Bremner, 2002; Scaer, 2005). This is consistent with the DSM-5 section on *Trauma and Stressor-Related Disorders*. To understand the role of adversity, trauma, and traumatic stress, as they relate to substance-related and addictive disorders, we must first address some essential issues about the experience of stress.

Following the lead of psychiatrist J. Douglas Bremner (2002), this chapter focuses on trauma and adversity as an inclusive category of *stress-related disorders*. Stress, as a psychobiological experience, is not limited to the diagnoses of acute stress disorder or post-traumatic stress disorder, however.[1] PTSD is only one possible outcome of toxic or traumatic exposures in people's lives, but there are others. There are varieties of stress-related, trauma-spectrum disorders to consider, including:

Acute stress disorder (ASD) and post-traumatic stress disorder (PTSD)
Depression
Anxiety
Somatic disorders
Dissociative disorders
Substance-related and addictive disorders
Physical and medical disorders such as heart disease, cancers, immune disorders, gastric ulcers, and so on.

This spectrum demands that we examine symptom clusters in context and within the scope of developmental milestones. Thinking about adversity and trauma in this wider context of stress-related disorders can help us to see more clearly that there is a common core underneath many of the behavioral, psychological, and health-related challenges we face: a *"stress-induced neurological deficit,"* (Bremner, 2002, p. 21). Toxic stress changes the brain and can have long-term neurological and physiological outcomes.

This perspective does not deny that other factors, such as genes or life circumstances, are involved in psychiatric or medical illness. It does challenge, however, all the health- and wellness-related fields to consider anew the impact of stress and coping on living. This has been a controversy in medicine and psychiatry for some time. What exactly is the role of stress (and adversity) in the instigation, occurrence, or maintenance of illness?

Is a 60-year-old woman struggling with lung cancer or heart disease viewed by her providers as having poor family genes, bad luck, or making poor lifestyle choices such as smoking or disordered eating? Do we ever consider that her smoking (or unregulated intake of alcohol or food), which began at 13 years old, was an adaptive response and a way to cope with sexual molestation from a stepfather that began when she was 12? Nicotine, alcohol, and food consumption ("stress eating") can be soothing elements in a stressful life, and their use may be a survival adaptation. What then is the cause of her disease . . . genes, bad luck, poor choices, maladaptive coping, or molestation and adversity? No physician is likely to diagnose her condition as a survival adaptation to trauma, but it is no less true. And if we fail to grasp the full causes, understanding and treatment may miss the mark.

Thinking in this way could help us to recognize and appreciate the tenacity with which people cling to their coping strategies, even if those strategies seem destructive or self-defeating. It might also help us to be more effective in our interventions. Beyond the adverse effects of nicotine, can we appreciate the neural and immunological toxicity of chronic but adaptive stress responses whenever she was home with her stepfather, or later when she was with her husband, a man who uncannily reminds her of her stepfather? Can we imagine that childhood adversity or ongoing toxic stress might be the hidden engines underneath her presenting illness today, or underlie what we see as "resistance" to change?

Some years ago, I saw a woman similar to this in psychosocial counseling. I remember the day she said, toward the end of a session: "Doc, I know my terminal cancer is the result of smoking so much, for so long. I have tried to quit many times. And yet, when I leave this office and go out to the parking lot today, I know I will light up a cigarette." This began a conversation about the onset of her smoking and weight gain, and the tenacity of these two adaptive behaviors. The age and timing of symptom onset suggested that she was coping with early sexual trauma. This interpretation became a new explanation of her story and opened up new avenues for us to pursue. She felt less ashamed and more able to manage the symptom. We felt connected.

Stress

In its most basic form, stress is an experience we have when under pressure. Something jostles us out of balance. We sense the approach of change or feel challenged in some way, and we feel stretched; we must exert energy to meet the challenge. Put simply, stress is an emotional or physiological challenge that triggers an adaptive process, so that balance can be restored. This can be good for us and can help us to grow. It is a normal part of development.

However, excessive or cumulative or untimely stress can be a catalyst for maladaptive coping.

Stress is a common experience among living things, and evolution has provided many creatures with mechanisms for coping with it. Biologist and professor of neurological sciences at Stanford University, Robert Sapolsky, in his delightful book *Why Zebras Don't Get Ulcers* (2004) provides a helpful perspective. Zebras, as prey animals on the African plain, have a finely tuned sentinel system that alerts them when danger is near. Sensing the approach of a hungry lion (who is also experiencing stress due to hunger, and needs to provide for her young), structures and processes in the zebra's brain react automatically. The amygdala, the brain's alarm system, sends signals to connected neural systems, such as the hypothalamic-pituitary-adrenal (or HPA) axis, flooding their bodies with chemicals and hormones, including adrenaline and the glucocorticoid cortisol, that assist in stress response.[2] Typically, they will run and live to graze another day. Assuming they survive, their stress response will return to its normal setting. Allied neural systems, such as the hippocampus, will store situational and environmental information about the encounter (smells, sounds) so that the response can be quicker next time. This is evolution's elegant design for survival, the fight, flight, (and in some cases) freeze stress response: Danger triggers neural and physiological responses that create stress and motivate action for escape. The system is quick and efficient.

Humans have similar biological stress response systems. Remember "Joe" from earlier? His alcoholic father's return home from work triggers a sense of danger and a similar zebra-like stress response prepares Joe for whatever may come. Hopefully, once the danger passes, Joe's stress system returns to normal. Many experiences in human living can be stressful (examinations in school, deadlines at work, illness, interpersonal encounters) and they do not have to be starkly horrifying events to trigger a response. They upset the person's psychobiological balance and trigger the accustomed stress response. A variety of such experiences can surface in the lives of individuals and can provide unique difficulties.

The situation is trickier for humans and some social primates. The basic physiological stress response systems are the same. However, a variety of psychological and social factors can precipitate our biological response all on their own.[3] Our more complex brains and interactive neural systems *remember* previous situations of danger and catalogue responses and reactions in memory; the intensity of previous encounters, enhanced by environmental cues, can form a searing memory and spark an over-reaction or paralyze us into inaction. When such experiences are unrelenting or overwhelming, or when a series of them pile up, they can be extremely difficult to resolve. Intrusive memories are often the most disruptive elements of stress disorders.

In addition, we can also *anticipate* the next encounter, and this may prompt the entire stress response again simply from a psychological memory. For example, Joe may lie awake all night worrying about what could happen with his father the next time, or environmental cues might trigger an intrusive memory to the past event in present time (flashback). His psychobiological systems may remain activated, as stress chemicals continue to operate, and his mind and emotions may replay the previous poisonous encounters. His stress response systems do not return to normal; they remain on alert.

Unfortunately, when our stress response systems turn on repeatedly or remain active, they can contribute to a great amount of physiological and psychological damage over time. We human beings are vulnerable to chronic and repeated activation of the stress response for many reasons. An overactive stress response can also exacerbate a number of physical illnesses, cause wear-and-tear on many systems (e.g. neurologic, cardiac, digestive), and deplete immunological systems, leaving us open to infections, inflammation, and illness (Geronimus et al., 2006; Sinha and Jastreboff, 2013).[4]

Stress and glucocorticoids also impact reward seeking, craving, and reward intake (such as high fat foods), as well as increasing the sensitization of reward pathways, which in turn heightens preference for, and reactions to, addictive substances and highly palatable foods (Harris, 2018). Coupled with the known increases in impulsivity and decreases in control that accompany stress and negative affect, the process becomes a highly charged minefield (Sinha & Jastreboff, 2013). This is some of the basic science behind excess reward chemical intake as well as obesity. The basic science also suggests potential methods for both lessening the impact of increased stress and enhancing processes for down-regulation. Mindfulness, meditation, physical relaxation (yoga, etc.), and a lifestyle balance that includes exercise, play and vacation can all become part of a therapeutic regimen.

Toxic Stress

The Center on the Developing Child at Harvard University describes different levels of stress, different kinds of stressors that can confront us, from "positive" and growth-producing, through "tolerable" stress that is buffered through supportive relationships, to "toxic" stress.[5] Stress can get us moving so that we overcome inertia and face the challenges in front of us, or it can be paralyzing, overwhelming, debilitating, and pose a threat to our well-being. Adversity and trauma can easily lead to toxic stress, especially in vulnerable individuals. Toxic stress is a threat to healthy functioning because it triggers excessive or prolonged activation of stress response systems in the body and brain.[6]

Typically, if a cohort of individuals are stressed by an event, many will experience transient symptoms but will recover without long-lasting effects. There will be a gradual decline in those experiencing symptoms, down to a residual affected group. For example, reports are that about 30 percent of the U.S. population had difficulty sleeping after the events at the World Trade Center, Pentagon, and Pennsylvania farmland on 9/11, but these numbers decreased to about 16 percent a few weeks later (Bremner, 2002). This is expected. However, some number of people had persistent symptoms, while a percentage will have lasting psychiatric or physiological dysfunction. While many of our animal cousins in the wild can release stress quickly once the threat or danger is removed, humans are able to "hang on" to stress and continue to trigger stress response systems. This is a human vulnerability and can occur long after the actual danger is gone, as our minds continue to (re)act as though danger is still present and real. Activating and reactivating stress responses is itself a threat to health and well-being (Sapolsky, 2004).

A SPECTRUM OF DISORDERS

What sort of experience gives rise to early relational trauma? Some difficulties occur unintentionally simply

> from problems and sometimes failures of everyday parent-
> ing, or from well-meaning, necessary, but intrusive medical
> procedures and hospitalization early in life. At such times
> an infant's simultaneous experience of intrusion and aban-
> donment may be overwhelming. There are also the well-
> documented difficulties that arise from early experiences
> that are abusive. Whether the abuse is psychological, phys-
> ical, or sexual in nature, if it occurs early in life the brain
> becomes hard-wired to cope in a hostile world. (WILKIN-
> SON, 2010, PP. 4–5)

Stress is a common human experience. From early in life, we learn to cope with it through a variety of strategies. Through connection and relationship we learn to withstand our stresses, and this very experience—bonding with another for calm and serenity, or seeking relief through buffering or allo-relationships—forms an adaptive template and becomes a lifelong strategy for coping. Even very young children learn to call out from their cribs when wet and hungry. A diaper change, a little food, and a warm snuggle makes everything okay. Asking for help in adult friendship or marriage can provide similar aid.

Research has uncovered several interlocking perspectives that can help us to understand trauma and adversity: First, we must attend to the *event* itself. What kind of occurrence is it? Is it a single instance or repeated situation? What is the level of danger or challenge it poses? Does the event itself carry any specific kinds of toxicity, such as the shame or loss of trust from intra-familial sexual abuse? Next, we must attend to the individual's *interpretation* of the event. What is the person's subjective assessment of danger and helplessness involved, and the *meaning* she or he attaches to the event? One person I interviewed long ago believed that her father's advances and her need for his attention were proof that she was a "bad seed." So great was her perfidy, she believed, that even God did not have the power to forgive her! Her interpretation of those events led to a lifetime of self-loathing.

Finally, we must also consider the individual's *reaction* to the event. Many people can marshal buffering resources of flexibility, creativity, and support and are able to move on without becoming bedeviled by a traumatic stressor or memory. Others, however, become fixated on the trauma, unable to integrate it into their personal identity; the traumatic *memory* and its concomitant toxic stress are split-off, stand alone, and cannot fit with the individual's internal working models. In this dissociated and isolated state, the memory continues to replay repetitively, in feelings, behaviors, and interpersonal relationships (van der Kolk & McFarlane, 2006). It takes on a life of its own.

We see another reaction to adversity far too frequently as well. Individuals trying to cope with toxic stress may reach for chemical or behavioral crutches ("chemical comforters") to help them cope. Wounded by trauma and feeling overmatched by adversity, it is a very human tactic to reach for an "other" as support in times of trouble. Attachment experience trains us to reach out for coping. If another human being is not available, for whatever reason, we will settle for something less. This is the beginning of "substitute relationships."

Multiform Stresses

Adverse and traumatic events are common, yet many people who experience trauma "do not seem to develop lasting effects" (van der Kolk, 2003, p. 169). They may experience stress symptoms, such as preoccupation, shakiness, anxiety, flashback or memory intrusion, or nightmares over several days or weeks following a trauma. Yet many recover naturally over time and do not experience extended psychiatric dysfunction (van der Kolk & McFarlane, 2006; Bremner, 2002). This is the good news.

Resilience in the present, however, is no guarantee of lifelong resistance. People can cope with acute stresses more or less effectively in the present and yet become ill or symptomatic, months or even years later. Memories of trauma, it seems, continually struggle to come alive, waiting only for opportunity and a trigger. The powerful emotions and meanings attached to the traumatic memory make it stand out. Remembrances of emotional tone and environmental cues (sights, smells, sounds) can be rolled into the memory as triggers. Even environmental cues from repeated instances of relived memory (flashbacks) can be folded in. Subsequent emergence of traumatic symptoms, even full-blown disorder, happens and is called "delayed" or "late onset" trauma (Bryant et al., 2013). This can occur in up to 25 percent of all PTSD cases.

For some, traumatic experiences lead to post-traumatic stress disorder, a diagnosable dysfunction in living; for others at the opposite end of the spectrum, the outcome may be "post-traumatic growth," an observable response of resilience in the face of trauma (Morrill et al., 2008). For still others, the outcomes are varied. A host of factors contribute to the ways in which the traumatic event impacts an individual: age of the person, developmental and psychological history, timing of traumatic occurrence(s), temperament, source of the trauma, previous exposures, length of the exposure, perceived sense of control, perception of the event's meaning, level of perceived life threat, availability and use of supports—all these contributing factors and more must be factored in.

Exposure most often leads to temporary preoccupation with the event and some level of memory intrusion immediately following the occurrence. Yet the full syndrome of post-traumatic stress disorder (PTSD) does not develop in all cases and simply from "extreme-magnitude events." Horrific events are over-represented among those suffering with PTSD, yes, but the extremity of the event itself does not easily correlate to major disability (Stuber, Kazak, Meeske, & Barakat, 1998). Research suggests that it is not the traumatic experience by itself that drives the development of PTSD, but "the persistence of intrusive and distressing recollections" or memories of the trauma (van der Kolk & McFarlane, 2006, p. 6). Persisting emotion- and body-based memories of the traumatic event are the culprits in PTSD and in the variety of symptoms that can give dogged pursuit to our consciousness, even below the threshold for full-blown disorder (van der Kolk, 2014).

Post-traumatic Stress Disorder

Of course, the most frequently discussed outcome of experiencing a traumatic event is the clinically diagnosable post-traumatic stress disorder (PTSD). This diagnosis includes exposure to, witnessing of, or extreme exposure to details of an overwhelming traumatic event or stressor, such as combat, natural or man-made disaster, and sexual assault (Criterion A). It is the outcome of what is called "event trauma" (Weinhold & Weinhold, 2015). The devastating nature of the event hinders integrating the event into a conscious memory or ongoing personal narrative, and creates difficulty in assimilating the trauma into self-identity. The event becomes a central defining moment in the person's life, drawing memories and consciousness back to it over and over again, like a lodestone.

At the extreme end of the spectrum, traumatic events break into a person's life, often without warning, and bring in their wake such distress and fear that life is forever altered. These events shake the core of the person and can overwhelm that individual's ability to cope, shifting the fundamental sense of self and others, and changing the ways that person perceives and moves in the world. They can alter the very ground on which we stand, making it unstable and unsafe. They can attack everything we know, or think we know, and affect our ability to trust others and seek help in renewing a sense of hope (Grant, 1996; Herman, 2012).

A number of symptoms are included in the full presentation and are arranged into symptom clusters:

- *Intrusion* or continual re-experiencing of the trauma (Criterion B),
- *Avoidance* or numbing of thoughts, feelings, or external reminders of the trauma (Criterion C),
- Negative *alterations in* cognition*s and mood*, including distorted beliefs, feelings, or blame, as well as diminished interest in previously valued activities, and feelings of disconnection from others (Criterion D), and
- *Alterations in* arousal *and reactivity*, including hypervigilance, irritability, or self-destructive behavior (Criterion E).
- The sixth criterion concerns *duration of symptoms* for one month or more (Criterion F);
- The seventh assesses distress or loss of normal *functioning* (Criterion G); and,
- The eighth criterion clarifies symptoms as not attributable to a substance or co-occurring medical condition (Criterion H).[7]

Post-traumatic stress disorder, as a diagnostic category, first appeared in DSM-III in 1980. Yet clinicians around the world are coming to see that the diagnosis may be inadequate for the full range of experiences and people affected, such as children, victims of spousal or child abuse, those subjected to acute hospitalizations, or those experiencing late-onset trauma-related symptoms long after childhood adversity ("developmental trauma").

As the numbers of qualifying events or circumstances continues to expand (see below), we are learning that adverse and traumatic occurrences are commonplace. The prevalence of adversity, trauma, and toxic stress far exceeds the numbers of those with PTSD. Post-traumatic stress disorder, while a predictable result of traumatic events, occurs only in a minority of those experiencing adversity. Logic suggests that some number of those who experience adversity, but who are *not* diagnosed with PTSD, might still experience harmful aftereffects. What might be the fallout for those with subclinical or "subsyndromal" post-traumatic symptoms? How might we understand their situation? Can lifelong emotional, relational, behavioral, or even physical dysfunction be conceptualized as the aftereffect of earlier trauma? Can toxic stress really affect us for a lifetime? Are life challenges such as substance-related and addictive disorders potential outcomes?

OTHER ADVERSE SITUATIONS

Over the last several years, I have come to see that, if we remain open to a variety of outcomes from toxic stress, we will appreciate the ubiquity of adverse occurrences and debilitating symptoms in people's lives. As I tell my students, *everyone* has a story. Adverse events and situations, as well as the toxic stress that trails behind, leave traces in that story, footprints made on soma, psyche, and spirit. The full spectrum of trauma or trauma-related disorders (Bremner, 2002; Scaer, 2005; Weinhold & Weinhold, 2015) is only now coming into view.

Following the work of Robert Scaer, physician and traumatologist, I will be laying out a variety of adverse situations that can have serious outcomes in their aftermath. Below is *"a continuum of variably negative life events occurring over the lifespan"* (Scaer, 2005, p. 2). This catalog of adversity is *not* exhaustive.

Attachment and Developmental Trauma[8]

Traumatization within attachment relationships has profoundly different impacts on affect regulation, self-con-
cept, and management of interpersonal relationships than
do disasters and motor vehicle accidents (VAN DER KOLK,
MCFARLANE, & WEISAETH, 1996/2007, P. X).

Many milestones, transition points, stages, and tasks are negotiated by
the developing individual, and the developmental point at which she or he
is traumatized or encounters adversity has a major impact on the degree to
which mind and brain are affected. Children rely on nurturing transactions
to form their brains, minds, and spirits; encounters with caregiving others
and affectionate relationships are the bread and butter of human attachment. The fact of simple attachment behavior, however, is a necessary but
not sufficient condition for positive development. It is the quality of attachment interactions, what developmental psychologists call attunement, that
really matters.

Developing humans experience stress when the relational connections
around them are less than satisfying or supportive. Insecure attachment and
relationship ruptures are traumatic. The accumulation of those experiences,
along with the individual's interpretation of those experiences and the availability of potential buffering resources and relationships, dictate whether that
stress becomes toxic or is ameliorated. This touches not only on the primary
attachment relationship but also on the wider network (for example, family)
in which children grow up. Intrafamilial resources (siblings, grandparents,
and others) can be a great additional asset in the wider attachment system.
Intrafamilial trauma, on the other hand, can produce complex symptoms
and ongoing traumatic "reenactments" (Weinhold & Weinhold, 2015, p. 3).

The public is still beguiled into thinking of trauma as overt acts of adversity, abuse, molestation, and so forth. This misleads us about the nature of
developmental trauma. We are speaking here of experiences, large and small,
that cause disruption in attachment, attunement, and bonding processes
during the early years of life (Weinhold & Weinhold, 2015). A child who is

not physically abused but is constantly told that he is "useless" (Joe) or she is "forgotten," and her needs consistently ignored in favor of others (think Cinderella), is one who is developmentally at risk. Every child has the right to experience that someone is "crazy about them."[9]

A core element of evolving and mature development is the formation of capacities for self-regulation and an integrated sense of self and positive identity amid satisfying interpersonal relationships. As Bessel van der Kolk writes: "our most intimate sense of self is created in our minute-to-minute exchanges with our caregivers" (2014, p. 111). Human identity is social and transactional (Cole & Putnam, 1992).

We have seen that affect and behavioral regulation are essential for self-identity to form. Self and social development are bound tightly together; they are psychological and social achievements. Van der Kolk again:

> "We are profoundly social creatures; our lives consist of finding our place within the community of human beings. . . . we get our first lessons in self-care from the way that we are cared for. Mastering the skill of self-regulation depends to a large degree on how harmonious our early interactions with our caregivers are." (2014, P. 112).

Sense of self and social development are also deeply biological. Early attachment caregiving occurs precisely at critical times in neural as well as psychological development (Schore, 2003a & b). Attachment transactions and attuned, synchronous give and take between caregiver and child build neural structures that are essential for self-regulation, stress response, and an ongoing capacity for further relating. This is the foundation for identity. Incest, child abuse, and early adversity interfere with necessary development in ways that increase the risk of serious psychopathology either in the immediate aftermath or later in life (Felitti, Anda, et al., 1998; Finkelhor & Browne, 1985). The loss of trust and fractured sense of safety undermine any sense of secure attachment.

Developing children form internal mental and behavioral representations of their world ("internal working models") through the interactions they have with significant others. These models constitute the background against which the child's expectations and desires form, and imprint into the biology of their brains. These processes—social, behavioral, psychological, biological—interpenetrate one another. When these interactions turn traumatic, these experiences can skew the child's expectations about the world, about the safety and security of relational life, and the child's sense of personal identity and integrity (van der Kolk, 2014).

In 1992 Cole and Putnam continued work initiated by Frank Putnam and colleagues into the impact of child abuse, irrevocably lifting the veil of secrecy and making an argument for a "developmentally sensitive model" of childhood trauma, particularly in the area of childhood sexual abuse. They documented "unique negative effects in the domains of self and social functioning, specifically in jeopardizing self-definition and integration, self-regulatory processes, and a sense of security and trust in relationships," as the result of childhood incest (p. 174). Their work began a long and painstaking study of self-regulation, cognitive, and behavioral problems as a result of early abuse and adversity (van der Kolk, 2014).

When caregiving is delayed or interrupted, twisted or nonexistent, the wiring of our "self-circuitry"—the images in our library of working models and our patterned relations with others—becomes distorted. Connections can help to restore the balance and provide resilience in the face of attachment wounds. But often this will take work and no small amount of luck.

Attachment-sensitive counseling can address these concerns in several ways. First, the welcoming and affirming attitude and caring stance of the counselor echoes the desire to be known and understood from our earliest days. The counseling alliance parallels this attachment dynamic and can provide corrective experiences. Second, the counseling process helps clients to understand and rewrite their stories in a new and empathic way while sharing it with another who can provide validation. Third, wise counseling assists the client in reaching out to original attachment and allo-caring relationships, so that new learning can be solidified within significant family and kinship connections as well as within the alliance. Each step in this therapeutic process deepens the healing.

Acute Childhood Illness, Medical Intervention, and Extended Hospitalization

Previously, chronic medical illness in children, and the treatment protocols for those illnesses, were not seen as sufficient to trigger traumatic stress, since they were not outside the range of normal expectancy (Stuber, Kazak, et al., 1998). Treatments for childhood cancer, for example, were "just the way we do things . . . never mind how uncomfortable or embarrassing those treatments may be for the young patient." Many physicians follow the normal protocols and pay scant attention to the psychosocial or even physical aftermath. If the child survives treatment and cancer, which they often do at present, all is well.[10] Nevertheless, with greater sensitivity to childhood development, we now suggest that notions of life threat and risks to physical integrity have been downplayed for too long in childhood medical care.[11]

Psychologist Anne Kazak and her colleagues at Children's Hospital of Philadelphia have pioneered utilizing the trauma model as a useful conceptual framework for childhood cancer, other chronic medical conditions, and their treatments (Kazak, Kassem-Adams, et al., 2006). There are significant levels of acute stress, and therefore the potential for post-traumatic and chronic toxic stress, as outcomes from these illnesses and their treatments.

While these experiences may not yield the full clinical disorder of PTSD in many patients, research studies are documenting clinically significant sequellae, or post-traumatic stress *symptoms* (PTSS), such as somatic complaints (e.g. stomach aches), bad dreams, intrusive memories, or repetitive play, in a number of child patients (Kazak, Alderfer, et al., 2004; Stuber, Kazak, et al., 1998; Kazak, Barakat, et al., 1997). Interestingly, once they began looking, researchers discovered that parents and even siblings of seriously ill children may also experience post-traumatic symptoms. This suggests that there is need for comprehensive, family-sensitive care in these situations.

There is also reason to suggest that more subtle psychological changes may be present, and that specific symptoms may not exhaust the full impact of stressful events. Childhood cancer survivors, for example, report that they are "changed" by the experience, often for the better, but not always. This suggests that there are subtle changes in personality or character such as "modulation of affect, maintenance of interpersonal boundaries, and intensity of interpersonal relationships" (Stuber, Kazak, et al., 1998, p. 175). Again, such changes affect emotional regulation, interpersonal relationships, worldview, and sense of identity. Trauma may also manifest itself through delayed somatic complaints, such as chronic pain, sleep disturbances, depression, and a variety of anxiety reactions, even into adulthood (Scaer, 2005). Behavioral disorders, such as substance use disorders, may also result.

I have engaged in counseling relationships with a number of young adult and several older patients who had previously been diagnosed and treated for serious childhood cancers. Interestingly, of the five patients I've seen who had struggled with childhood cancer, two were in middle adulthood (forties) and had recurrences of cancer, while three were still in early adulthood (twenties) and, while they had no current cancer symptoms, their life trajectories were stalled because of anxiety, depression, substance misuse, or amotivation. In none of these cases did a patient acknowledge the role of previous cancer or treatment, or the psychological impact of childhood cancer, in their current stressful situation, feeling as though they had "moved on." Yet there was something unresolved about the past that they instinctively shied away from. It was as though they had determinedly moved on from their previous illnesses and left them behind, but those illnesses still cast a shadow. Changes in attitude and behavior in counseling came, however, when they were willing to look at the past and confront it. Childhood illness seems to act like an invisible ball and chain in the life trajectories of some patients.

The Childhood Cancer Survivor Study (CCSS) has documented substantial information about survivors of childhood cancer.[12] As follow-up, a number of researchers including Bradley Zebrack, Lonnie Zeltzer, and others have studied the long-term impact of childhood cancer and its treatments and have published findings about psychosocial and physical effects of childhood and adolescent cancer and its treatment (Stuber et al., 2010; Zebrack, 1999; Zeltzer et al., 2009).

With improvement in treatments for childhood cancer and other illnesses, affected children have a good chance at physical survival into adulthood.

This does not mean, however, that they have no long-term impacts from the experience. In fact, while many survivors of childhood cancer report good quality of life and ongoing health, some subgroups of survivors need greater understanding and long-term support. Research has documented risk factors for ongoing distress, including low educational attainment, unmarried status, unemployment, lack of health insurance, or the presence of a major medical condition. Behavioral risk factors and poor health behaviors, including smoking and risky alcohol use, fatigue, and altered sleep, also interact with psychological distress (Zeltzer et al., 2009).

Motor Vehicle, Occupational, and Household Accidents, Particularly if they Involve Significant Medical Intervention and Hospitalization, Acute and/or Chronic Illness

"Distressing or harmful events can lead to negative outcomes, such as post-traumatic stress symptoms (PTSS), but they can also lead to positive outcomes, an experience termed post-traumatic growth (PTG)" (MORRILL, BREWER, ET AL., 2008).

Television has accustomed us to the drama and expertise involved in emergency, trauma, and critical care medicine. The plot lines of our favorite medical sitcoms often focus on urgent procedures and follow-up care, as well as potential medical residue, such as extended wound care or post-concussive syndrome (PCS). The fictional characters become involved in the complications from trauma, and a good word from the medical specialist often brings a convenient resolution, all within an hour.

Television is not a good medium, however, for presenting the real-life complications that we know exist and that cannot be managed by the *bon mots* of a caring physician. These are the lengthier psychosocial dilemmas that can follow trauma and adversity.

Cecilia, a 35-year-old schoolteacher from a small town in New England, was driving home from local errands. It was a beautiful autumn day. She stopped to make a turn onto her street and was immediately struck by the distracted driver from behind her. She found her car pushed to the side of the road. Except for bumps and bruises, no one seemed seriously injured. Nevertheless, over the next several months Cecilia continued to have symptoms, such as flashbacks, anxiety, hyperventilation about driving, and sleeplessness. These continued to interfere with the smooth functioning of her life.

Traffic accidents, major and minor, are a staple hazard of modern American life.[13] Some can be quite horrific, with loss of life or limb; others have a variety of physical and psychiatric outcomes. Most of us don't pay attention to the ongoing or delayed occurrence of stress- and trauma-related symptoms from motor vehicle or household accidents. It is the price of modern living, and we expect that once the accident is over it is time to move on. But for some, "moving on" is the one thing they cannot do. For example, a significant percentage of those involved in motor vehicle accidents—approximately one-third—have persistent psychiatric symptoms related to stress and adversity (Mayou, Bryant, & Ehlers, 2001).

Repeated Traumatic Exposure, such as First Responders, Soldiers, Abused Children, and Others

Not long ago, I worked with someone who had been a policeman and then ambulance driver for most of his working life. He was referred to my cancer service for psychosocial support of a systemic cancer. One day he acknowledged that for years he had had difficulty sleeping through the night, and still did. He had never told anyone except his wife about this. He would wake up with gruesome images from dreams that reflected his working activities. Sometimes he awoke while sleepwalking with thoughts of "trying to escape." His ambulance often reported to house fires, motor vehicle accidents, and local disasters; he replayed in his mind gathering up human body parts and disfigured torsos for transport. Being a trauma survivor himself was the last thing he thought about, although his lack of sleep, compulsive smoking, and cancer may have resulted from ongoing, unresolved toxic stress.

Unrecognized Societal Traumas, Including Preverbal or Neonatal Trauma, as well as Medical Practices that may Cause Adversity, such as Fetal and Infant Surgery, Birthing, Isolation, Poor Pain Management, Infant Delivery

"One controversial but critical example . . . is preverbal trauma, which includes, among other things, in utero exposure of the fetus to the stress hormone cortisol from the distressed mother, in utero fetal surgery, medicalized, technologically advanced and intrinsically traumatic birthing procedures, and exposure of preemies in neonatal ICUs to isolation and inadequate pain management" (SCAER, 2005, P. 97).

Physician Robert Scaer offers insights into the wider trauma spectrum in his disturbing chapter, "Preverbal Trauma," as part of his book *The Trauma Spectrum* (2005).

Beginning this chapter of his book with a brief discussion of neonatal pain perception and preverbal sentience, Scaer sets the stage for understanding neonatal medical procedures from the fetal infant's point of view. He makes a convincing case: Infants and neonates can experience trauma from a variety of sources, including from invasive medical procedures, from sterile intensive care environments, from insensitive birthing procedures, and from the mother's own experiences of stress. The potential impacts can be far-reaching.

For instance, commenting on the impact of maternal stress, emotional health, and mental illness on the wellness and neural development of the fetus, Scaer comments:

"Newborns from depressed mothers had lower APGAR scores, were more irritable, cried more, and were more difficult to console and quiet. . . . In other words, exposure of the mother to stress during the pregnancy contributed to changes in the autonomic status of the fetus and to behavioral abnormalities in the infant after birth . . . Spikes in maternal cortisol are also correlated with increased miscarriages in early pregnancy . . .

Finally, exposure of the fetus to the stress-related hormones of the distressed mother is likely to alter the infant's adaptive capacity to further life stress through sensitization and reprogramming of the fetal HPA axis" (2005, PP. 106–107).

We are reminded again that the maternal caregiving environment, within and outside the womb, is a primary system for shaping infant development (Karr-Morse & Wiley, 2013). Dysregulation of affect and behavior in infants exposed to prenatal and infant stress, especially those affected by maternal depression, is an ongoing field of study (Burke, 2003; Field, 1998; Field et al., 2006).

In addition, we now know that prenatal and early maternal stresses can affect the development of infant neuroendocrine and immunological systems. The effects of adversity and toxic stress can become biologically embedded as stress responses are recalibrated, sensitized, and overall health is altered (Johnson, Riley, et al., 2013).

"Delayed Trauma" or "Delayed-onset" Reactions

Memories are at the core of trauma reactions. Many different kinds of traumas, from natural disasters and accidents to various kinds of abuse, to kidnapping and torture, have eventuated in trauma reactions and to amnesias that can be triggered back to life at a later time. There are those with traumatic events in their history who have memory recurrences 10 to 20 years later. This is the most common pattern in adult trauma, and some persons have worsening symptoms over time (McFarlane, 2016).

Trauma specialists are learning that "the memory system is made up of networks of related information, and that activation of one aspect of such a network facilitates the retrieval of associated memories" (van der Kolk, et al.,1996, p. 284). Studies indicate that some proportion of those affected have total amnesia for traumatic events while others have significant amnesias for details of those events. The relevant triggers for memory retrieval, however, seem to be the emotions and sensations attached to particular experiences.

Bessel van der Kolk and others have hypothesized that, in specific cases, the emotional and sensory input from traumatic events is unable to be integrated into the individual's personal narrative and hence remains in a kind of split-off, dissociated state. When it is triggered by emotional or sensory cues later in life, it returns in its undigested state to plague that individual. This is the essence of the pathology of PTSD (van der Kolk, et al., 1996).

Cultural Trauma, Including Exposure to Violence in the Media and Popular Entertainment

Robert Scaer and others speak about cultural trauma as a group of manufactured stresses and tensions that make a population feel afraid and endangered. Terrorism and modern media's inflation of terrorism's effects, as well as a government's authoritarian response, can be part of this pattern. Civil unrest can also reach threatening proportions. Many have become all too familiar with these traumatic occurrences in our cultures. Critiques of the media and modern entertainment are available for readers. Below, however, I want to address a different kind of cultural trauma.

In *Hillbilly Elegy*, author J. D. Vance (2016) describes the heartbreak and resilience of a subculture within America: the white, Scots-Irish, Appalachian "hillbilly" culture. Their story, as told by Vance, is a parable of the deleterious effects of cultural fragmentation and societal disconnection. It is a cautionary tale for what can happen when people are left with lack of connection to the wider society, with little social capital, with few mainstream cultural resources, and with loss of hope. Vance describes the plight of hillbilly culture seen in social and familial dissolution as well as the trauma and substance abuse that plague Appalachia.[14]

The societal deterioration Vance describes, however, does not just affect marginalized white folks. Localized cultures can have profound effects and create situations of collective toxic stress and concentrated adversity. In his own powerful book, Gregory Boyle, a Jesuit priest working with Latino gangs in Los Angeles, lays out similar dynamics.

Tattoos on the Heart (2011) tells the story of Boyle's ministry, running Homeboy Industries, the largest gang intervention program in the United States.[15] Homeboy offers a variety of opportunities, such as locally run job training, tattoo removal, and employment assistance to former members of enemy gangs and incarcerated women and men in Los Angeles. It encompasses a variety of facilities and services from education and parenting classes, to bakeries and restaurants, to groceries, silkscreens, and embroideries, as well as counseling and job search services.

While these are all opportunities for former gang members to acquire skills and social capital, which in turn increases access to the mainstream culture and a helping hand out of neighborhood crime and violence, they are also opportunities to encounter Boyle's ministry of kinship. Homeboy creates an environment of kinship in which former enemies can reach across the divide and engender an atmosphere of hope that can revitalize the spirit. Not taking the narrative approach of *Hillbilly Elegy, Tattoos* is a collection of essays describing the gang members and families whom Boyle has encountered and the power of universal kinship and redemption.[16]

Both *Tattoos* and *Elegy* offer inside looks at localized American subcultures that, while clearly different on the outside, are not so different within. These microcultures—Scots-Irish working class and urban Latino gangs—surround people and provide a sense of identity and belonging, but ultimately do not serve the greater needs of their members, particularly as people attempt to integrate into the larger society. The attitudes and values these cultures engender are ultimately stress-producing, self-defeating, and toxic. They provide little of the human and social capital needed for success and healthy living. Immersions in these cultures can predispose for alienation, addiction, and violence.

Both books, however, also provide a sense of strategies that can address the problems. J. D. Vance, author of *Elegy*, describes his good fortune in the loving care and support of people who nurtured him. They provided a way for him to move up and out. Now an attorney and venture capitalist, as well as bestselling author, Vance has become an important voice in our society's reevaluation. Boyle's ministry provides the same kind of redemptive service through Homeboy Industries, what he calls "a community of compassion from which no one is excluded." It is a ministry of "mutual kinship." He continues his wide-ranging ministry, both at Homeboy and in his publications and lectures that provide a similar reevaluation of our modern society.[17]

Both real-life stories of marginalized subcultures offer a glimpse into dynamics that can be catalysts for cultural trauma, leading to individual and family dysfunction. Depression, anxiety, substance misuse and addiction, physical and mental illness, even suicide, are often not far behind. Yet both narratives also provide insights for ways forward. Building social capital in the form of community inclusion and access to community resources (employment, education, housing, and financial support) are critical. Homeboy Industries is a very useful model here. It is also interesting to note that J. D. Vance has recently returned to his roots in Appalachia to begin Our Ohio Renewal (OOR), which envisions building employment, supported housing, job training and educational opportunities, and community at the local and state level.[18]

Both *Tattoos* and *Elegy* offer welcoming and challenging community as a form of treatment for alienation and disconnection. Care and connection are essential elements for addressing trauma and addiction. Toward the end of this book, I will draw some conclusions about the social and ecological implications of these stories. Attachment-sensitive counseling cannot simply be a psychotherapeutic intervention. Practitioners must also become advocates for building healing and recovering systems of care. Discovering a renewed sense of meaning and experiencing inclusion within a welcoming society is as important for full recovery from substance disorders as restructured neurobiology and psychological wellness. Connection is powerful.

WHAT ARE THE PATHWAYS FROM STRESS AND TRAUMA TO ADDICTION?

Unfortunately, stress and trauma are all too common and appear to be a hidden engine underneath many different manifestations of addictive outcomes (such as chemical addictions, behavioral compulsions, and "a-holias"). Some events that trigger trauma are clearly horrific, and we have finally come to understand that they can leave psychic and emotional scars along with the physical ones. In addition, toxic stress may not be tied to specific events but to patterns of adversity and relationship failure. These too can leave their marks, large and small. Individuals can encounter adversity in their initial maternal care and familial environments, and in ongoing ways throughout their development. Memories, sensations, and details of previous adversity can be retrieved inadvertently, if the relevant cues re-emerge. We are also learning that some events and behavioral patterns, while seemingly less catastrophic and more "normal," can leave footprints on the bodies, brains, psyches, and emotional life of vulnerable persons who require support and understanding.

Stress, adversity and trauma—whether they encounter us prenatally, in childhood, adolescence, or in adulthood—have the potential to skew hormonal and neural formation and development, to affect emotional regulation and reactivity, and to disfigure our perceptions of self, others and the world. So far, we have seen that those with a history of trauma have a greater likelihood of utilizing psychoactive substances and compulsive activities, and those who struggle with addiction have a high probability of involvement with trauma.

Addiction is not the only negative outcome from trauma, of course. We know that adversity and toxic stress have an impact on a number of medical, psychiatric, and behavioral health risks. The focus of this book on addiction, however, raises the question about pathways from adversity to addiction. How does trauma "get under the skin" to create the conditions for substance-related and addictive disorders?

Adversity and trauma are catalysts for toxic stress. Experiences of stress trigger a cascade of biological responses, flooding our bodily systems with hormones and chemical messengers. These chemicals initiate physical actions and reactions, as well as functional and even structural changes that help to meet the dangers brought by stress and adversity. This is the way our systems are designed. When the danger passes, our bodies should return to balance (homeostasis). However, adversity also sensitizes stress response systems and engraves the experience into learning and memory so that the occurrence of similar situations triggers the stress response more quickly. Memories and their environmental triggers help us to respond. Linking of memory and situational awareness with stress-responsive systems provides real survival value through rapid behavioral and psychological responses. An alert and sensitive sentinel system is essential for survival in the wild and in the jungle of human relationships.

The focus for much of this activity is a highly interactive stress response system connecting the emotional limbic system, HPA axis, hippocampus, vagal safe/not safe complex, and neocortex. Stimulation of these systems, either by external cues or internal states, creates emotional arousal, visceral activation, and when needed, neuromuscular activity (Everly & Lating, 2013).

As we have seen, two of the main psychobiological pathways to addiction are (1) the Pleasure-Reward-Motivation track through the mesocorticolimbic system, utilizing dopamine and endogenous opiates, and (2) the stress and adversity track, employing the extended stress response systems (HPA and SAM axes) and neurochemicals such as adrenaline, cortisol, and glucocorticoids.

With the advent of psychobiological studies we are learning that what began as a social and interpersonal process (trauma and adversity) is transformed over time into a physiological process as well, and becomes more deeply inscribed or embedded into the brain. Environmental elements are folded into the traumatic memories as triggers and augmented in memory; they can become catalysts for increasing reactivity. Allied to this neurobiological process is a sensitive psychological process. Hormones flooding our biological systems trigger the emotions of anxiety, panic, and a need to act defensively that are complemented by fight-or-flight behaviors.

In optimal (attached and attuned) development this is how it proceeds: Connection and biography become biology, creating the fertile soil out of which regulation, identity, and relationship capacity emerge. However, when development does not progress well, cracks open and holes or ruts appear, the individual is unable to adjust or adapt, and feels the need for substitutes. Toxic stress enters the picture when expected attachment relationships do not materialize or are distorted. Affect and stress dysregulation and inability to turn to others for co-regulation (emotional soothing and comfort) contribute to the onset, continued use, and relapse into drug use and addictive behaviors (Daily, 2012).

However, it is important to remember that the physiological development of humanity also leads to a second outcome. The social brain becomes the catalyst for a social and cultural environment that continues human and neural development. We affect our own growth and development. In particular, the process of co-regulation by turning to others can become enshrined in cultural assumptions and societal mores surrounding love, friendship, and community. Rules of conduct and laws regulating behavior, public and private, can codify a sense of identity and mutual belonging. Art and literature can be drafted into a common enterprise for celebrating these cultural values. The self-regulating social brain can give birth to these many ways of being together.

The next section will focus on ACEs as a case study for the role of toxic stress and substitute coping in addiction.

7

❖❖❖

Impact and Implications of Childhood Adversity: The ACE Study

"It is easier to build strong children than to repair broken men."

—FREDERICK DOUGLASS

"Society reaps what it sows in the way it nurtures its children."

—MARTIN H. TEICHER

NEW RESEARCH IS REGULARLY COMING to light that can help us understand the pervasiveness and wider implications of early adversity in people's lives. Adverse childhood experiences, or ACEs, are understood to be trauma exposures that constitute a frequent and common pathway to "social, emotional, and cognitive impairments that lead to increased risk of unhealthy behaviors, risk of violence or re-victimization, disease, disability, and premature mortality as people age and develop" (Anda, 2008, p. 3). That is, ACEs are understood to be a "hidden engine" underneath many of the nation's leading health and social problems.

ACEs predispose for maladaptive and risky coping mechanisms and behaviors (for example, smoking or opioid misuse) that can become auxiliary pathways to other problems (overdose) and chronic illnesses (cancers). The ACE studies, then, broaden our understanding of traumatic experiences *and* their sequellae (Cronholm et al., 2015). They can help us to unravel the complex and intertwined effects, short- and long-term, as well as the connections and potential pathways of trauma, adversity, and toxic stress.

In the words of Frank Putnam, professor of pediatrics at the University of Cincinnati, the ACE studies have "changed the landscape" in public health, pediatric, and even adult medicine. ACE is fueling an emerging field of trauma-informed understanding, treatment, practice, and prevention.[1]

Currently, researchers, practicing physicians, prevention providers, and others are concentrating their work on several elements of developing ACE knowledge, including (a) the neurological impact of ACEs and toxic stress on children's developing brains; (b) the effects of ACEs on overall health; (c) on genes and intergenerational transmission of ACEs; and (d) on resilience research. The more we know about the effects and reach of adversity, the better informed we can be for intervention, treatment, and prevention.

ACE science also addresses major questions in this book: What is the role of trauma in disease and health, broadly? Is early adversity a catalyst for substitute relationships and addiction? Is trauma a leading factor in individuals' liability for addiction? Can harmful use of chemicals, addiction, and engaging in compulsive behaviors be understood as potential solutions to other problems, as adaptations to adversity? A growing consensus sees addictions, even harmful use, as a predictable result of childhood trauma (Anda, Felitti, et al., 2006).

Evidence from a wide variety of sources indicates that America's addiction health crisis—and specifically its current prescription drug and opioid crisis—has roots in childhood and later adversity. This insight does not deny that other factors, such as genetics, temperament, or comorbid mental illness, are important, but it does insist that developmental trauma, toxic stress, and social ecology are major players in public health. The evidence also indicates that improvements in the nation's health and addiction crisis must involve intervention and prevention regarding adverse childhood experiences and transformation of the nation's families and other social systems (Dubé, Felitti, et al., 2003). Childhood adversity is a premier predisposing risk factor for vulnerability to substance-related and addictive disorders.

The original and follow-on ACE studies find that most people (64 percent) have some burden from ACE, while 12 percent of the population have an ACE score severity of 4 or more (Harris, 2018).[2] This score doubles the risk of later heart disease and cancer along with greatly increasing the risks for alcoholism (700 percent) and attempted suicide (1200 percent). "Compared with people who have zero ACEs, people with ACE scores are two to four times more likely to use alcohol or other drugs and to start using drugs at an earlier age. People with an ACE score of 5 or higher are seven to ten times more likely to use illegal drugs, to report addiction and to inject illegal drugs" (Stevens, 2017, p. 3).[3] Additionally, people with histories of childhood trauma often have more chronic pain and use more prescription drugs, making them more likely to engage in doctor-shopping and drug-seeking with opioids. Those with ACE scores of five or higher are three times more likely to misuse prescription pain medications.

A BRIEF LOOK AT THE EVOLUTION OF ACE

The ACE studies broaden our understanding of traumatic experiences and toxic stress in several ways. With a basic cohort of over 17,000 respondents, the initial study—one of the largest of its kind ever undertaken—occurred between 1995 and 1997 in two waves, to allow for midcourse corrections. The first wave responded to survey questions and follow-up regarding eight categories of adversity. Two additional categories of neglect were added in the second wave.

The ACE categories on which the scoring is based include such things as growing up abused or neglected, witnessing parental marital discord or domestic violence, or living with substance abusing, mentally ill, or criminal household members. The effects of these experiences are seen to be powerful, long-term, and cumulative; often, in childhood, adverse experiences are not isolated events but rather co-occur, and the cumulative effect can be daunting. The initial ACE study assessed the prevalence and impact of the full

10 categories of traumatic childhood experiences and cross-referenced them with a variety of later health and social consequences (Anda, 2008).

It should be noted that the original list of 10 adverse experiences was already larger and more encompassing than a typical list of traumatic events at that time. The previous literature on trauma, up until World War II, had been limited to adult stressors and adversity, and even then listed trauma as a catastrophic "event" in a person's life (combat, natural disaster, and later, rape). It was not until after the Vietnam War that researchers and clinicians began looking at child maltreatment as a different category of adversity from "event trauma." Childhood adversity predisposes for a different kind of impact, named "developmental trauma" (Weinhold & Weinhold, 2015).

With further experience and international consultation the list continues to expand, adding adversities that occur in both the developed and developing worlds. Experts now consider that, when we are dealing with children, a wider range of traumatic experiences can be equally devastating and produce debilitating outcomes even years later. Consequently, further expansion of *categories of adversity* has continued. Adversities such as major accidents, acute and serious illnesses (such as cancer, autoimmune or seizure disorders), childhood hospitalizations, involvement with the foster care system, bullying, or loss of a sibling can be stressful for a child (see previous chapter). In addition to the 10 original categories, adversities from a global context, such as child kidnapping and conscription, forced marriage, genital mutilation, or losing a parent to deportation, have been added. In this regard, expanding categories of adversity provide a catalyst for deeper consideration and appreciation of social, cultural, and ecological dimensions of adversity and the effects on children. Further discussion may suggest that other adverse experiences should also be considered, such as experiences of discrimination, community violence, or police brutality.[4]

Over the last decade there have been accelerating efforts to gather and use the ACE data for public health purposes. The Centers for Disease Control and Prevention (CDC) has incorporated ACE-related survey questions into its ongoing surveillance system, the Behavioral Risk Factor Surveillance System (BRFSS), and has helped states to conduct the surveys.[5] Currently there are more than 30 U.S. states involved. Use of similar surveys in public health surveillance has also occurred in developing countries in Africa and Asia; the data suggests similar relationships between adversity and health risk, comparing the original ACE cohort outcomes with further studies and populations (Brown et al., 2009). Collaboration with the World Health Organization (WHO) has begun.

> It has been shown that considerable and prolonged stress in childhood has life-long consequences for a person's health and well-being. It can disrupt early brain development and compromise functioning of the nervous and immune systems. In addition because of the behaviours [sic] adopted by some people who have faced ACEs, such stress can lead to serious problems such as alcoholism, depression, eating disorders, unsafe sex, HIV/AIDS, heart disease, cancer, and other chronic diseases[6]

Another element that broadens our understanding involves the *mechanisms* by which ACEs exert their effects. Not so long ago, experts believed a simple narrative, namely that child mistreatment arrested psychosocial development, or fostered tainted psychological defenses, and warped internal images of self, others, and the world. This view was almost entirely social and psychological. We now know that this narrative needs augmentation with neurobiological sophistication. Over the last twenty years or so, a "reasonably clear picture" has emerged of the relationship between adversity and alterations in neural structure and function (Teicher & Samson, 2016).

Additionally, adversity science is revealing the broad diversity of *outcomes* from child maltreatment and toxic environments. For example, contrary to expectations, ACEs appear to have similar psychobiological impact regardless of category. Surprisingly, verbal shaming or humiliation can be equally damaging when compared with physical or sexual abuse, or neglect. Physical, sexual, and psychological trauma and neglect can lead to psychiatric or medical challenges that show up in childhood, adolescence, or adulthood and assume many forms, including substance-related and addictive disorders. Medical illnesses (such as cancers, heart disease, autoimmune disorders), psychiatric illnesses (such as anxiety or depression, somatoform disorders, or a variety of personality disorders), and behavioral difficulties (such as suicidality, violence, addiction) can all emerge within a history of trauma and toxic stress. ACEs can also lead to problems with emotional regulation, impulse control, relationship difficulties, and social judgment (Shonkoff & Garner, 2012). This helps to explain why so many children are misdiagnosed with ADD/ADHD when the real challenge may be adversity. Post-traumatic stress disorder (PTSD) and the lesser but still debilitating post-traumatic stress symptoms (PTSS) may also complete the picture.

ACE RESEARCH: WHAT HAVE WE LEARNED?

ACEs sought to fill the conceptual gaps in our understanding of child development. Converging information from multiple studies and a variety of disciplines has become the landscape for a new adversity science, an emerging field of trauma-informed understanding, treatment, and practice.

Some observations:

1. ACEs are common, but unrecognized.

Many individuals experience adversity and/or maltreatment over the course of development. The fingerprints of these experiences not only shape our psychology and spirit, they also sculpt our neurobiology and other physical systems. There is a slowly evolving picture regarding the impact of these changes on psychopathology, the role of resilience, the roles of family and genetic influence, and patterns of expression (Teicher & Samson, 2016). A major task of the new adversity science is to pursue these impacts and influences, specifying how they interact and mutually affect one another.

ACE findings confirm that risks for trauma experiences and toxic stress are neither evenly nor randomly distributed over the population, but rather tend to occur in clusters. Those who experience developmental adversity tend to experience more than one kind, and in fact can experience multiple exposures ("doses") that have a cumulative impact on development. As the ACE score increases, so does the risk of numerous health and social problems throughout the lifespan. That is, larger doses of ACE have a cumulative impact and form a graded, dose-response relation to outcomes. Those with four or more ACEs (one in six of the people studied) were twice as likely to be adult smokers, 7 times more likely to be alcoholic, 10 times more likely to have injected street drugs, and 12 times more likely to have attempted suicide. People with high ACE scores are more likely to be violent, to have more marriages, more broken bones, more depression, more suicide attempts, more drug prescriptions, more auto-immune diseases, and more work absences (Harris, 2018).

As a relevant example for our interests, 81 percent of those who grew up with household substance abuse reported at least one (and often more) additional ACEs (Anda, 2008). The relevant childhood stressors are interrelated, often co-occurring in the same homes and increasing the "dose" of trauma to family members. Outcomes such as heart disease, addiction, depression, or suicidality increase in likelihood as the ACE score increases.

Moreover, once someone has grown beyond childhood, her or his cumulative adversity is often hidden due to the passage of time, to social taboo, to shame, or to a legitimate desire to move on from a distressing past. The impact of their burden of adversity, however, although dormant, does not dissipate. It may lie in wait until called forth by triggers from within the person or in the external environment, or it may emerge in a mutated form as a biological illness (cancer, autoimmune disorders, stress-related conditions), or mental health problem like depression, anxiety, or in behavioral disorders such as harmful substance use or addiction. The emerging problem may then require a substitute strategy for coping that can lead to additional risky behaviors, particularly given the individual's prior vulnerabilities and deficits in self-regulation. Individuals drag around their ACE experiences like a ball and chain.

"Joe" (from earlier chapters, with an estimated high ACE score of 4-plus), for example, moved on from an adverse childhood and adolescence, and established a family and career. However, the seeds of adversity gave rise to anxieties, particularly around issues of social competence and self-worth. He coped with these anxieties through increasing use of alcohol and overwork. This led to a slow-growing negative outlook and depression, along with high blood pressure and pre-diabetes. As Joe's substitute relationship to intoxication and tuned-out defensive living became more pronounced, it led to further difficulties, creating more anxieties, exacerbating his medical conditions, and enhancing needs for substitute coping.

Is it fair to say that Joe's problem was the brain disease of alcoholism? Or, is a better explanation the ongoing impact of childhood adversity and faulty coping, and did this play as much of a role as the chemical (alcohol), both in his neurobiological vulnerability and in his psychosocial impairments? Thinking this way would likely impact the choice of therapy for Joe. Is a twenty-eight day inpatient rehabilitation for addiction (which Joe's family clearly wanted) the treatment of choice, or an outpatient course of attachment-sensitive counseling that could address his traumatic past, current anxieties, and use of alcohol?

2. ACEs continue to have a large effect decades later.

ACEs are relational experiences of adversity that miswire and distort neural circuits, psychosocial mindsets, capacities for self-regulation, and sense of self. This creates vulnerabilities and it may well be that adversity wires the brain and related systems for survival and functioning in a (perceived) more hostile environment, keeping the individual keyed up, excessively alert, and living defensively (Teicher, 2000, 2002). Left to fend for themselves, ACE-affected children seek ways to adapt and survive. Of course, this constant adaptation to adversity, a positive from an evolutionary point of view, comes with a price.

ACE researchers are uncovering evidence of an association between these social and environmental experiences (trauma exposures) and the process of neurodevelopment. Neuroscientists now link childhood maltreatment to long-term changes in brain structure and function.

- Early stress is associated with lasting alterations in interconnected neurobiological systems, including the prefrontal cortex, hippocampus, amygdala, corpus callosum, and cerebellum (Teicher, 2000, 2002). These form an interconnected circuit that monitors and reacts to environmental danger (Danese & McEwen, 2012).

- Early stress is also associated with alterations in stress-responsive systems, such as the hypothalamic-pituitary-adrenal or HPA axis, making it both hypersensitive and hyperreactive (Danese & McEwen, 2012; Anda, 2008).
- These effects on the developing brain and connected hormonal and immunological systems affect many human functions into adulthood including emotional regulation, immune response, endocrine function, memory, aggression, and substance misuse (see Anda, 2008; Baylin & Hughes, 2016).

These exposures can also lead to unwanted experiences with post-trauma symptoms. Take, for example, the observation that there appears to be a split within the brain/mind that occurs in response to a trauma that is not fully resolved (van der Kolk, 2014). As a result, memories are not fully integrated, while emotions are left intact and take on a life of their own. This forms "states of mind," that is, networks or patterns (schema) of thinking/ feeling related to the trauma. These schemas contain dissociated aspects of the original experience such as memories, thoughts, emotions, and somatic symptoms, which are easily reactivated in response to mental images, sensations, and internal and environmental cues. Smells, sounds, sensations directly or indirectly related to the original trauma can all be triggers for a defensive or coping response. It is not uncommon for coping to involve adaptive use of "painkillers" (alcohol or other drugs), distractions (gambling, sex), attachments (to power, or fame, or wealth), or other ultimately counterproductive strategies (substitutes) that can make negative schemas disappear for a time.

In other words trauma can set the stage for later difficulties. It sets the terms of engagement for struggling with ongoing development, maturity, and personal and spiritual growth. There is also evidence that a history of trauma and adversity can complicate the relationship with healthcare providers and inhibit sufferers' consistent engagement in disease management (Korhonen et al., 2015).

3. ACEs underlie much of the health and well-being of the nation but do not function in a straightforward manner.

ACEs are transformed from psychosocial and behavioral experiences of adversity and toxic stress (attunement ruptures, caregiving deficits, attachment failures, physical or emotional brutality) into relational impairments, risky behaviors, and substitute adaptive solutions to stress that can lead to medical and psychiatric disease, health complications, disrupted social functioning, and addiction. The route of transformation, the mediating factor from ACEs to adult dysfunction, is disrupted neurodevelopment, the misshaping of brain circuits, structure and function, cumulative effects on endocrine and immunological systems, and distortion of psychosocial experience (Anda, 2008). These function in a graded, dose-response relationship with health outcomes and health-risk behaviors.

We are learning more all the time about the "plasticity" of neural and biological development both in utero and beyond (Karr-Morse, 2012). Children are vulnerable to the distorting influence of adversity because their young systems are incomplete and still developing. A complicating developmental factor is the enduring impact of stress and adversity that occurs during "sensitive" (times of increased sensitivity to environmental influence) or "critical" (period of time beyond which environmental influence will not matter) developmental periods. These are windows of vulnerability or opportunity. Potential alterations in psychobiological, neural, endocrine, and immune systems are mediated by a number of factors, but the timing of exposures to adversity, as well as the severity and duration of exposures, and the presence or absence of environmental buffers, are important to consider (National Scientific Council on the Developing Child, 2007).

It is worth noting here that ACEs are also disturbances in family relationships and deprive children of the security and emotional support they need for healthy development. ACEs do not just happen to individuals, but affect the family system as well. They disrupt and distort family relationships; they can also inhibit the protective buffering that family members might provide to one another.[7] ACE burden appears to transmit across generations in family ecologies (Noll, Trickett, Harris, & Putnam, 2009). Not surprisingly, while individuals with significant ACE histories are more likely to experience physical and mental illness, relationship difficulties, and substance abuse, they are also more likely to expose their own offspring to similar forms of toxic stress. Just as attachment insecurities can replicate across generations, so too can ACE burden seed the next generation with adversity.

The intergenerational mechanisms appear to be both behavioral and epigenetic. As attachment theory reminds us, parents' behaviors toward offspring echo the patterns of the parenting they received, creating templates for their children's later parenting practices (Chapter 4). The interactions of insecurely attached parents with their offspring can replicate these insecurities, especially if the child is difficult to handle. For example, a beleaguered caregiver who needs affirmation and support may seek it from a fussy or distracted child, and then become dismayed or angry when the child is not sufficiently pleasing. This dynamic can be replayed over and over again. But, that's not all.

We also now have convincing evidence that there is a "vital synchrony" between environment, experience, and our genetic code. "Environment and experience play a huge role in determining which parts of your genetic code are read and transcribed in each new cell your body creates," Nadine Burke Harris states (2018, p. 83). This insight is the basis for the science of epigenetics. Epigenetic influences are handed down from parent to child side-by-side with DNA. We are learning that the mechanisms of epigenetic transmission and regulation involve DNA methylation (methyl groups added to DNA can change its activity), histone modification (altering proteins that can affect gene expression), and the lengthening or shortening of DNA telomeres (protective caps at the ends of DNA strands that reduce fraying). Telomere shortening facilitates cell aging and hastens "weathering," the wear-and-tear degradation of physical systems due to ongoing stress (Boeck, Krause, et al., 2017; Drury, 2015). Each of these processes involves biological changes to DNA, rooted in experience with the surrounding environment. These changes affect the transcription and replication of DNA, which affects in turn the individual's responses to the environment. Not surprisingly, these processes are highly responsive to stress and the impact on individuals' stress response and health-illness systems can be profound (Harris, 2018). This influence of environmental (ecological) factors on DNA biology is currently a very active area of scientific research (Geronimus et al., 2015; Park et al., 2015).

These initial results of ACE science remind us that the stakes are high for understanding adverse child experiences which play an outsized role in health and wellness. The responsiveness of these systems holds promise as well as caution, however. Yes, experience can predispose individuals for trouble, but these systems also respond to environmental enhancement over time. Providing ameliorative external and internal conditions can make a difference. Focused modification of the environment facing recovering addicts, for example (such as recovery group participation, or building "recovery capital") can alter DNA expression as well. Learning meditation, stress-reduction, and other techniques can also help (Hoge et al., 2013; Jacobs et al., 2011). Attachment-sensitive counseling and advocacy can contribute.

Correspondingly, it appears that the burden of disease and adversity also tends to cluster, particularly in disadvantaged communities. There is a "concentration of the burden of disease in disadvantaged populations" (Kinner & Borschmann, 2017, e342). And, lest one think that this clustering of adversity around disadvantage involves only people and communities of color, it is well to remember that the original ACE cohort was largely middle- to upper-middle class, highly educated, and Caucasian. Also, the clustering and localization of adversity may have as much to do with geography and socioeconomic status as with race.

4. ACEs are a catalyst for new approaches in assessment, treatment, and prevention.

ACE science calls for an integrated approach to intervening early with children and families.[8] Prevention and treatment of one ACE frequently can mean that similar efforts are needed to treat multiple persons with multiple adverse experiences in affected families. Childhood stressors are interrelated and usually co-occur in homes. These experiences can also eviscerate the ability of families to support and comfort members. The nexus of adversity, development, attachment, and addiction can be understood, related to, and folded within an overall family and ecological model.

Nevertheless, we must remember that, while early experiences of abuse and adversity can play a significant role in later illness and risk for behavioral disorders, ACEs are not destiny. There is also a role for resilience, for prevention efforts aimed at supporting children and families, for supportive and buffering communities and civic organizations, for responsive adults. Because adverse childhood experiences and family dysfunction can play such an outsize role in illness and health, it is important here to mention societal initiatives that have been proven to affect the prevalence of adversity. This will preview later suggestions for a social ecology approach to prevention and healing. One such initiative involves home visitations.

Reducing exposure to trauma and adversity for the nation's children and families cannot help but decrease risk for harmful use of substances and addiction, as well as for the burden of physical and mental illnesses and behavioral difficulties that result from ACE exposure. A pioneer in this endeavor is David Olds of the Prevention Research Center for Family and Child Health at the University of Colorado Denver, and his Nurse-Family Partnership program.[9] This was the original home visitation model of prevention for reducing child abuse, neglect, and family violence. Begun over 30 years ago, it has a long track record and was designed to (a) improve prenatal health; (b) improve sensitive and competent care of the child; (c) lessen the risks of child challenges and mental health problems; and (d) improve parental life-course by helping parents attain self-sufficiency, plan future pregnancies, complete their educations, and find work (Olds, 2008). It was adapted and utilized both nationally and internationally.

The Nurse-Family Partnership directly addresses the conditions that underlie adverse childhood experiences. Olds created supportive connections and relationships between trained nurses and first-time, at-risk moms. These relationships not only help to improve children's health and lives, but also help to sustain parents as they take a more positive course in their lives.

The Nurse-Family Partnership has demonstrated effectiveness across a range of positive outcomes, from reducing verified rates of abuse and neglect to decreasing the number of emergency room visits and hospitalizations and increases in school readiness (Campaign for Trauma-Informed Policy and Practice, 2017).[10]

Nurse-Family Partnership and the Home Visitation model on which it is based are a powerful anti-ACE preventive and social-ecological intervention. They are examples of systemic and societal interventions that complement attachment-sensitive counseling practice. They alter the environment around young families and provide opportunities for attachment-sensitive child care that can affect the burden of adverse child experiences. This in turn alters risk for trauma and toxic stress that may lead to medical, psychological, or behavioral risks, not only for children but for later adults. Systemic programs can set the stage for virtuous cycles in prevention and community-based intervention.[11]

5. ACEs challenge our current understandings of addiction and lead us in a two-fold direction of neurobiological and social and ecological conditions and their impact on neurobiology.

The Adverse Childhood Experiences paradigm demands several shifts in the ways that we think about health, illness, and addiction.

First, there is a shift in the way we view life problems. Problems are not always what they seem. Disordered eating, alcohol and other drug use, and other compulsive behaviors can also be adaptations or solutions to a problem. If utilizing a chemical or behavior is a coping strategy, even though unconscious, and assuming that those chemicals or behaviors "have what it takes" to help one cope, then perhaps the individual does not view her or his "problem" as the chemical or troublesome behavior. Others around that person might see the harmful use or unsafe behaviors as the problem, but the individual does not. The problem is the original stressor, but it may be obscured. This "hidden engine" drives the seeking and use of a substitute relationship.

"Jane" was a bright and talented little girl born, along with her older brother and younger sister, into poverty and disadvantage, family struggles, and a parental civil war. Her father was a drinker, and fought frequently with Jane's mother, but Jane was the apple of his eye. Coming home from school one day when she was nine years old, her older brother and several of his early teen friends tricked her into a compromising situation in which she was sexually molested. Her brother begged her to keep the incident a secret, citing their father's temper and volatility. Confused, and wanting to protect her father from himself, she kept the secret.

Within that year, her mood and outlook on the world began to change. By the time she was 11 years old, she had begun smoking cigarettes with several girlfriends and drinking in an abandoned barn near the project where she lived. By the time she turned 17, she herself was pregnant with her first child and just barely finishing school. She states that at that time she was well on her way to alcohol and drug addiction. Looking back, she acknowledges that the dramatic change in her life was a consequence of keeping the secret of an unacknowledged trauma. Childhood trauma set Jane up for a lifetime of suffering.

ACEs produce neurodevelopmental damage and attachment-based emotional deficits, impairing life-function. Neuroscientist Martin Teicher starkly states the case for this assertion:

> Society reaps what it sows in nurturing its children. Whether abuse of a child is physical, psychological, or sexual, it sets off a ripple of hormonal changes that wire the child's brain to cope with a malevolent world. It predisposes the child to have a biological basis for fear, though he [sic] may act and pretend otherwise. Early abuse molds the brain to be more irritable, impulsive, suspicious, and prone to be swamped by fight-or-flight reactions that the rational mind may be unable to control. The brain is programmed to a state of defensive adaptation, enhancing survival in a world of constant danger (2000).

A second insight may be helpful here: How does someone cope with dysregulated emotions, with the inevitable stresses that come with living, or with the intolerable stress that lies hidden deep within from previous experiences of childhood adversity? We think of fight-or-flight—and in extreme situations, freeze—as classic responses to stress or danger. But what if there are other alternatives?

We know that evolution has provided another avenue for coping with danger and fear. The tend-and-befriend response is one of the biobehavioral strategies that allows humans not only to survive but thrive in hostile environments (Taylor, 2006; Taylor & Master, 2011). Banding together to care for the young of a troop when in hostile territory or while other members of the troop are off hunting or protecting is an efficient use of resources under stress. Typically, among mammals and primates, these responsibilities are divided up by gender.

Perhaps another alternate response to chronic or extreme stress, however, involves substituting a relationship with a chemical or compulsive behavior in order to self-medicate in the face of stress, even if the relief or actual coping is only temporary. Turning to substances or compulsive behaviors may be an auxiliary self-regulation strategy. This insight changes the addiction calculation. Someone may be reluctant to give up a solution to a problem that seems to work.

Let's take a simple example. Nicotine "has what it takes" to become a coping solution. Neurobiologically, it works in the reward, stress response, and self-regulation neural pathways to reduce anxiety, adapt to stressful situations, and ameliorate depression. It can serve the purpose of reducing anxiety, and is quite effective. Smoking brings with it a host of negative potential consequences over time, to be sure, but the capacity for emotional regulation in the present can outweigh the cognitive awareness of those negative outcomes. When coupled with aggressive and targeted social marketing that emphasizes psychosocial desires, such as looking more mature or being slim and confident, the combination of neurobiological effect and social ecological cues can be difficult to resist for those who need the substitution.

Parallels to the current opioid crisis are difficult to miss. Opioids are potent relievers of pain and social discomfort. Complemented with aggressive marketing and oversupply in vulnerable areas of the country, the combination of neural effect and ecology can be dynamite. This creates a crisis. However, what if those areas had initiated alternative means of coping? Programs of healthy care for persons seeking stress or pain relief, particularly if allied with local and affordable, easily accessible physician practices, hospitals, or rehabilitation facilities can be part of a full-bodied societal response. This can be a social-ecological intervention that can complement one-on-one approaches.

Third, the ACE framework and the new science of adversity also challenges the current dogma about addiction as a disease. Clearly, addiction changes the brain through neuroplasticity, but perhaps not only in the ways suggested by the brain disease hypothesis.

Substance-related chemical use and addiction do affect elements of neural function and dysfunction. Resort to chemical and compulsive behaviors can be seen as reaching for functional prosthetics that address emotional needs. They can help people cope. Yet we also have growing evidence that childhood adversity and toxic stress, particularly when experienced during "sensitive periods" or "windows of vulnerability," hijack the brain and predispose individuals for developmental disorders by altering the trajectories of brain development. This creates vulnerabilities that can be partially corrected by drugs or behaviors that "have what it takes" to provide regulation (Felitti, 2003).

> "Addiction is not a brain disease, nor is it caused by chemical imbalance or genetics. Addiction is best viewed as an understandable, unconscious, compulsive use of psychoactive materials in response to abnormal prior life experiences, most of which are concealed by shame, secrecy, and social taboo." (FELITTI, 2003, P. 9)

Warning Signs

Widespread resort to coping behaviors, then, can be understood as signals of challenging adversity.

> ". . . psychological [and existential] pain is at the heart of addictive behavior . . . vulnerable individuals resort to their addiction because they discover that the addictive substance or behavior gives short-term and otherwise

unobtainable relief, comfort, or change from their distress" (KHANTZIAN & ALBANESE, 2008, P. XVI).

Do current smokers, harmful and addictive drinkers, drug and opioid
users represent a primary group of Americans with profound needs for the
psychoactive benefits provided by alcohol, nicotine, and other drugs? Is it
possible that this vulnerable cohort demonstrates the amount of emotional
suffering, affect dysregulation, and need for self-medication that arises as a
result of nationwide adverse childhood experiences and toxic stress? What if
we came to understand mistreatment of children as itself the sign of a society
that has lost its moorings? Are those with vulnerabilities the "canaries in the
coal mine" that point to the dark underbelly of a culture in trouble?

Perhaps it is time for us to begin examining our contemporary drug issues
through a lens other than the disease or choice models. Using our current
opioid and prescription drug crisis, I want to suggest that moving into other
areas of thought beyond the neurobiological or medical can offer us some
important ways forward.

Substance Use Disorders and Addiction

Trauma (and PTSD) and addiction (SUDs) are seen as co-occurring often;
many times they set the stage for one another. Practitioners are coming to
expect one when discovering the other. And yet, even up to the present day,
trauma and addiction are perhaps the two most under-diagnosed and misdiagnosed conditions we face as clinical practitioners. Counselors and other
clinical providers often miss the hidden suffering of trauma and/or addictions as they encounter it.

One suggestion for attachment-sensitive counselors, given the frequency
of ACE exposures and subsequent outcomes of co-occurring substance use
disorders, is a recommendation for *universal screening* for adversity and difficulty with substances. In my counseling practice, providing psychosocial
support for oncology patients, we began insisting on universal ACE screening
with patients and complemented it with substance use screens. We learned a
great deal about what we didn't know, and the information assisted immea-

surably in providing care.[12] Given what we are learning from ACE science, it seems likely that methods and tools for assessing trauma exposures and outcomes will continue to appear.

It is interesting to note that "adverse childhood experiences" have been found to have a "particularly strong association with alcohol abuse" (Anda, 2008, p. 9), and in fact account for a large portion of risk for adult alcohol abuse regardless of parental alcoholism. It is not surprising, then, that Felitti (2003) and other ACE researchers (see Felitti et al., 1998) have demonstrated the relationships between ACEs and smoking (250 percent increased risk over children without ACEs), alcoholism (500 percent increase in self-acknowledged alcoholism), and injection drug abuse (46-fold increased risk). Opioid misuse is a current topic of research in ACE science (Stein, Conti, et al., 2017).

The lifestyle of active addiction is in and of itself traumatizing, of course. In coping with their own pain, loneliness, isolation, and shame, persons struggling with harmful use and addiction reach out and cling to anything that promises an end to suffering. These persons experience a sense of alienation, estrangement, loneliness, unlovability, and hopelessness, often feeling a sense of being "different from" or "less than" others. In the face of this pain of living, they turn to pills, bottles, needles, sex, and the like as "magical solutions"; they turn to chemical or behavioral crutches. Persons who have experienced trauma and been unable to resolve its after-effects often turn to substances or addictive processes to cope with the lingering consequences of trauma exposure.

ATTACHMENT-SENSITIVE COUNSELING

When he came for counseling, "Joe" from Chapters 1 and 2 had emotional and neural systems trained for living defensively. The abusive relationship with his father and dysfunctional home environment mangled Joe's primary attachment experiences, oversensitizing his neuroceptive safe/not safe defensive systems and inhibiting his social engagement systems so that social learning became difficult. When a person is living defensively, it is difficult to utilize the relationships and care that surround her or him. Assessing for adverse childhood experiences, Joe gave evidence of repeated emotional abuse and dysfunction in the home environment with alcohol abuse, mental illness (Mom's depression), and marital discord as factors (ACE score of 4). Joe's was a case of "earned defensiveness" (Baylin & Hughes, 2016, p. 2).

Once he became an adult, the repercussions of his adverse childhood experiences and ongoing defensive living became more prominent. His resort to alcohol for coping as a substitute relationship affected all the significant relationships in his life. His interpersonal problems heightened his experience of stress and his social relations of family and work became increasingly problematic. His negative outlook in life and ongoing depression sapped his energy and optimism, making change difficult. His physical illnesses, high blood pressure, and pre-diabetes—themselves predictable outcomes of adverse childhood experiences—were complicating factors.

Attachment-sensitive counseling, much like the "attachment-focused therapy" of Daniel Hughes (2007; Hughes et al., 2019), would focus on these issues through an attachment and adversity lens and concentrate on the twin goals of calming and retraining his defensive systems while simultaneously reinvigorating the social engagement systems. Treatment would focus first on welcome and safety, inviting Joe into a reliably safe environment, then attend to repair through social experiences that enhance safety and attunement, facilitating a psychobiological shift toward greater openness and trust. Calming defensive circuitry and providing experiences of acceptance and empathy, creates space for increasing self-awareness and relational thinking. It provides buffering for sensitive circuits and allows them to react differently. Listening and learning become available. The client can then use the relationships— first with the therapist, and then with family, kin, and others—the test, modify, and absorb lessons from new action.

Looking back on this case, I have renewed appreciation for why counseling was successful. Treatment slowly disarmed Joe's defensive systems and removed the blocks to care and attunement. I was able patiently and consistently to send messages of safety, approachability, and care to Joe. With Joe's alarm and protective systems less reactive and more calm, his social engagement systems could begin to incorporate new learning and use it to soften his defensiveness and allow love into his life again. The ability to utilize P.A.C.E.

as a therapeutic attitude (playfulness, acceptance, curiosity, empathy) was essential for this practice.

P.A.C.E. and welcoming are not sufficient, however. The therapeutic process begins there, but expands through attachment learning into self-regulation and creativity (Baylin & Hughes, 2016).

BUILDING AND REMEDIATING HUMAN CAPITAL

"The most reliable way to produce an adult who is brave and curious and kind and prudent is to ensure that when he is an infant, his hypothalamic-pituitary-adrenal axis functions well. And how do you do that? It is not magic. First, as much as possible, you protect him from serious trauma and chronic stress; then, even more important, you provide him with a secure, nurturing relationship with one parent and ideally two." PAUL TOUGH

As more people learn about adverse childhood experiences and their impact, more disciplines are beginning to appreciate the need for consilient study in this area. ACEs science has reached into neurobiology and is learning about the formation of neural systems based on attachment experience. There is also work being developed into the neural impairments fostered by adverse experiences, trauma, and toxic stress in childhood (Anda, 2008; Dubé et al., 2003; Felitti et al., 1998).

Contributions to ACEs science from economics are also emerging. One thread of this work is the study of human capital that relies on children's neural development from very early in life. John Tomer is among those economists who believe that work on human capital has been limited by too narrow a focus on school-age children (five years and older) and ignoring the emotional, noncognitive development and brain maturation that occurs in early childhood (Tomer, 2015). These economists echo the work of Allan Schore and other neuroscientists in proposing the foundations for optimal human and neural development from the time in utero to four years of age. Their work also builds on what Eisler calls "a caring economy," one in which the full development of human capital in all people is valued and supported, and based on actions that address concern for human welfare and optimal human development (2012). For Eisler, economics must reflect and value "the most essential human work: the work of caring for ourselves, others and our Mother Earth" (2012, pp. 12–14).

The development of a caring economy would enable us, as a society, to attain "a future where all children have the opportunity to realize their potential for consciousness, empathy, caring, and creativity—capacities that make us fully human" (Eisler, 2012, p. 82). This requires investments in human capital development across the board.

In these analyses, too many children come to school already at a disadvantage from poverty, stress, neglectful childcare, poor parenting, and increases in adverse childhood experiences (Tomer, 2016). Their emotional and cognitive difficulties are exacerbated by exaggerated reactivity, poor emotional regulation, and dysregulated neural systems. They are unable to participate in social enterprises since their challenges indicate an inability to regulate their own emotions and manage their relationships with others. They lack the human and social capital that comes from emotional intelligence. These abilities emerge as a set of personal and social competencies rooted in early neural development.

The work of James Heckman (2007, 2008) documents deficits in human capital formation due to adverse family environments, low motivation, and deficient self-regulation. These deficits begin in early childhood and affect the child's ability to utilize school and other social learning experiences for development. From an economics point of view, he maintains that early childhood investments are both a matter of fairness and smart productivity. Adverse development is far too costly to society to ignore. However, Heckman also argues that school and post-school programs (e.g. public job training, remedial education) cannot fix all the damage done in childhood. The best interventions may involve supplementing childcare services, parenting interactions, and family environments.

A number of approaches have been proposed, discussed, and implemented to address these concerns and begin to build a more "caring economy" and "compassionate social ecology." These include paid parental leave, methods for improving parenting (such as the Nurse-Family Partnerships and home visitation), involving extended family members in childcare, providing support in the instances of divorce/separation, enriched preschool, and other similar programs (Karr-Morse and Wiley, 2013).

Societies must invest in building human and social capital in order to help children survive and thrive. These investments will help to curtail the incidence and prevalence of adverse childhood experiences, and foster healthy neural, personal, and familial development for all our children.[13]

8

◈◈◈

Recovery Ecologies: The Road to (Re)Connection

"Recovery-oriented care . . . takes on a much broader scope, and involves a much broader repertoire of interventions and supports, than conventional disease-based models of acute treatment followed by so-called "aftercare." The majority of recovery processes, like the majority of a person's life, take place outside of acute care or other treatment settings in the community-based contexts in which people pursue their desires to life, love, learn, work and play."

WILLIAM L. WHITE (2008)

"We must begin to create naturally occurring, healing environments that provide some of the corrective experiences that are vital for recovery."

SANDRA BLOOM (2013)

In order to be fully effective, attachment-sensitive counseling with addictive and trauma-spectrum disorders cannot remain solely within the counseling room. It must be fully relational. This means that the therapeutic alliance opens out into the recovery-oriented systems and relational ecologies that are available. The counselor will be attentive to opportunities that present themselves and the systems that can assist in fostering new perspectives and skills for the recovering person. The counselor will also advocate for the creation and enhancement of recovery-oriented systems.

Barbara was in recovery but miserable. Life had not been kind to her. She had serious adversity in her life history: born with a chronic illness that required frequent visits to doctors during childhood and a strict regimen of medications that often made her nauseous; adopted away from an absent biological father and a teen birth mother who could not care for her adequately; oppressed by anxiety and depression that were rooted in early attachment difficulties and trauma, she had a problem-saturated story.

When I saw her in counseling, she was 26 years old and 120 days sober. Frightened by watching a friend overdose, she had made an impulsive decision to enter inpatient addiction treatment, but had trouble hanging on to a commitment to stay for the full course of treatment. Barbara had many dreams, but few life skills, and a history of troubled relationships. She had achievements and some successes, but downplayed them, believing the worst about herself and experiencing herself as alone and abandoned in a hostile world. She had matriculated at a number of elementary, middle, and secondary schools, always sensitive to how she was treated, feeling bullied by her peers and neglected by those around her. She had attempted college several times, but was unable to stay engaged. She had just started a new low-wage job, having left the last one in a fit of temper. Things never went her way, and it was always someone else's fault.

Her problematic use of pills (benzodiazepines, opioids)—Barbara's way of coping when stressed, depressed, and overwhelmed—did not last long, but it was accelerating when she finally tried to stop. She lasted about a week in inpatient treatment due to conflicts with the treatment center rules and expectations, as well as conflicts with fellow patients. Barbara moved to an outpatient setting and continued to live at home with her mother and older siblings. Life at home was turbulent, yet she was consistent with her attendance at recovery meetings, continuing to attend after completing the traditional "90 meetings in 90 days." She did engage several recovery sponsors, finally settling on one, and had a regular routine of 12 Step meetings and outpatient therapy appointments.

Barbara's developmental trajectory was arrested, and it could be said that she needed habilitation as much as rehabilitation. This is a common picture for substance using or addicted 20-somethings trying to make progress in early or mid-recovery. For those of us working with them professionally, the challenge is to help them move forward into recovery with an agenda that is bigger than "don't use drugs, and go to meetings." We often see them after several years of problematic or harmful use, but without significant time in hard-bitten addictive use. We also see them post-treatment, often still in post-acute withdrawal, and in early recovery but still hurting (Gorski & Miller, 1986).

Post-acute Withdrawal Syndrome (PAWS), a prolonged cluster of unpleasant symptoms, is mostly psychological and emotional (irritability, anger, frustration, impatience, sadness, inability to think things through, poor planning, fatigue), that results from cessation of drug use or compulsive behavior. Mood-related symptoms come and go unexpectedly. PAWS makes life miserable for former users trying to change, and can precipitate relapse. The emotional and neurobiological underpinnings of post-acute withdrawal are well explored by George Koob and colleagues (Koob, 2009a & b; Koob & Le Moal, 2008). It can affect users at any stage along the continuum of use. With the development of dependence and addiction, however, disrupted and dysfunctional neural systems leave "residual neuroadaptive traces" that can levy a weighty emotional burden on patients and predispose to relapse even months and years following abstinence (Edwards & Koob, 2010, p. 2).

WHERE TO BEGIN?

The wise counselor will remain a reliable and empathic presence throughout the PAWS period. The goal is to help the client to be patient and roll with the ups and downs of early recovery. There will be good days and bad days; early recovery is a rollercoaster. The counselor will remain a proponent of commitment and self-care as well as continued focus on recovery tasks.

The overall goal for treatment of substance-related problems and behavioral compulsions is *recovery*. Whether we are talking about intervention into harmful use of psychoactive chemicals, engagement with compulsive behaviors, or full-blown chemical or behavioral addiction, the long-term goal remains: a recovery life that is healthy, productive, free of obsession and compulsion, and a lifestyle that allows for integration into relationship and community (Best & Laudet, 2010; Betty Ford Institute Consensus Panel, 2007). Nevertheless, while we know a great deal about addiction, we know much less about recovery and the ins and outs of the recovery process. But we are learning.

New Science

Today, there is a paradigm shift occurring in recovery science. For several years there have been calls for change, and dissatisfaction with the results of traditional addiction treatment (Institute of Medicine, 2001, 2004, 2005; McLellan et al., 2000). There is also greater appreciation of various methods and tools used by those seeking relief from substance use problems, including "unassisted means" (natural recovery), "assisted means" (formal treatment, inpatient, residential or outpatient; participating in mutual help and support), and "maturing out" of a problem lifestyle (Kelly et al., 2017, p. 163). More research into the dynamics of seeking and sustaining recovery is leading the way (Best & Lubman, 2012; White 2008).

The shift is long overdue. Recovery science is pivoting from a pathology and intervention acute-care focus, primarily on addiction (stabilize, rehabilitate, discharge), toward a wider and more inclusive "continuing care" or "recovery management" focus (McKay, 2009a & b; White, 2017; White & Kurtz, 2006a & b; White & Cloud, 2008). There is a growing consensus that achieving and sustaining recovery, whether from harmful use or full-blown addiction, requires flexible and adaptive, strengths-based approaches to continuing care beyond the confines of traditional treatments. Models of integrated and sustainable care are emerging (Dennis & Scott, 2007).

Research is also concentrated beyond narrow drug-related outcomes, such as abstinence, moderation, or harm-reduction. Broader functioning is highlighted. With a recovery focus, researchers can expand beyond minimizing harm and cessation of drug use to now include global health, wellness, and community participation and contribution. As a recovery framework takes center stage, research is demarcating stages of the recovery process and recovery-promoting factors that can be aligned with specific stages and needs over time.

In addition, a growing public recovery movement is taking place nationwide, as recovering people feel empowered to engage around issues of recovery advocacy (Williams, 2013), and the experience becomes contagious across society (Christakis & Fowler, 2009; Best & deAlwis, 2017).[1] Evidence and accumulated knowledge about recovery from multiple disorders are emerging and the good news about the possibility of recovery from addiction is being widely disseminated (U.S. Department of Health and Human Services, 2016).[2] New recovery support institutions and structures are emerging to put flesh and bone on recovery visions (White, Kelly, & Roth, 2012). These developments are similar to, and complementary with, the contemporary social trends in the mental health recovery movement (Best & Laudet, 2010); and there is a synergy between these two movements (White, 2007a & b; White, Boyle, & Loveland, 2003).

In the past, the term "recovery" was used to indicate general improvements in health status and overall functioning following abstinence from substance use. Today, the word is being used in a more targeted way (1) to counteract stigma and instill hope in the possibility of broad-spectrum remission (not simply abstinence-based) from substance-related disorders, and (2) to establish an "organizing paradigm" for research and clinical practice in addiction as well as a central framework for the growing recovery social movement (U.S. Department of Health and Human Services, 2016). The initial steps in this new recovery science identify promising target goals, such as (a) formulating "recovery management" strategies, (b) designing and implementing "recovery-oriented systems of care," and (c) building personal and communal "recovery capital" with the means to assess and enhance it.

For ease of understanding, we will consider *recovery management* (RM) as an overarching philosophy that supports long-term personal and family recovery, an approach that can help to integrate addiction treatment with a diverse menu of recovery support services and activities (Kelly et al., 2017; Zemore et al., 2018). RM incorporates themes of empowerment, connectedness, self-help, self-determination, civil rights, and social recovery awareness (McKay, 2009a & b). *Recovery-oriented systems of care* (ROSC) describes an array of professional, non-professional, and volunteer services and relationships that support long-term recovery, while at the same time constituting an overall ecology in which recovery can flourish. On one side, ROSC is the environmental pole of recovery; the term highlights linked systems and networks that can collaborate in support of recovery (White, 2008). Building and enhancing *recovery capital* (REC-CAP) is the individual/family/relational pole of this equation. REC-CAP describes internal and external resources or assets that individuals and families can bring to bear in support of recovery. This terminology recognizes that recovery is about more than drug use; it is about elevating overall health and quality of life as well as the social contributions of recovering people. Enhancing recovery capital is also a skillful clinical or mentoring strategy that builds on strengths and focuses resilience (White, 2017). Wise counselors choose to concentrate on building recovery capital as a strengths-based path to recovery.

Interventions designed to amplify recovery, including those that aim to provide continuing care outside of and beyond formal treatment, need to be located in an ecology of recovery, utilizing resources that are at hand. They need to harness the power of community and connection. Formal treatment settings, inpatient or outpatient, may be (re-)structured as anchors for this wider recovery environment and its systems, extending treatment services into the community and reciprocally integrating community resources into treatment programming. Alternatively, a network of potential recovery-facilitating systems within local communities—

such as drug courts, county agencies, law enforcement or social service programs, colleges and universities, or voluntary associations—may coalesce in other ways and work to link treatment and the community.[3]

What is Recovery?

> . . . the essence of recovery is a lived experience of improved life quality and a sense of empowerment; that the principles of recovery focus on the central ideas of hope, choice, freedom and aspiration that are experienced rather than diagnosed and occur in real life settings rather than in the rarefied atmosphere of clinical settings. Recovery is a process rather than an end state, with the goal being an ongoing quest for a better life (BEST & LAUDET, 2010).

Recovery is more than sobriety or cessation from drug use; it is multidimensional and encompasses health, well-being, and social engagement (Betty Ford . . . , 2007; U.S. Department of Health and Human Services, 2016). The treatment industry and the specialized addiction service provider community remain focused (and rightly so) on primary treatment, relapse prevention, and retreatment when needed. Grassroots recovery leaders, advocacy groups, and organizations, however, are calling for more, that is, reconnection between processes and systems of recovery and a *transformed* or "radically redesigned" model of intervention and treatment (White, 2017). They are signaling a needed adjustment of focus from individuals to include recovery systems. Attachment-sensitive counseling is an appropriate clinical model for addressing harmful use and addiction, but ought not limit its purview to therapy with individuals and families. It can be used in both inpatient and outpatient settings. There is also a proper role for engaging with wider recovery resources and local advocacy activities.

The recovery advocacy movement is clamoring for a revision of the wider treatment-community relationship and a deeper appreciation for the needs of a broad spectrum of recovering people. There are questions about the existing professionally facilitated and specialty treatment structures as currently configured, and their ability to adapt to contemporary needs. Hence the calls for transformation and a new vision of "treatment and recovery without walls" (Miller & Carroll, 2006; White, 2009). Are present-day treatment and rehabilitation institutions prepared for the adaptations that this changing vision entails?

Many treatment centers and agencies have grafted continuing outpatient and other care services onto their lists of offerings (aftercare programs, family programs, trauma or co-occurring disorders work, and the like). These add-ons, however, are only partial measures that have their own difficulties (such as high dropout rates, or lack of financing and trained staff) and may inhibit a thoroughgoing look at the full paradigm change that is needed (McKay, 2009a & b; McKay, 2006). These ancillary offerings need further research on outcomes and benefits. Recovery-seekers need more than initial treatment, but what should the next steps look like?

ROLE OF COMMUNITY AND CONNECTION IN ADDICTION RECOVERY

Current acute-care models used by the addiction treatment industry focus on the individual struggling with harmful use or addiction, and sometimes also with his or her family system. Treatment here is an opportunity for "recovery initiation," helping to destabilize the addicted lifestyle while providing psychoeducation, counseling, and support for new recovery behaviors and attitudes. It can place a fledgling recovery on firm footing and influence entry into recovery management, and is an important first step. Alone, however, it is inadequate for what comes next: the challenges of living a recovery life in natural environments, and building on individual, family, community, and ecosystem resources. It is also often a mismatch for addressing the needs of harmful or problematic users.

Treatment outcome studies are often flawed and have consistently reported a full remission rate of only approximately 30 percent for acute-care interventions, including residential and outpatient treatment (White, 2012). While a majority of addicted individuals, roughly 58 percent, will ultimately achieve lasting remission—that is, those who previously met the criteria for substance use disorders no longer do, and are in stable remission for a year or longer (U.S. Department of Health and Human Services, 2016)—only a small percentage enter recovery through formal inpatient or outpatient treatment. The majority of professionally facilitated addiction treatment occurs in outpatient settings (Best & Lubman, 2012; McLellan, McKay et al., 2005).

Nevertheless, following initial intense treatment of whatever kind, extended treatment regimens such as (a) low-intensity but assertive and low-cost recovery monitoring through tools such as email, social media, or phone, or (b) in-person checkups along with follow-up and early reintervention when needed, show promise as more effective treatment and long-term recovery options (National Institute on Drug Abuse, 1999; HHS, 2016). These approaches need further study but do extend the dosage of treatment beyond initial or repeated episodes of acute care. Adequate length and dosage of treatment is a necessary component of effective recovery initiation and later maintenance.

An example of the transformative effectiveness of this kind of thinking is the set of healthcare professionals' programs for physicians and medical professionals, as well as uniformed professionals' programs for those in law enforcement, firefighters, and first responders that have begun at the more savvy treatment centers. These programs are posting impressive rates of success (DuPont, McLellan, et al., 2009a & b; White, DuPont, & Skipper, 2007). They utilize combinations of (a) longer and more intense initial treatment, recovery introduction with professional colleagues for mutual support, and relapse prevention on an inpatient/outpatient basis; (b) trauma- and grief-sensitive individual and group work; (c) intensive reentry planning and networking, along with linkages to referring boards and unions for ongoing supervision; and then (d) extending recovery into the patients' natural environment through years of monitoring, intensive case management, network support, aggressive follow-up—with and without drug testing—and when needed, early reintervention. These programs appear to be an "evidence-based prescription" for recovery success (Gold & Frose-Pineda, 2006; Merlo & Gold, 2008, 2009).

However recovery begins, individuals and their families need assertive support and relationship involvement for a significant period of time. The transition into a recovery lifestyle is a significant challenge, requiring sensitivity to, and engagement with, natural healing factors within the ecology of the patient (McKay, 2009a & b). Recovery success here takes addiction seriously as a "chronic illness" (McLellan et al., 2000; White & McLellan, 2008).

A New Key

The current DSM-5 spectrum diagnosis of substance-related and addictive disorders challenges us to assist those struggling with "harmful use" as well as addiction. I propose a slightly different model for meeting this challenge than has been used previously. For example, abstinence as a way to initiate the basic condition of sobriety was understood to be necessary for those who were formerly dependent: "sobriety is most reliably achieved through the practice of abstinence from alcohol and all other drugs of abuse" (Betty Ford, 2007, p. 222). This has been the position of traditional treatment through the years. However, this standard may be too stringent a measure of sober living, especially for those struggling with harmful use or mild to moderate substance-related disorders. The potential mismatch between an abstinence-only model and the needs of those with mild to moderate substance-related issues may be not only off-putting—keeping them away from healing resources—but inaccurate as well (White, 2008).

There is now evidence that other forms of initiating and maintaining recovery may be more helpful for nondependent but troubled users, and perhaps even for some dependent users (Heather & Robertson, 1983; Miller & Caddy, 1977; White, 2007a). We know that "treatment-facilitated recovery" (versus "natural" or "unassisted" recovery) accounts for a small percentage of those who actually recover. For those at the most severe end of the substance disorder continuum, who likely have additional medical and psychiatric complications, have a history of adversity, need significant support and supervision, and have fewer personal and social resources (or "social capital"), treatment-facilitated recovery and its focus on abstinence is likely the best and most effective treatment alternative over the long term (White, 2008). However, there are other alternatives, other paths to recovery, especially for those who reside at the mild and moderate regions of the continuum.

We know that many people who incur significant negative consequences from alcohol and other drug use also do not meet the full criteria for diagnosis of addiction (Kelly et al., 2017). For example, 12.5 million people reported misuse of pain-relieving medication in 2015, yet only three 3 million met the criteria for prescription medication disorder (HHS, 2016). Can (Should?)

we continue to require abstinence from alcohol and other drug use—or gambling, or food, or sex addiction—as the sole criterion for sober recovery from people at all levels of risk and severity on the addiction spectrum? Medication-assisted and replacement therapies, such as utilizing Suboxone or methadone for opioid addiction, in tandem with counseling and less risky use, are helping us to understand alternative recovery strategies (White & Mojer-Torres, 2010).[4]

Recovery from opioid addiction, particularly through medication-assistance and replacement, has been a challenging issue in the field of addiction. It calls into question long-held assumptions and definitions of recovery, and forces all those involved to debate, examine, and justify their personal interpretations. Yet, especially now, as we face a contemporary opioid crisis and hope for broad-based recovery from opioid addiction, this is a challenge that demands resolution.

> Can a methadone patient who has achieved long-term dose stabilization, uses no other nonprescribed opioids or other intoxicants (including alcohol), and has achieved significant improvements in psychosocial health and positive community integration be considered in recovery or recovering? (WHITE & MOJER-TORRES, 2010, P. 48)

White and Mojer-Torres (2010) present a well-researched analysis—historical, clinical, and scientific—of medication-assisted recovery, and come to the conclusion that "methadone [or by association, naltrexone or buprenorphine], provided under competent medical supervision at proper dosages with appropriate ancillary psychosocial support services, aids long-term recovery from opioid addiction and should be so recognized" (p. 62).[5] They believe that medication-assisted recovery should be accepted as one of the legitimate varieties and diverse pathways of recovery (Rush & Urbanoski, 2019; White & Kurtz, 2006a & b). While there is active debate in the field about this position, there is movement toward consensus (White, Parrino, & Ginter, 2011).

Remission is a term of art used in psychiatry and addiction medicine to indicate that the diagnostic criteria for addiction are no longer met or have been greatly diminished. In this view, the person, not the drug, is the focus; the person is *in remission*. The main pathology, drug misuse, has been ameliorated. Abstinence, however, is not the only criterion; rather the "absence of drug-related clinical pathology," such as obsession, compulsive use, loss of control, and social or legal consequences, is the holistic goal. Non-use of all drugs, including alcohol, in ways that lead to intoxication, as well as active abandonment of the process of intoxication-seeking, is required. "Remission is about the subtraction of pathology; recovery is ultimately about the achievement of global (physical, emotional, relational, spiritual) health, social functioning, and quality of personal/family life" (White & Mojer-Torres, 2010, p. 49). Recovery is about more than the removal of drug use from a life that is otherwise unchanged.

Replacement pharmacotherapy—medically supervised, regularly administered, utilizing the proper doses, and accompanied by other clinical interventions, including psychotherapy and ongoing case management—may be considered an approved medical treatment and not illicit drug use. It can assist in lessening of cravings, and reduction or even eventual cessation of harmful drug use, and engagement in broader psychosocial rehabilitation. Medication-assisted therapy also contributes to social stabilization and allows patients to engage in building recovery capital, securing employment, housing and financial contentment, and seeking reconnection to community resources and relationships.[6] These positive consequences lead to increases in overall health, wellness, and improvement in personal and family life. In this sense it is no different from a person in abstinent recovery taking Prozac, or Zoloft, or Abilify. Experience indicates that in stable and optimal doses, orally administered, methadone and other replacement medications do not produce euphoria (Senay, 1985). In short, seekers who utilize medication-assisted or replacement therapies under supervision are *in recovery*.

Among the diverse and varied pathways to living a recovery life, each one is judged by its ability to facilitate wellness. Experience suggests that medication-assisted treatments in combination with social, psychological, and spiritual processes can achieve a synergy that accelerates outcomes greater than either one in isolation (White & Mojer-Torres, 2010). Attachment-sensitive counseling in the context of substance use disorders can be open to alternative pathways into recovery.

The intentional pursuit of personal and social rehabilitation, a symptom-free life, and the achievement of global health and social functioning are necessary components of recovery. The person's identity is no longer defined by drug use or misuse, nor does it involve the medications she or he takes. Self- and social identity formation is an intentional achievement of the whole person. Recovery as a process of renewing identity is an active and committed pursuit of living "weller than well" (Brown, 1985).[7]

Recovery and Family

> . . . the only path to long-term recovery is through family recovery, not just individual recovery. Alcoholism [addiction] affects the family and the family can positively affect recovery from alcoholism (LANDAU & GARRETT, 2008).

With new research and clinical practice, we know that individual and family recovery are deeply entwined (Morgan & Litzke, 2008), but we were not always so well-informed. In fact, for many years counselors and treatment centers actively discouraged family members from their attempts to help loved ones. We told them to take care of themselves and leave the treatment of addiction to the experts. In the process, those struggling with addiction and harmful use, as well as their loved ones, suffered and were unable to use their love as a force for healing. Their mutual connections went unused as motivational forces for intervention, treatment entry, and recovery enhancement; the process of longer-term recovery was put at risk, since the natural family environment went essentially unchanged.

Initiation into recovery-seeking can occur out of a "moment of clarity" (Lawford, 2009), or a "jolt to self-image" (Satel & Lilienfeld, 2013, p. 55); there are many points of entrance and many different styles of recovery participation (White & Kurtz, 2006a & b). The peer-support tools for recovery-seekers, for example, cover a wide spectrum of approaches and styles (Zemore et al., 2018).[8] However the transition begins, the individual starts down a path of more moderate, less harmful use, or abstinence from use, and pursues a path to health.

However, it is not just the individual's path. We have known for some time that other individuals and systems in close relationships with addiction-struggling persons make their own adaptations to the lifestyle of addiction and harmful use (Brown & Lewis, 1999; White & Savage, 2005). These adaptations can be costly and destructive. While all chronic disorders can take a toll on families and kinship networks, few disorders are more pernicious than the potential effects of addiction on these same networks (Conyers, 2003). Not only do family dynamics (boundaries, roles, rules, perceptions, rituals) suffer under the distorting impact of addiction, but there is ample evidence that addiction in relational systems is often accompanied by adverse, abusive, and oppressive behaviors, with parents and caretakers themselves sometimes acting as the perpetrators (Dubé, Anda, Felitti, et al., 2001a; Magura & Laudet, 1996).

In addition, addiction impacts a number of neural areas, as we have seen: the prefrontal and orbitofrontal cortices, the limbic system, anterior cingulate, and the striatum. These are critical areas for learning, social action, reward, and executive functioning. With neural degradation, the affected person becomes increasingly irrational, irresponsible, and impulsive. These changes impact the behavior and personality of affected persons and transforms them into virtual "strangers" in the family's midst (Landau & Garrett, 2008). The person is present to the family but only tentatively so; present, but also vitally absent. Consequently, the family cannot fully embrace or fully grieve; this has been called "ambiguous loss" (Boss, 1999, 2006). It infects all the relationships with tinges of grief, sadness, shame, guilt, anger, and helplessness. These increase as the addiction increases its grip and deterioration of the brain continues.

The family is not only a victim, however; it is also a critical resource for healing this downward spiral. The brain-wise therapist will assist concerned family members to understand what is happening, providing context and some buffers for their guilt and anger. The counselor can also remediate their sense of helplessness and strengthen their resolve. There is a role for family participation and neuroeducation can lead the way.

Working with clients' addiction, then, must include assessment, psychoeducation, and treatment of family dynamics (Morgan & Litzke, 2008; Roberts & McCrady, 2003). This is also an ethical responsibility. Contrary to common belief, entry into early recovery does not immediately guarantee positive rewards. In fact, at least for a time, it can provoke heightened stress and conflict ("sober but miserable"). Some years ago Stephanie Brown and Virginia Lewis laid out the developmental terrain for recovering individuals and families. Early recovery, they said, is often a time of heightened stress and dysfunction (1999). The initial ending of drug use does not end the family's problems. Each family member experiences something like a trauma; each member, the addict, and the family environment as a whole, ‚needs attention. Helping individuals and families come to terms with change and the post-acute withdrawal that follows, with the alterations of family relations and dynamics that recovery initiates, and with the demands of attachment repair in frayed relationships, are critical elements of attachment-sensitive counseling (Brown & Lewis, 1999; Schmid & Brown, 2008).

In order for the family and addicted individual to recover, the dysfunctional family system often needs to collapse. Helping the family members to understand and prepare for this collapse is a necessary step in attachment-sensitive counseling. They must also proactively engage meaningful support persons and systems, along with the counselor. The wise counselor will seek support as well, in order to tolerate the pain and chaos that often ensue during treatment. Once begun, the counseling process follows a series of stages that involve well-timed application of person-centered, psychodynamic, cognitive-behavioral, supportive, and educational approaches. Entry into a firm recovery allows family members to move forward in their lives, separately and together, without reliance on substitutes for coping.

How can treatment providers, recovering people, and supportive families utilize the best evidence-based science to support recovery management over the long term? It is incumbent upon us to work with families, not only to help integrate recovering addicts into support and recovery resources, but also to assist family members and systems in the transition into their own recovery status (Roberts & McCrady, 2003). Addiction and recovery science need ongoing research into effective models of kinship and family intervention (Morgan & Litzke, 2008). As individuals are embedded within family and kinship networks, so these networks themselves are embedded in larger community systems (Brown & Lewis, 1999; White & Mojer-Torres, 2010). We are learning that individual/family recovery and change often require complementary support from social, communal, and cultural factors, if it is to be sustained (White, 2008). With increasing awareness that people do recover, addiction science is now imagining the active social ecological ingredients that enable recovery and the tools and practical applications of this vision (U.S. Department of Health and Human Services, 2016).

RECOVERY CAPITAL REVOLUTION

In the monograph, *The Mobilization of Community Resources to Support Long-Term Addiction Recovery*, William White (2009) describes the mismatch of many current acute-care models of addiction treatment with the long-term needs of problematic users and addicted recovery-seekers. White has been a leading voice in the renewed appreciation of recovery and its power to transform contemporary life. He trained and honed his skills in the acute-care model of addiction; he also became one of the top historians of addiction and recovery. Gradually he came to understand the need for research and scholarship in the area of recovery and began writing about "recovery management" as a living solution to alcohol and other drug problems (White, 2017). He is a strong advocate for linking recovery-support counseling and other services with supportive structures within recovery-oriented systems of care, and developing the active pursuit of recovery capital into all levels of recovery.

Initiating treatment and recovery is often prompted by emotional or psychological change and by significant life events (Best, Irving, et al., 2017; Morgan, 1995). However, current research documents that recovery maintenance and sustainability come with changes in significant relationships, social networks, involvement in pro-social groups, and the shaping of a new social identity (Best, Irving et al., 2017; Best et al., 2016). Individual recovery alone is insufficient. Stephanie Brown pointed to the necessity of identity change for enhancing and maintaining addiction recovery (Brown, 1985). David Best and his colleagues in the United Kingdom have picked up this idea and promoted a "social identity model of recovery" (SIMOR), stating that:

> ". . . identity change that is linked to recovery is as much social as personal in nature and is largely managed through group connections . . . engagement in recovery groups leads to the internalization of the rules, norms and values of these groups . . . creating a form of informal social control that increases the motivation to be in recovery and access to supports that help to sustain it" (BEST, IRVING, ET AL., 2017).

Best and his colleagues advocate for the power of social influence in maintaining recovery. They also suggest that increasing the availability and accessibility of community-based resources promotes environmental "capacity" for recovery (Best & Lubman, 2012). These resources include informal assistance organizations and role models, mutual help organizations and group supports, community volunteer groups, even sports affiliations (Landale & Roderick, 2014)[9] and other options. Best and his colleagues also suggest a number of social-clinical tools, such as "social identity mapping," a variety of recovery capital assessments, and assertive linkage to community resources. Several conceptual models and tools for assessing and mapping the process and elements of recovery capital are now available (Best et al., 2016).

Recovery Capital Defined

Recovery capital informs both the individual and community levels of care and self-change. Linked to natural recovery, recovery management, and resilience, recovery capital is defined as "the breadth and depth of internal and external resources that can be drawn upon to initiate and sustain recovery from severe AOD [alcohol and other drug] problems" (White & Cloud, 2008, pp. 1–2; Granfield & Cloud, 1996; Cloud & Granfield, 2004). Different types of recovery capital come into play in the recovery journey and are influenced through continuing care:

1. **Personal recovery capital** includes the client's *physical* stamina and health, medical and emotional; it also involves assets that can increase

recovery options, such as income, safe housing, health insurance, food, clothing, and so forth. *Human* capital is a broad area that includes the client's values, knowledge, skills, education, intelligence, self-esteem and self-awareness, and their sense of meaning and purpose.

2. **Family/social recovery capital** reflects the quantity and quality of intimate, family, and kinship relationships that support recovery. It is a measure of mutuality, a give and take of supports and obligations in functioning relationships. It is characterized by the willingness of partners and family members to be actively involved in the process of recovery; it involves the interconnections of the individual and family to community organizations and institutions (church, workplace, school, community organizations, etc.) that nourish relationships.

3. **Community recovery capital** embodies the values, resources, and attitudes toward recovery within the surrounding local community and the resolve to overcome AOD problems. It includes the emergence of treatment and mutual aid resources, the presence of supportive structures such as recovery homes and schools, recovery industries, and recovery ministries, and the creation of sustained recovery supports such as recovery community organizations, recovery checkups, drug courts, and the like.

> The community is not an inert stage on which the trajectories of addiction and recovery are played out. The community is the soil in which such problems grow or fail to grow and in which the resolutions to such problems thrive or fail to thrive over time. That soil contains promoting and inhibiting forces for both addiction and recovery. The ratio of such forces can tip the scales of recovery initiation efforts toward success or failure . . . As such, the community itself should be a target of intervention into AOD problems (WHITE, 2009, P. 13; EMPHASIS MINE).

3a. **Cultural capital** is aligned with community capital and is signified by the individual's ability to fit in and the availability of culturally specific supportive pathways into recovery, such as faith- and culture-based ministries for African American or Native American recovery seekers, or local support groups for recovering pastors or health professionals. These can become prescriptive pathways for subgroups of those seeking recovery supports and their family members.

It is helpful to remember that the availability of recovery capital in a community not only supports those emerging from traditional treatment venues but can also support those primarily utilizing natural paths into recovery (spontaneous self-change, mutual support groups, outpatient counseling). It can also activate "turning points" or triggers for those attempting to moderate or manage their drug use, by providing a next step. Recovery capital informs the larger local community with recovery-based values and activities, shaping the overall environmental climate toward health and wellness.

Attention to recovery capital also influences and augments service delivery overall. In particular, a relational ecology that is aware and supportive of recovery capital can champion "connectedness" as an agent of change. With an understanding that connection and relationship among people can foster health, then assertive community-based outreach, fostering of family and community connections, maintaining supports for early screening and brief interventions even at the community level, and working to build a milieu of acceptance and welcome for recovery seekers can become a community's distinctive features. This is truly contagious (Best & Lubman, 2012). "Long-term recovery is about more than a relationship between an individual and a treatment center; it is about altering the complex relationships between individuals and the multiple layers of the ecosystem in which individuals and families are nested" (White, 2008). Recovery-focused thinking, visioning, and planning must target all the layers of this wider ecosystem.[10]

Recovery Capital: Practical Applications

Recovery capital describes the sum of resources available to initiate and sustain recovery as well as effectively cope with the stress of recovery and living. Each individual's quantity and quality of recovery capital facilitate recovery success. Each community's building and investing in recovery resources creates a healing relational ecology. Building recovery capital can be a clinical strategy, a bridge to self-directed and peer-assisted planning and execution of recovery, and a process of community enhancement. Clinically, helping the individual client to access and increase recovery capital enables the growth of recovery. Societally, it can inspire the development of resources for nourishing and sustaining the recovery of many. Consequently, assessing recovery capital and building on capital strengths are critical tasks for counselors, sponsors, coaches, recovery-seekers, and others who are trying to engage in and support the recovery process. The long-term goal is to empower recovery-seekers to take charge of their own recovery (Best & deAlwis, 2017; Best, Irving, et al., 2017; Best, Beswick, et al., 2016).

Recovery Capital is an evidence-based model for enhancing recovery success. It is currently being used in several localities and has broad applicability in peer-based and self-directed settings. Best and colleagues' *Assessment of Recovery Capital* (ARC) model has inspired clinical work and research at several sites in the United Kingdom and United States (Best, Edwards, et al., 2016).[11] Ecologically, it is becoming an essential task for community leaders to assess and enhance recovery support systems, both formal and informal. The current opioid crisis is driving examinations of available recovery supports across communities.[12]

Recovery Capital Matrix

White and Cloud (2008) have constructed a matrix that shows the balance of capital and problem severity (Kelly & Hoeppner, 2014). Their easily used quadrant model can assist in explaining the concept to those involved and can describe how the concept might help in self-directed planning (Best & Laudet, 2010).

Those with high recovery capital (employment and job support, active family relationships, friendship connections, high intelligence, spiritual or religious involvement) and low problem severity may respond to brief interventions or informal alerts, while those with high recovery capital and high problem severity (intense or long-term use, multiple drug use, or loss of control, employment, family connections) may respond best to outpatient inter-

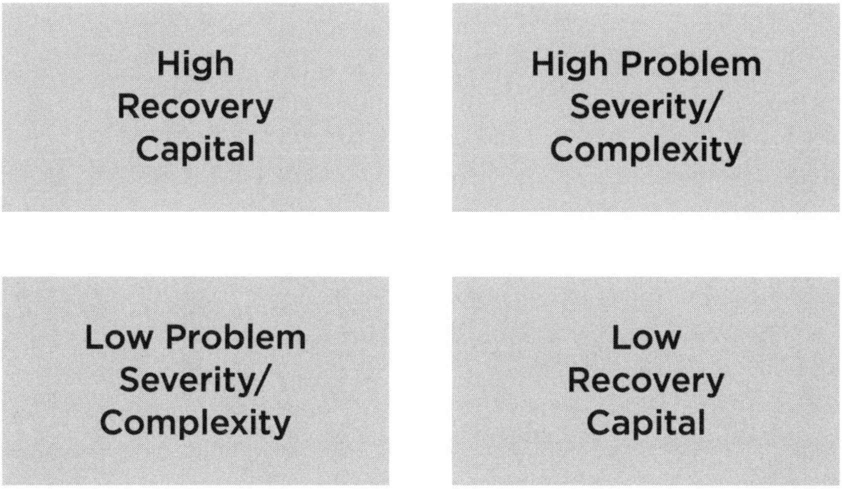

High Recovery Capital	**High Problem Severity/ Complexity**
Low Problem Severity/ Complexity	**Low Recovery Capital**

Figure 8.1.   Recovery Capital Quadrant Model. *Used with permission from William L. White*

vention combined with intense community support. Those with low problem severity and low recovery capital (isolation, low self-esteem, anxiety, spotty employment or school history) may benefit from residential rehabilitation and follow-up, while those with low recovery capital and high problem severity will likely need intensive interventions.

Barbara, for instance, came to the tasks of treatment and recovery initiation with low recovery capital (few life skills, attachment challenges, a lack of "stick-tuitive-ness," impulsiveness, turbulent relationships, frequent turnover in job and education history), and moderate problem severity (escalating use of pills but limited time of use). She also carried the scars of "negative recovery capital," such as a history of trauma and childhood adversity and co-occurring mental health disorders. She is a likely candidate for either inpatient or intensive outpatient treatment, with ongoing counseling, assertive recovery monitoring, and "recovery capital enhancement" for a prolonged period. Building on Barbara's interest and motivation for recovery, the counselor focused on establishing a welcoming and affirming alliance, traditional recovery tasks (meetings, use of a sponsor, service), and on building recovery capital (employment, housing, life interests), along with continuous counseling.

While improving in traditional recovery, Barbara was also encouraged to begin a new job within an industry she aspired to join. She found this work rewarding, with fellow employees who shared her interests. She got along well with her manager and slowly became a valued employee. She felt more stability in her life and experienced affirmation in her new workplace. Barbara also returned to an athletic hobby she enjoyed. At the same time she continued 12 Step involvement, and with the help of an effective sponsor celebrated one year of recovery. All these infusions of recovery capital into her life improved her mood and stabilized her recovery.

Ecological Implications

British psychologist David Best believes that "focusing exclusively on individuals underestimates the impact of key icons of recovery and of recovery communities . . . there is evidence for the social transmission of some of the key elements of recovery capital, and we do not have to conceptualize it exclusively as the property of an individual" (Best & Laudet, 2010).

What might these observations mean in practical terms? Every local grouping of recovering persons knows of people—"recovery champions," we might call them—who speak and live with a kind of *gravitas*, an attractive and inspirational voice for recovery. These people are often charismatic and connected. They are often sought out as "sponsors" in recovery circles. Barbara found such a person as her sponsor. In the same way, most locales have one or two vibrant recovery groups and systems of care that provide support and hope. In many communities, the local drug court and its allied groups have become recovery-fostering connections and important community health assets. For some communities, the local treatment center functions as an anchor and beacon for recovering people and systems. Barbara's outpatient therapy was part of such a community asset. Some communities benefit from colleges and universities that function as workforce training platforms, research hubs, and centers of advocacy for sobriety. Sober housing and recovery homes as well as employers and businesses that seek out recovering people are part of this landscape, often funded by county agencies or private enterprise. Finally, there are localities and regions where recovering people participate actively and publicly in civic and

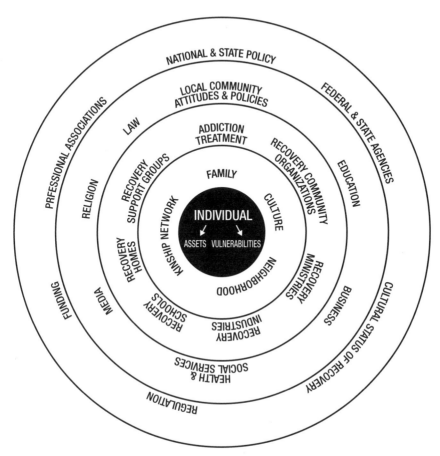

Figure 8.2. The Ecology of Recovery. *Used with permission from William L. White*

community life. This may be individually in small groups, or collectively, and those in recovery are seen as a positive social influence.

Attachment-sensitive counseling with substance use, addictive, and trauma-spectrum disorders works best when it is connected and integrated with community-based resources. This widens the healing field into a fully relational context. Recovery does not happen in a vacuum. This broader approach provides multiple benefits:

- It provides a space within which recovering persons can belong and become "part of" something greater.

- It weaves together recovery services and supports into a strong holding environment.
- It allows persons to discover, enact, and strengthen a new social and personal identity as "recovering" and valuable.
- It provides opportunities for fledgling recovering persons to participate and make a contribution. Service is essential in recovery.

Context Matters

Achieving long-term recovery is about more than an individual's relationship with a drug or behavior, more than his or her relationship with family and friends, more than a relationship with a particular treatment center or recovery program. It is about altering the complex relationships between individuals and the multiple layers of a relational ecosystem within which individuals and families live. As such, all layers of this ecosystem are targets of recovery-focused interventions.

A graphic depiction, based on the ecological theory of Urie Bronfenbrenner and reproduced below with complements of William White, shows the breadth of possible interventions (White, 2008, pp. 19–21).

9

Social Ecology and Poverty of the Spirit

"Explaining the rise of addiction in modern societies requires looking beyond the brain to the environments that shape it."

KEITH HUMPHREYS

"When it comes to health, your zip code matters more than your genetic code."

ANTHONY ITON

ADDICTION HAS MANY FACES. It is a great chameleon. Driven by invisible forces, it disguises itself by hiding in plain sight. In one corner are the attachments to alcohol, nicotine, opioids, and other drugs we know so much about. In another are the behavioral compulsions, such as gambling, online gaming, disordered eating, and sexual excess. In a third corner are the "-aholias," such as workaholia and addiction to wealth, or power, or fame. Addiction is not just about "demon drugs," brain chemicals, and faulty neurons. Addiction is also about adaptive solutions and attempts to cope with adversity, trauma, and toxic stress. Much of this remains concealed from the untrained eye.

As we saw in Chapter 3, the process of intoxication—the high we experience when "under the influence"—is similar across the range of addictive activities. Nevertheless, the *objects* of addiction vary. Psychoactive chemicals and compulsions like gambling or compulsive sex are the expected objects or activities in addiction; they "have what it takes" to serve as addictive objects. On the other hand, other objects and experiences can also be recruited to serve in the role of alternative mood-regulators or substitute regulatory relationships. These are the "-aholias."

Philosophical, ascetical, and spiritual traditions have long identified "disordered attachments" or addictions to wealth (money or possessions), power, status, fame, and a host of other experiences as dangerous activities (Alexander, 2008/2011). Ancient wisdom traditions point to disciplines such as *apatheia* or *indifferentia*—the seeking of spiritual peace and freedom from disordered entanglements with created things and possessions—as crucial for healthy human development. A peaceful life and the end of suffering often come as we relinquish worries about attachments.[1]

Intuitively, we know this. Many of us have already learned that our possessions sometimes also possess us. Whether it involves worrying about where the next paycheck will come from, or where the next million dollars will come from, money can be a ferocious taskmaster. Power, social status, celebrity can exercise the same control over our lives. However, I want to note that classic and "scientific" views of addiction do *not* commonly examine these experiences as addictions. We overlook them; perhaps we do not want to know too much about them. Perhaps drug or gambling addiction helps to distract our attention. In many ways, however, these "-aholias" may be our most dangerous addictions. Writer Tian Dayton reminds us that money or possessions can become a primary relationship, shunting all other relationships to the side.[2] They can provide a core sense of identity for some people, and provide ways to manipulate or control others as well as modulating emotions.

Finally, the *context* of addiction is crucial to understanding its true nature. Addiction is a unique threat to the relationships that anchor our lives. Interdependence is our special advantage as a species, our secret sauce for survival. Addiction imperils not only our health and happiness, but also menaces our connections to one another.

Addiction is embedded within social ecology, that is, within the set of relationships, systems, and interactions that are the substance of our daily lives. All the way from family and friends, to kinship networks, to the neighborhoods and workplaces that we inhabit, to the community institutions in which we participate, to the historical and cultural trends we experience, and even to Twitter and Facebook—each level of connections and influences has its impact. Our genes and our brains are open to these influences; our psychology and attitudes, our values and beliefs, are profoundly affected as well. High risks for substance misuse and addiction adhere to each of these levels of influence. Research into social and cyber dynamics, environmental justice, and fair distribution of resources and risks holds promise for comprehending these complex, interactive, and multilevel influences (Mennis, Staher, & Mason, 2016).

In this chapter, I ask that we stretch our thinking beyond the usual explanations for addiction, harmful drug use, and behavioral compulsion. We will turn from neurological, psychological, and trauma-centered accounts to the relational and social-ecological landscape within which those factors reside. Social forces and culture are powerful, and can "get under our skin," affecting the formation of the neurons, neural and hormonal structures, psychobiological systems, and relationships on which our identity and self-awareness rest (Cozolino, 2014; Harris, 2018; Iton, 2016). Conversely, we are often unaware of the powerful influence of social forces on our values, beliefs, and attitudes. Those around us and the cultures in which we are embedded shape the kinds of relationships we have with others and with the myriad of objects in our lives.[3] Addiction isolates us, turning us inward and hardening our hearts to one another.

SOCIAL ECOLOGICAL FRAMEWORK

The traditional models of addiction—disease, choice, learning—rely on good evidence that addiction has psychobiological and (epi-)genetic contributants. More recent research into the interpersonal neurobiology and social ecology in which addiction is embedded provides a different way to think about the addiction dilemma. Social ecology incorporates concepts such as interdependence and dynamic homeo-(socio-)stasis from systems theory to characterize reciprocal and vital person-environment transactions. Ecosystems thinking argues that the only way to fully understand some-one-thing or occurrence is to view the parts in relation to the whole. A relational ecology can help to frame new and different approaches to healing. It is a framework that pays explicit attention to the social, systemic, institutional, cultural, and moral/spiritual contexts of people-environment relations.

The concept of "social ecology," as used in this book, derives from several different sources. The term "ecology" refers to more than our connections with the "green" natural world. A human ecology is the network of relationships, including relationships with nature and the environment, which facilitates human flourishing. The primary relationships, however, are social ones. We are born into relationships with others; we come to awareness within relationships and systems that precede us and endure long after we are gone. Community (communion) among persons is the foundational context for development of the self. The individual self is "embedded within communities of communities" and dependent on our communal relationships (Wimberly, 2009, p. 35). We are resolutely social animals.

The natural world and our communal, social connections are not two detached and isolated realms. They are profoundly linked. As humans, individuals are nested within a social world, which is itself nested within a natural environment. Our ways of acting in one domain affect the quality of our actions in the other; the natural and social spheres are deeply connected, interpenetrating, and mutually interacting. Most social ecologists believe that "the restoration of harmonious relationships among human societies is a prerequisite for achieving harmony with nature" (Wimberly, 2009, p. 36).

> . . . it is incumbent upon us as individuals, families, and communities to quickly recognize and acknowledge our creatureliness, to accept our species-derived need to principally care for self and others like us, and thereafter to understand that our future upon the planet is entirely dependent upon our readiness to extend care and consideration for all around us that is not human but upon which our very existence depends (WIMBERLY, 2009, P. 205).

This harmonious relationship among different elements of our interdependent ecology is sometimes called "humanization" or an "integral humanism." It is an achievement of "psychosocial integration" (Alexander, 2008/2011).

Origins of Social Ecology

The investigation of social ecology emerges from a confluence of philosophies and social commentary, and has an eclectic pedigree. Below, we will briefly examine several of these influences. Urie Bronfenbrenner (1981, 2004) is perhaps the most recognizable contributor. His ecological model of development provides the structure and scaffolding for my view of social ecology. Murray Bookchin, often described as the "father" of social ecology, was a social and political theorist who wrote from the 1960s through the 1990s. He adds a decidedly political and economic flavor to our understanding. Pope Francis provides the spiritual and theological tone that pervades my view. Bruce K. Alexander's work shapes the concept of social ecology as it intersects with addiction studies, and adds his own political and economic twist.

1. Urie Bronfenbrenner

Social Ecology blends systems thinking with the ecological proposals of Urie Bronfenbrenner (1981, 2004). Bronfenbrenner proposed that in order to understand human development, the entire ecological system in which it occurs needs to be taken into account. The complexity and interactivity of relationships between individuals, the social environment, and nature is emphasized, along with the importance of establishing more mutualistic social structures.

At the core of Bronfenbrenner's ecological model is the child's biological and psychological makeup, based on individual and genetic developmental history. It continues to be affected and modified throughout the lifespan by the individual's immediate physical and social environment (family, kinship networks) as well as interactions among the systems (schools, workplaces, and so forth) within that environment. Other broader influences impact the structure and availability of surrounding systems and the manner in which they affect the child. Finally, social, political, and economic conditions are themselves influenced by the general beliefs and attitudes shared by members of the society.

The graphic that ends the previous chapter describes an ecological interpretation of recovery from addiction, for example, that utilizes Bronfenbrenner's model, visualized as concentric circles. Nested and interacting levels of experience form each individual's ecosystem. Recovery from substance misuse and addiction depends on assets and vulnerabilities that each individual brings to the task. At the *individual* level, personal history and biology influence how individuals behave and increase their likelihood of drug use or compulsive behavior. Among these factors, for example, are being a victim of child maltreatment, psychological or personality disorders, and a history of behaving compulsively or impetuously. At the same time, other factors can guide the individual toward recovery. This individual level of influence can be transformed into a positive asset with entry into treatment, maintenance of recovery, and cultivation of recovery capital.

Surrounding the individual is an embracing near-relational environment of kinship, family, neighborhood, workplace/school, and local culture that can inhibit or support problem resolution (*microsystem*). Personal relationships such as family, friends, intimate partners, and peers may influence the risks of drug use, but also the initiation and maintenance of recovery. For example, having friends who use drugs may influence whether a young person engages in compulsive or addictive behavior, while seeking out friends who support recovery (an element of recovery capital) can be an asset. The framework also presents professional services and local recovery supports and resources that are available to the recovering person (*mesosystem*).

The larger community environment of attitudes, accessibility of human services resources, and key community institutions (police and courts, medicine, religion, media, business) forms the *exosystem* of recovery. Risk factors here may include the level of unemployment, unsafe housing, lack of education, and the existence of a local drug or gun trade. Community contexts in which social relationships and systems occur, such as schools, neighborhoods, and workplaces, also influence risk for drug use and potential recovery.

The *macrosystem* of recovery in this model consists of state, national, and international trends as well as research and education resources in service to recovery. Large societal factors influence whether addiction is encouraged or inhibited: economic and social policies that maintain socioeconomic inequalities between people, the availability of and access to drugs, public policies about alcohol, tobacco and drug advertising and availability, and social and cultural norms, are all influences at this level.

This overall ecology of recovery is a critical set of influences to consider in thinking about the addiction and recovery process (White, 2009). Clinical intervention is one level of treatment; other levels need to be considered as well for comprehensive action. This framework views human phenomena, such as addiction and recovery, as the outcome of interaction among many factors at all four levels—the individual, the near-relational, the community, and the societal (White, 2008, p. 19).

The ecological model treats interaction between factors at the different levels as having equal importance to the influence of factors within any single level. Social policy and distribution of risks/resources can be as important to addiction (or recovery) as genes, or neurons, or behavioral contracts. The framework also acknowledges that effects of interventions (and risks, benefits) can reach across levels to impact multiple dimensions simultaneously. The levels are permeable and interpenetrate one another. This framework can be useful to identify and cluster risks, benefits, and potential intervention strategies. For example, home visitation interventions (Olds, 2008), used to support child development and prevention of family violence or adverse childhood experiences (ACEs), act in the relationship level to strengthen the bond between parent and child by supporting positive parenting practices. Yet home visitor programs can also emerge from larger civic concerns for the strength of families and the health and welfare of children. Or these visitors can embark on a new professional career and stimulate new social policy. A single intervention can have diverse effects at multiple levels.

2. Murray Bookchin

Philosopher and social critic Murray Bookchin (1996, 2004, 2005, 2007) focused his work on the ways in which human relationships and social systems are organized, and the impact they have on the natural world. He viewed natural environmental problems as rooted in market economic, ethnic, cultural, and gender conflicts. Disordered power relations and how these organize social life are at the core of his view.

Bookchin believed that the roots of ecological problems lay in deep-seated issues of scarcity, hierarchy, and domination. For him, the domination of nature mirrors the domination of humans by humans (2005). People are converted into commodities; natural resources are also "commoditized" and flagrantly merchandized. The pursuit of financial capital and the power status it brings becomes paramount. The planet itself and all the creatures within it become resources to be exploited through unjust market relationships, reflecting the ways in which individuals and countries exploit one another. The epitome of this dynamic lies in unbridled capitalism and brutal market relationships, what Bookchin called "the plundering of the human spirit by the market place," which mirrors "the plundering of the earth by capital" (Bookchin, 2004, pp. 24–25).

> Social ecology is based on the conviction that nearly all of our present ecological problems originate in deep-seated social problems. It follows, from this view, that these ecological problems cannot be understood, let alone solved, without a careful understanding of our existing society and the irrationalities that dominate it. To make this point more concrete: economic, ethnic, cultural, and gender conflicts, among many others, lie at the core of the most serious ecological dislocations we face today—apart, to be sure, from those that are produced by natural catastrophes (BOOKCHIN, 2007, P. 19).

Bookchin believed that the current social order must relinquish hierarchy and domination by developing a new political and ethical movement between humanity and nature (Bookchin, 2005). In an early publication he stated: ". . . in the final analysis, it is impossible to achieve a harmonization of man [sic] and nature without creating a human community that lives in a lasting balance with its natural environment" (Bookchin, 2004, p. 58).

Humanity's relationships became crippled by domination of some over others in his view, while similar power-dynamics are at play in relationships to the natural world. This has created the ecological ("green") crisis. Humanity can no longer allow societies that seek to dominate the social and natural realms; we need social arrangements devoted to an ethic of "complementarity."

> Ecology, in my view, has always meant social ecology: the conviction that the very concept of dominating nature stems from the domination of human by human, indeed, of women by men, of the young by their elders, of one ethnic group by another, of society by the state, of the individual by bureaucracy, as well as of one economic class by another or a colonized people by a colonial power. To my thinking, social ecology has to begin its quest for freedom not only in the factory but also in the family, not only in the economy but also in the psyche, not only in the material conditions of life but also in the spiritual ones (BOOKCHIN, 1996, P. 76).

Bookchin's critique undergirds the thinking of many contemporary social commentators. His view finds echoes in both contemporary and ancient voices, including unlikely support from the current Pope, Francis, in his recent encyclical letter, *Laudato si* (2015), subtitled "On care for our common home."

3. Pope Francis

> We urgently need a humanism capable of bringing together the different fields of knowledge, including economics, in the service of a more integral and integrating vision. Today, the analysis of environmental problems cannot be separated from the analysis of human, family, work-related and urban contexts, nor from how individu-

> als relate to themselves, which leads in turn to how they
> relate to others and to the environment (POPE FRANCIS,
> 2015, CHAPTER 4; EMPHASIS MINE).

Pope Francis advocates for what he calls a new humanism rooted in an "integral ecology." For him, such an integral human ecology is the opposite of our current fragmented and dislocated world. Francis is echoing the sentiments of deeper and richer spiritual and religious traditions of ecology and justice from across the globe and down through the centuries. What Bookchin calls our social "irrationalities" (see quote above) can be reconfigured, following the great religious traditions, as moral and spiritual blindspots.

In biblical terms, the ultimate moral and spiritual context for human living, decision-making and action is the essential goodness of all created things (Genesis 1 and Psalm 104). Human beings are meant to live in harmonious relationship with creation and to interact with creation's gifts through rightly ordered relationships. The ethic that guides harmonious relating is care (complementarity) not domination; we are created to be a supportive, collaborative species, not a dominating one. We use the gifts of creation as they were intended. Bookchin calls this a "natural spirituality."[4] The biblical-theological term for healthy and right relationships, as well as inter-relationship with all creation, is *shalom*.

Humans are to exercise caring stewardship toward the whole of creation in collaboration with the Creator. This maintains creation's *shalom*. Care for self, for the other, and for the world is a core ethical principle, an imperative that is rooted in our very existence. Care makes a claim on us. However, humans are also capable of injuring or destroying the natural order of creation through misuse of created gifts. Compulsive, addictive behavior is one form of such misuse. Visiting harm on self, neighbors, the community, or creatures fractures *Shalom*. We can become "estranged" from a proper relationship to the Creator and creation. In biblical terms, this is the first and primary dislocation, a primordial or original sin.[5]

Francis' diagnosis of current social problems sees the human focus on unbridled acquisition of capital, domination, and power over the environment as wounding both our world and relations with one another.

. . . [Mother Earth]) now cries out to us because of the harm we have inflicted on her by our irresponsible use and abuse of the goods with which God has endowed her. We have come to see ourselves as her lords and masters, entitled to plunder her at will. The violence present in our hearts, wounded by sin, is also reflected in the symptoms of sickness evident in the soil, in the water, in the air, and in all forms of life. This is why the earth herself, burdened and laid waste, is among the most abandoned and maltreated of the poor . . . (FRANCIS, 2015, PARAGRAPH 2).

Francis' ecological diagnosis has a silver lining, however. Because so much of what is being done to the planet reflects how we treat one another, it can also be transformed through a conversion of the heart, extended throughout human systems and mechanisms.

The urgent challenge to protect our common home includes a concern to bring the whole human family together to seek a sustainable and integral development, for we know that things can change. . . . Humanity still has the ability to work together in building our common home (2015, PARA-GRAPH 13).

In this view, addiction is not just a problem carried within an individual, but is best understood as a communal problem within the full context of human living. Human ecology is itself embedded (nested) within a wider natural and terrestrial environment, a living system that can only be maintained in a healthy state when all participants exercise an ethic of complementarity and the virtue of care. We rely on this larger ecology for our very lives. Any kind of fracturing or fragmentation within this intricate network of living systems leaves us wounded and unable to cope. Addiction is a harbinger of a fragmented world.

4. Bruce K. Alexander

For Canadian psychologist Bruce Alexander, addiction is a "window onto modern society" (2015). As we saw earlier, traditions in East and West were long concerned with "addiction" to riches, power, fame, drunkenness, social status, gluttony, and other excesses. In some traditions these were seen as disordered attachments and paths to the dark side of human personality and behavior, "deadly pitfalls for the human soul" that were also understood as threats to society and civic culture. Alexander returns to this classic view of the full range of destructive addictions.

For him, contemporary chemical and behavioral addictions are only one example of these attachments. Alexander makes the case that addiction to wealth and power through rapacious market capitalism, as well as modern technocratic living that increases societal fragmentation, is our current downfall. He sees societal fragmentation that has led to individual dislocation and alienation on a grand scale. Alexander believes that this has three interlocking implications. In *social* terms it leads to "absences of enduring and sustaining connections" between individuals and their most intimate relationships. In *existential* terms, the absence of feelings of belonging, of identity, and purpose is a deadly impact. In *spiritual* terms it is an experience of "homelessness of the soul," of "poverty of the spirit."

Alexander has published his more developed thinking in *The Globalization of Addiction: A Study in Poverty of the Spirit* (2008/2011). Addiction is not only a characteristic of individuals, he says, but can become part of an organized and systemic social force. People can create structures and systems that serve the needs of a few at the expense of others. Alexander has opened a window into these dynamics through his examination of globalization and market forces:

> . . . worldwide rending of the social fabric ultimately results from the growing domination of all aspects of modern life by free-market economics. . . . Free-market society subjects people to unrelenting pressures toward individualism, competition, and rapid change, dislocating them from social life. People adapt to this dislocation by concocting the best

substitutes that they can for a sustaining social, cultural, and spiritual wholeness, and addiction provides this substitute for more and more of us (ALEXANDER, 2011, P. 3).

Alexander believes that we are so accustomed to looking at addiction through an individualistic and near-relational lens—individual brains and biology, close and family relationships—that we miss the systemic, ecological, and spiritual connections. Our vision is limited. However, contemporary toxic distress is also grounded in fragmentation and profound dislocation. Lack of supportive and rejuvenating connections evolves into life among a community of strangers and vanishing neighbors (Dunkelman, 2014). Without real community and connection, we wither and seek substitute relationships. Our hectic, dislocated, caffeinated existence exacerbates these stressors. Living in chaotic and fragmented environments that are not supportive of human flourishing adds extra stressors.

Unfortunately, this is not the only limitation to our vision. As a society, we also insist that investigation of addiction limit itself to alcohol, drugs, and troublesome behaviors, while virtually ignoring powerful attachments to other forms of excess, such as addiction to power or wealth. Were we to examine these "-aholias" honestly, many unspoken rules shaping individual and societal behavior would be laid bare.

It is not difficult to hear echoes of Murray Bookchin, Pope Francis, and many other modern social critics in these words. As we will soon see, social fragmentation and dislocation also lead to loss of hope and optimism, which in turn lead to a variety of social pathologies, including addiction.

ENVIRONMENTAL ADVERSITY

If we look beyond our limited vision, what will we find? What challenges are at work in the wider social and systems environment that create the conditions favorable to drug misuse, behavioral compulsion, and addiction? If we examine the systemic and social environments surrounding people who struggle with addiction and harmful use, we will find conditions of toxic stress that exacerbate their risks.

There are many potential points of entry for studying social ecology and its relation to addiction. Previously, I chose *interpersonal adversities* (trauma, toxic stress) as a lens to examine the experience, development, and neurobiology of addiction. Now I want to examine social ecology and addiction through the window of *environmental adversity* (Hamoudi et al., 2015; Murray et al., 2015).

Many Americans today live in "chronically precarious" and challenging environments. These produce stressful living conditions, and often the most easily accessible, adaptive options for coping are a variety of unhealthy behaviors, such as smoking, drinking, drug use, sexual promiscuity, and so on. Psychoactive substances and compulsive behaviors often have a short-term adaptive, "stress-buffering role" in the lives of many people (Jackson et al., 2010). These behaviors may alleviate symptoms of stress for a time, but simultaneously have debilitating effects on physical, emotional, and mental health. These activities emerge from, and interact with, difficult living environments to create disparities in mortality and health: "Those who live in chronically stressful environments often cope with stressors by engaging in unhealthy behaviors that may have initially protective mental-health effects. However, such unhealthy behaviors can combine with negative environmental conditions to eventually contribute to morbidity and mortality disparities among social groups" (Jackson et al., 2010).

Health disparities are one kind of environmental adversity. They are not just generic health risks but "systemic health inequities" focused on groups with low social status, located in contexts and locales that are already prone to adversity. This is a function of unequal distribution of risks as well as social, economic, and environmental resources. Looked at in this way, health disparities are a social justice issue.

Conditions in adversity-prone places include such elements as neighborhoods with high crime rates; lack of fundamental resources, such as medical care, economic stability, access to employment, safe housing, and fresh food; persistent and chronic poverty; and a pervasive "psychology of scarcity" (Murray et al., 2015). Cumulative disparities create health vulnerabilities and can reduce one's ability to focus, plan, and problem-solve, making effective social action to correct or rebalance disparities impossible. Taken together, detrimental health conditions predict "poor mental health, low psychological well-being, and short life expectancy" (Rivera, 2014, p. 2).[6]

Nevertheless, it is important to remind ourselves that precarious and challenging environments are not restricted to the lives of the poor or economically disadvantaged. As we learned from looking at the ubiquity of trauma and the prevalence of "adverse childhood experiences," toxic stress can affect children and parents in any family, any community. There are children and families with similar risks in Westchester, New York, or Beverly Hills, California as well as Ramp Hollow, West Virginia. How else do we account for poor health, addiction, and opioid overdoses among the wealthy and famous? We need more research into the ways that toxic stress patterns itself.

Environmental Health Disparities

Since the 1990s, the environmental justice movement has fostered an emerging science of environmental health and cumulative risks. This approach is one of the new consilient sciences and is helping us to understand addiction risks in an ecological context. The wise attachment-sensitive counselor comes to understand that, while good clinical care must rely on attachment repair and reconnection with caring relationships, truly *comprehensive* care necessitates addressing social and ecological ruptures as well. There is a valid role for systemic awareness and political action as well as advocacy. Assisting in the creation of common healing strategies and nurturing environments for recovery is also required.

Health disparities reflect social inequalities. They are a tenacious and powerful element in many neighborhoods and locales. Barriers to understanding and intervening, such as (a) blindness to the disadvantage of poor and middle-class folks as well as the rich and famous, (b) blaming disadvantaged people for their ill-health, (c) unequal distribution of risks and resources, (d) relying solely on biomedical approaches, (e) political short-termism, and (f) the current political and economic climate—to name only a few—keep these persistent gaps in business. Interventions into the health of the public require attention to both health-related *and* social-political concerns. Addiction prevention and intervention can benefit from these insights. Ameliorating disparities and boosting the health of individuals and communities are twin strategies.

Geography and ZIP Codes

Health disparities, risks for illness, and potential predisposing factors for substance use and addiction come from many directions, but they also seem to cluster by location. A social ecological view needs to begin with a sense of "place."[7]

Dr. Anthony Iton, physician and public health specialist,[8] addresses a variety of health disparities across the United States. He does this through a two-pronged approach: (a) improving direct, patient-focused healthcare in affected communities, which he believes accounts for only 20 percent of overall health status, but also (b) by attacking the poverty, racism, lack of opportunity, and loss of hope—the overall social and cultural ecology, or societal environment—that impacts the other 80 percent of health. He has led a number of efforts to address those ecological disparities by addressing the underlying "social compact" in various cities and rural locales.

Iton and other creative thinkers who have studied these issues, are reaching consensus regarding how to account for these health disparities (Commission on Social Determinants of Health, 2008; Marmot & Bell, 2009; Marmot, Friel, et al., 2008). Most all of them acknowledge that the relevant issues regarding health are more than behavioral choices, genetics, or toxins, more than even poverty and racism. Other important factors include societal forces that can separate and disconnect us from others and fragment us into pockets of difference, by social class, societal and educational opportunities, availability of meaningful employment, affordable housing, public safety, transportation, recreational services and facilities, the overall environment and community resources available, and so much more. These "social determinants" of health can be more impactful than genetic history or access to quality healthcare (Iton, 2016; Slade-Sawyer, 2014; Wilkinson & Marmot, 2003). And, social determinants tend to cluster by geographic location; they can certainly be the subtext for social and geographic disparity.

Ecological ingredients located in specific places and locales affect poor health and the prevalence of chronic illnesses, such as cardiovascular disease, obesity, diabetes, depression, abuse of prescription painkillers and drug overdose, and of course addiction. Community poverty as well as issues of class and race are important factors, so are transportation (some families spend more on driving than healthcare, education or food), access to healthy food (low-income neighborhoods offer greater access to food sources that promote unhealthy eating, like the densely packed fast food outlets in poor areas), educational disparities (linked to longevity, heart disease, types of cancer and the like), even income inequality.[9] Neighborhood design and rural planning play a role as well.

This suggests that health concerns need actions that will encompass more than disease care. Effective strategies must also focus on "an upstream approach that ultimately reduces healthcare burdens and improves population health" (Slade-Sawyer, 2014, p. 394). Increasing public health may be as much the province of city and urban planners as physicians and urgent care centers, of the Chamber of Commerce as much as the local medical society.

Once health scientists began to look, the geography of poor health and behavioral dysfunction began to reveal itself. A case in point, as it relates to substance use and addiction, may be the current opioid crisis. To understand harmful drug use and addiction, as well as the opioid crisis, we need to understand and evaluate the context in which drug use takes place. The application of a social ecological framework to this task would have several goals: to explain the person-person and person-environment interactions involved, to improve people-environment transactions, to nurture human growth and development in particular environments, and to improve and support healthy and safe ecologies. This is important work for purposes of prevention, intervention, treatment, and recovery. As well, it is critical for policy and services in addition to promotion of public health and wellness.

Case Study: The Geography of Desperation

In a recent set of reports from The Brookings Institution (2017, July 24), titled *The Geography of Desperation in America*, Carol Graham and her colleagues document relationships between premature mortality—from heart, liver, and lung disease as well as from preventable causes (suicide, opioid, and other drug overdoses)—and differences in optimism, worry, and pain in the U.S. Their report also documents the clustering of lost hope and its relationship with troubled pockets of suffering by geographic location.[10] In other words, they wrote about the significance of *place* for health and illness.

Graham and colleagues focused on racially diverse, low-income, high-stressed groups (less than $24,000 annual income for a family of four) and document that, while poor minorities (Black and Hispanic) face similar poverty-related challenges, they also have higher levels of resilience; non-Hispanic poor whites seem less resilient overall. Depression, suicide, and less optimism are more typical for poor whites than for minorities. The authors attribute this to higher levels of community and family support (connection) in minority communities as well as higher optimism and aspirational levels. Poor whites, and particularly rural poor whites who also tend to have lower educational attainment, are caught in a downward spiral, that is, lack of social mobility with weakened family structures and poor employment prospects. This plagues their future and saps their hope, leading to a spiral of premature "deaths of despair," driven by depression, suicide, drug abuse/addiction, and overdose (Graham et al., 2017). In other words, *The Geography of Desperation* paints a clear social ecological picture of place-based vulnerability for addiction and other health challenges.[11]

Similar work by Case and Deaton (2015, 2017) examines marked changes in US mortality among poor, less-educated (high school degree or less), non-Hispanic whites. Leading causes of death appear to be drug and alcohol poisoning (or overdose), suicide, alcohol-related liver mortality, and chronic diseases. These outcomes accompany significant decreases in coping ability with self-reported lessening of health and mental health. Case and Deaton also report extension of these troubling trends beyond rural areas to include smaller cities and suburban locales.

When combined with mortality data from the Centers for Disease Control and Prevention (2011), the information from these researchers offers a "robust association" between lack of hope, high levels of anxiety and stress, and premature mortality rates. However, note that these characteristics cluster by *place* and social location. Graham and her colleagues call these "pockets of desperation and despair" (Graham & Pinto, 2018). Different communities and their cultures share common identities, economic conditions, community traits, cultural assumptions and beliefs, and physical environments

(Graham & Pinto, 2017). Adverse child and family toxicity permeates these environments.

While the social compacts among residents in these places can vary widely, Graham and her colleagues see the starkest markers for desperation as preventable and premature deaths, suicides and drug overdose. Granted, desperation wears many faces and not all of them are poor and uneducated, but social fragmentation and dislocation share certain hallmarks in common.

Ground Zero

The map below (Figure 9.1), from the NCHS National Vital Statistics System of the Centers for Disease Control and Prevention, shows the rate of drug overdose deaths in 2016. Notice where the highest levels of overdose occur (darkest areas).

Currently, we live in a nation afflicted with an opioid and prescription drug epidemic. There are 142-plus opioid-related deaths daily in the United States. This number is the equivalent of those lost on 9/11 every three weeks! Drug overdose is the leading cause of accidental death in the U.S., greater than death from guns or auto accidents, with opioids accounting for more than half of that number.[12] Overdose deaths among women and teens have risen dramatically. Four in five heroin users began by misusing prescription painkillers, and a large amount of available heroin is adulterated with fentanyl, a potent and potentially lethal painkiller. The combination is a leading cause of overdose deaths.

While overdose from prescription opioids may be leveling off, deaths from heroin and fentanyl are rising. Prescription opioids appear to be the "gateway" to further abuse. Nationally, the majority who use illicit narcotics began with a prescription. Seventy-five (75 percent) to eighty percent (80 percent) of heroin users are hooked initially on prescription painkillers. One hundred million Americans took prescription painkillers this past year; at least 12 million did so without physician prescription. Overdoses appear to cluster by region, with the highest rates in Appalachia, the former Rust Belt, the Lower West, and parts of New England (Sanger-Katz, M., 2018).

Graham's Brookings reports draw a bright line from disadvantaged econom-

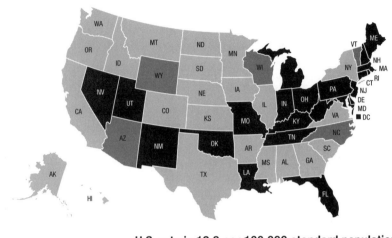

U.S. rate is 19.8 per 100,000 standard population.

- Statistically lower than U.S. rate
- Statistically the same as U.S. rate
- Statistically higher than U.S. rate

Figure 9.1.   Map of U.S. Drug Overdose death rates, 2016. [Darkest states have higher than US death rates]. *Source: NCHS, National Vital Statistics System. Public domain.*

ics and loss of hope (declining incomes, chronic unemployment, family dysfunction) in specific locales to mappable rises in preventable chronic illnesses, premature mortality, deaths of desperation, and addiction. One prime example is Appalachia. In his book, *Hillbilly Elegy,* author J. D. Vance (2016) offers a vivid portrayal of the fortunes of the Ulster-Scots or Scots-Irish, non-Hispanic poor whites who are a major segment of the population in Appalachia. He documents in detail many of the characteristics that are being uncovered about the communities that share family and cultural roots in this area. Journalist Gwynn Guilford (2017) documents the ecological and business decisions that have affected Appalachia in her article, "The 100-year Capitalist Experiment that Keeps Appalachia Poor, Sick, and Stuck on Coal." The region's declining health, poverty, and loss of hope rests not on moral failings of individuals and families, but at least in part from reliance on a failed business ideology that insists "profit equals prosperity, regardless of its true costs."

1. Role of Toxic Stress

Dr. Iton states: ". . . when people don't see a future for themselves, they blunt the stress and pain of the moment with drugs, alcohol and comfort food." These are adaptive, substitute methods. Stresses in the environment and life space of individuals "get under the skin and change physiology" (Iton, 2016). It is fair to say that social- and communal-level stresses play a significant role in predisposing to illness and addiction.

An overall contributing element in health disparity, premature mortality, quality of life, and well-being is the cumulative impact of toxic stress on individuals and communities (Solomon et al., 2016). We now know that the weight of individual adversity, traumatic occurrences, and toxic stress on individuals is higher than we previously imagined. This also appears to be true in specific locations (Harris, 2018). As Iton says, low-resource and low life-expectancy communities function like "incubators for chronic stress." Certain ZIP codes carry with them a double-whammy: higher risks of stress, personal and systemic, *and* a paucity of resources for coping.

Risks and opportunities tend to pattern themselves. Chronic stress influences risks, changes physiology, and can even change how genes express themselves (Dick et al., 2015; Gatzke-Kopp, 2011). This increases the total allostatic, or stress-related, load carried by community members, who can find themselves craving high fat, high salt, and high sugar foods, leading to diabetes or obesity, as well as alcohol and other drugs, leading to addiction and overdose (Devine et al., 2006; Tryon et al., 2013; Yau & Potenza, 2013), or coping with chronic stress in multiple other ways.

We have seen that in the case of Adverse Childhood Experiences these risks are more common than previously suspected and tend to cluster together. We now know that they also cluster by place; those places can be in the "hollers" of West Virginia, or the barrios or penthouses of Los Angeles. These clusters represent an iceberg of multiple health-related risks and stresses, and signal the stress-related burden of specific locales and communities.

2. Stress is Contagious

The impact of disparities can be contagious and spreads beyond low-resource communities to affect the overall population as well. As we have seen throughout this book, chronic stress increases risks for chronic medical illness, particularly for obesity, diabetes, asthma, certain types of cancer, and heart disease; it also increases the overall load for behavioral and mental illness, including substance misuse and addiction (Mennis et al., 2016). These are expensive conditions, personally and financially, not only in terms of healthcare but also in family dysfunction, community fragmentation, lost worker productivity, and employer costs. These outcomes stress the entire societal and medical system. We are so accustomed to thinking about health and illness in purely medical or biological terms that we often skirt or give short-shrift to social factors and social justice (Farrer et al., 2015). Downstream medical and psychiatric outcomes can be caused by upstream social conditions, burdens, and toxic stress.

However, beginning to examine the impact of a wide variety of community-based environmental factors, such as geographic location, social relations, elements of marginalization, and unequal distribution of economic opportunities can open our horizons not only to new insights but also to new possibilities for comprehensive healthcare as well as drug misuse/addiction prevention, intervention and treatment. Transformation of traditional public roles (police, judges, teachers, counselors, physicians) and the forging of new pro-health alliances and connections in communities is required. No single-issue approach is sufficient. A deeper understanding of the neurobiology and relational ecology surrounding stress and health can take us to a nexus of multiple factors, where wellness, societal circumstances, toxic stress, and social justice meet (PolicyLink, 2007).

Bruce K. Alexander (2001) states the case for significant societal change, based on this data:

> Addressing the problem of addiction will require funda-
> mental political and economic changes. The beginning of
> political change is a realistic discussion of addiction that
> recognizes that addiction is mass-produced in free mar-

ket society, and that society, as well as individuals, must change. It requires moves towards good government and away from policies that undermine our ability to care for one another and build sustainable, healthy communities.

THE OPIOID CRISIS AS A "WICKED PROBLEM"

America today is as divided as it has ever been, in terms of incomes and opportunities, politics, and, perhaps most importantly, hopes and dreams. Hope matters. . . . individuals who do not believe in their futures are much less likely to invest in them—as in education, health, and job training. This increases the odds of America becoming even more unequal in the future. These divisions are corrosive to our society, our polity, our civic discourse, and to our health (GRAHAM, PINTO, & JUNEAU, 2017. BROOKINGS INSTITUTION).

One way to think about the opioid and prescription drug crisis is to imagine it as a "wicked problem."

In a 2008 *Harvard Business Review* article, Professor John Camillus points out that "wicked problems" cannot be solved, but they can be tamed.[13] "Wicked problems" are confounding and defy definitive answers. What makes a problem "wicked" is not just that it is tough to handle or resistant to resolution, but rather that traditional processes cannot put an end to the problem. A wicked problem is difficult to describe fully. It is dynamic and does not have one right answer, no clear solution. Its roots are tangled and difficult to ferret out. It has multiple causes and there is no consensus about what the causes might be or the priority of their impact. It is socially complex and involves many stakeholders, individuals, groups, and systems with different values, opinions, and priorities. It appears to be intractable, with many attempted solutions but no clear successes, no "righteous" solutions. It morphs when acted upon, presenting unforeseen difficulties, unintended consequences, and challenges. There are few ways to judge whether a proposed solution is on the right path or even achievable.

While there may not be clear solutions, wicked problems can be brought to heel. To do so, however, often requires courage, a willingness to act when all the pros and cons are not clear or even known. Experiments, pilots, prototypes, sometimes called "robust actions," may be the best way forward. Promising moves forward and alternatives will present themselves, once risky actions are taken. Resolving to learn from these actions, revising and then acting again along the way, may be the best strategy. Determination, tenacity, and imagination are required.

In business, "robust actions" involve utilizing social planning processes, such as brainstorming, retreats, focus groups, and visioning exercises among stakeholders. The goal is to create a kind of intentional and action-oriented community, with a shared understanding of the problem and a joint commitment to possible ways of resolving it.

The opioid crisis conforms to many of the criteria for a wicked problem. Because the causes and contributing factors for wickedness are multiple, one can begin from several different starting points and get to some ideas about potentially "righteous solutions." A set of national and regional strategies have already begun to address the opioid problem.[14]

- Improving nationwide and state-by-state surveillance and reporting of the opioid problem is an essential first step.
- Expanding treatment capacity is already underway. Providers, insurance, and third-party payers need to get on board and think creatively about reimbursement.
- Increasing access and insurance coverage for non-opioid, even non-pharmacological treatments for pain. Alternative and complementary medical approaches can be helpful (yoga, acupuncture, meditation, etc.).
- Law enforcement and first responders are already receiving more resources, such as emergency deliverable Narcan and drug-specific overdose training, as well as support for burnout and "compassion fatigue." These resources need to be expanded, particularly in rural and out-of-the-way places.

- Training and retraining medical providers, especially primary care providers, needs to intensify and move forward. Screening, Brief Intervention, and Referral to Treatment (SBIRT) is being implemented across a variety of "settings of opportunity" (trauma centers, emergency rooms, prisons).[15] Moving initial assessment and intervention into primary care and first-responder settings can help to address substance problems before they become intractable.

- Support for medication-assisted treatment and a range of psychosocial treatment options and peer-based recovery support is ongoing, but needs expansion.

- We need to curtail diversion of narcotics to non-patient users, encourage more cautious prescribing of opioids for pain (while insuring that those who need medication receive it!), better monitor the pain levels of patients and offer alternative pain treatments, and interrupt the supply of heroin and synthetic opioids.

- Communities must continue to fight stigma (and the racial and class bias that lurk beneath) and reach out to those who still struggle. We must help communities to support individual and family recovery, and build recovery capacity.

These are standard actions often encouraged in previous antidrug efforts. However, other ways of thinking and acting must be brought to bear as well:

- Too many Americans struggling with drug use are overlooked in our communities and treatment systems. Only a small percentage of those who need help—not just those struggling with addiction but the even bigger population of "harmful users"—actually receive any kind of treatment. This is a treatment secret: Millions (!) of people who struggle with drugs, and could benefit from earlier intervention and treatment, receive no professional help. This must change. We need new protocols, enhanced capacity, easier access, earlier intervention, updated reimbursement protocols, and revised social marketing to capture and assist those who need help.

In addition, too many people with an opioid or other drug problem are incarcerated and languishing in our jails and prisons. These drug sufferers are often off our radar and outside our circle of care, but they also need access to high-quality treatment.

- We must finally acknowledge the inadequacies of many current treatment programs. This is another little secret that the treatment industry wants to keep hidden. There is no organized, system-wide implementation or assessment of evidence-based practices in addiction treatment, and many current practices have little research supporting their efficacy.[16] Much of the marketing is based on anecdotal evidence or financial greed. Too much treatment is geared to an acute model of care, more appropriate for a broken leg or diseased appendix than for a chronic illness like addiction or harmful use (McLellan et al., 2000; White, Boyle, & Loveland, 2005. In addition, while inpatient and outpatient facilities give lip-service to individualized treatment planning, this is not often available. There are many wonderful people involved in helping those struggling with addiction, but the systems in which they work need serious revision.[17] Centers of excellence do exist, but many systems require overhaul.

- Thinking of opioids as a "wicked" and *chronic problem*, addressing the need for long-term *recovery management* (not "graduation from treatment"), aggressively *linking* recovering people with community resources, *assertive follow-up and continuing care* (often for years following treatment), *proactive re-intervention when needed*, and helping to build *recovery capital* for individuals and communities, could help to reframe a more modern approach and offer people the length and quality of treatment they need (Laudet & White, 2008; White, 2008; White & Cloud, 2008). The traditional drug treatment and prevention strategies of the past are woefully inadequate. We must revise these strategies with a social-ecological approach.

Additional Strategies

In order to confront the wicked crisis of drugs, we need creative thinking and a willingness to invest in experimental programs that offer the promise of success. We must be willing to explore new options and be committed for the long term. I suggest that we pay attention to several factors among others that are crucial from a social-ecological point of view: (a) an "adverse childhood experiences" understanding of trauma and addiction vulnerability (that is, "full-spectrum trauma-informed treatment"), and (b) addressing the wider social, cultural, and economic environment in which addiction is embedded. Not surprisingly, these two factors are interrelated.

We know that substance misuse and addiction take root when the soil is right. This is another way of saying that a significant factor in vulnerability to addiction is its social ecology (Alexander, 2008/2011). This goes beyond the traditional view of disease, genetics, and psychological vulnerabilities. Research is revealing a powerful vulnerability that involves the interplay of early childhood experiences, adversity and trauma, family dysfunction, neurobiology, and psychological impairment. Each of these factors is intertwined and operates simultaneously to place the (potential) addict or harmful user at a serious disadvantage. Histories of physical and sexual abuse and co-occurring mental disorders are associated with opioid trajectories (Stein et al., 2017; Tilson, 2018). Adverse Childhood Experiences are a crucial "upstream" factor in overall health and vulnerability to later drug misuse, behavioral compulsion, and addiction.

We need to consider multiple investments in family and kinship supports. Home Visitation programs to support young families and new parents as a way to prevent adverse experiences are an evidence-based methodology. Social science research also indicates that the wider societal, cultural, and economic environment has profound effects on the ecology in which opioid addiction is imbedded. Family, social systems, safe and sober housing, and employment support can facilitate recovery (Hser et al., 2015). While we consider doubling-down on traditional strategies to combat opioids, we should also consider newer social-ecological interventions. Because the causes and contributing factors for "wickedness" are multiple, one can begin from several different starting points and explore "righteous solutions." Traditional *and* more radical ecological strategies must be attempted.

In the 1990s, many countries in Europe had serious addiction problems and a runaway opioid crisis, but were willing to try something different.[18] Several EU members, including Portugal and Switzerland, attempted decriminalization of drug use and experienced some successes. The important thing about Portugal and Switzerland, however, is that they did not stop there. They added something even more powerful than decriminalization to their drug strategies. They added strategies to catalyze active and inclusive social connections within their populations. They strove to invite and reintegrate recovering citizens back into the civic culture. They worked hard to make opioids a public health, not law enforcement, problem and invested in public health strategies.

Both countries de-emphasized the punitive role of law enforcement and promoted health-related services, working to provide medication replacement and therapeutic alternatives (drug and non-drug) for people struggling with addiction. Police, along with social workers, therapists and locally based accessible facilities, became points of contact and agents of outreach to addicts. The government helped to provide social services, employment and safe housing assistance, and reintegration into mainstream society, even going so far as investing capital in start-up business ventures by recovering people. In other words they assisted "drug outsiders" to find paths of (re-) inclusion into their society, bringing them "out of the shadows" and offering a sense of meaning and purpose.

Now, more than a decade later, the results in both countries indicate that they have made great strides in overcoming their "wicked problem." Journalist Johann Hari recounts the basic stories of Portugal and Switzerland in *Chasing the Scream* (2015), and in an op-ed in the *Los Angeles Times* (2017) titled, "What's really causing the prescription drug crisis?".[19]

While it is likely that neither model is a perfect fit for the United States, and decriminalization is only a far-off possibility, nevertheless the ingenuity and courage of these approaches can give us hope. Strategies of healing and reconnection need to be considered. We must find ways to pilot alternatives and learn from them. Robust and courageous actions are needed to catalyze hope.

If we take seriously the social-ecological approach examined here, then it is clear that simple clinical, legal, educational, and preventive interventions have always been insufficient. Comprehensive strategies to transform the ecologies surrounding affected individuals and families must also be utilized. Changing the ecology around addiction must be our mantra. But what does this look like? Chapter 10 suggests something of a vision.

10

A Circle of Compassion

"The most reliable way to produce an adult who is brave and curious and kind and prudent is to ensure that when he is an infant, his hypothalamic-pituitary-adrenal axis functions well. And how do you do that? It is not magic. First, as much as possible, you protect him from serious trauma and chronic stress; then, even more important, you provide him with a secure, nurturing relationship with one parent and ideally two."

PAUL TOUGH

"Spirituality is recognizing and celebrating that we are all inextricably connected to each other by a power greater than all of us, and that our connection to that power and to one another is grounded in love and compassion."

BRENÉ BROWN

THE SUBTITLE OF THIS BOOK, *The Power of Connection*, provides a powerful metaphor for understanding addiction and recovery. Connections bind our world as one. They knit together the neurons and systems that anchor our neurobiology. Relationship connections and social systems are the mainstays of our social brains. Reliable relationships ground our social and psychological abilities. When connections are frayed or broken—when persons experience trauma, social fragmentation, and disconnection—illness and addiction often ensue. The remedy is (reconnection and community.

Bruce K. Alexander, whose work helped to inspire this book, tells a story relayed to him by an indigenous healer in Northern Canada. It portrays the current dilemma we face in the Americas regarding drug misuse and addiction. She told him the story of a tribe of healers that rescues drowning people from the swift-running river nearby. These healers bravely swim to those in trouble, avoiding the rocks and currents they have learned are ever-present, and bring the victims to safety. They deposit those rescued onto the shore, where they learn to fend for themselves; some do, some don't. The tribe celebrates their victories and mourns those who cannot be rescued. The tribe knows that they are warriors; however, the tribe also knows that "some sonofabitch upstream" continues to throw people into the water, even more people than last year. As long as this persists, nothing will change.[1]

Who is this "sonofabitch upstream" and what is his role in the drama of addiction? The forces of disconnection, trauma, toxic stress, and social dislocation are the soil of addiction; they have the power to create victims and toss them overboard. They are in cahoots with individual and systemic adversity, with wounded neural systems, as well as with individual and family vulnerabilities. Together, they create an ecology of suffering. Addiction and harmful use—with substances, with compulsive behaviors, with attachments and - aholias (wealth, celebrity, power, and so forth)—take firm root in toxic soil. Substitute attachments are adaptive solutions to human suffering and they will remain potent as long as the misery endures.

Addiction has many faces and utilizes many elements of our humanity, including our neural structures, genes, psychological working models, relationships, and psychosocial needs. It is a multidimensional phenomenon with layers within layers of mutual influences, internal and external, all interacting concurrently, leading to a pathological outcome. And it has a common core: Adversity, disconnection, and fragmentation are the mothers of addiction. We often fail, however, to acknowledge fully the social and systemic, ecological context that is involved.

People cope as best they can. Misuse of chemicals, of behaviors, of attachments often begins as an adaptive solution and advances into addiction when misuse proves itself useful. It serves a function. Once ingrained as a substitute relationship, it takes on a life of its own. Personal and familial adversity play a critical role on the path to misuse and addiction. Adversity and trauma in our surrounding relationships distort our neurobiology and mangle our sense of ourselves. Systemic adversities such as family dysfunction, divorce, racial discrimination, economic hardship—and in a global context, adversities such as forced family separation, even terrorism or child conscription—become part of our damaged ecology. But it takes another step to understand how overall economic hardship, health disparities, social-political upheaval, cultural disenfranchisement, and societal loss of meaning and purpose also create the kinds of alienation and dis-ease (poverty of spirit) that can lead to "desperate substitutes."

Nevertheless, coming to such a comprehensive understanding is essential if we are to address successfully the "wicked problem" of harmful use and addiction. For decades, we have utilized the best antidrug measures available (law enforcement, education, treatment, prevention) with limited success. The successes are worth celebrating but they are insufficient. More of the same, by itself, will not avail us. Antidrug strategies are essential of course, such as wise (and transformed) use of law enforcement and drug courts; new methods of screening, assessment, and treatment accessibility; increased research into effective treatments and use of medication-assisted treatments; supplying Naloxone to emergency personnel, and syringe/needle exchange programming to curb infections.

We also need better science-based drug education for kids, parents, and affected families. We need recognition of the extent of our harmful use and addiction problems and the universal screening/assessment protocols that should result. We need better, evidence-based, trauma-informed, attachment-sensitive treatment, as well as more consistent, aggressive, and far-reaching follow-up (and reintervention as needed) when people leave treatment and begin recovery living. But more importantly we need to change our attitudes as individuals and as a society.

The complementary key to successfully addressing harmful use, addiction, and our current opioid and prescription drug crisis is creating and maintaining a society in which human beings are valued, not commoditized; where compassion and creating genuine community guide our choices; where people can belong and make a contribution. This is what Alexander calls "psychosocial integration," an essential part of human well-being (2011). I prefer the term "humanization" (Martin-Baró, 1994, p. 109), or even better, "radical kinship" (Boyle, 2017).

The core of addiction is lack of connection, loss of meaning, and social fragmentation . . . in short, poverty of spirit. Recovery, then, for individuals and families struggling with addiction and for our society as a whole, is a restoration to connection, to life-giving relationships and a sense of belonging. People find purpose and value within human community. They "feel felt" and discover that their lives have worth, that they are part of something larger, with a reason to achieve and maintain sober living. Their vulnerabilities are met with compassion and an ethic of care. Community and society become a "circle of compassion from which no one is excluded" (Boyle, 2011).

Compassion (complementarity, care) is an essential ingredient of a new social ethic that can foster healthy living as well as recovery, and flies in the face of society's usual misapprehensions about those struggling with addiction. If more struggling persons were treated as "kin" rather than "other," we could remove many barriers, including stigma, from successful recovery. Imagine a society built around compassion and kinship. Without it, addiction will be an ever-present risk, at least for some.

Once the individual is able to acquire some time away from drugs or compulsive behaviors and learns strategies for healthy coping with triggers and cravings, recovery largely involves (a) remaining free of addiction pathology and disordered attachments, (b) reintegrating into relationships with family, friends, and the communal institutions that provide meaning, and (c) reorientation into a non-addictive lifestyle with purpose. There is a critical role in this picture for family, friends, and society; the vast majority of recovery takes place in everyday life. The day-to-day, back-and-forth of relationships is the milieu of everyday recovery. The individual assumes a "renewed stake" in conventional life and in social relationships. This becomes the catalyst for a new identity and sense of worth (Alexander, 2008/2011; Cloud & Granfield, 2004, p. 200). Social engagement and community help to maintain identity as a recovering person.

Sustained long-term recovery often (but not always) requires counseling, inner work, and relationship repair to assist in making a start. This is the role of attachment-sensitive counseling. But recovery also requires the mending of broken and frayed connections among people and finding the means to live without substitutes. This requires a vital social ecology. Caring communities can be augmented with recovery-oriented systems that make compassion concrete, that provide opportunities to engage with other recovering people and structures/resources to meet their needs.

Addressing the modern crisis of addiction and the current opioid crisis is an enormous undertaking, but it is impossible to comprehend the full size and scope of the challenge until we take this final step. Nothing less than a full transformation of human society will eradicate the problem. This is not a cause for despondency. The magnitude of the task should not deter us. Imagine that we can begin—one decision at a time, one relationship at a time—to build a more humanized, caring, and compassionate world, a world in which no one is left behind. All of us, not just those who struggle, will benefit.

This vision is worth fighting for.

Acknowledgments

No author writes alone. Yes, there are isolated (and isolating) moments. It is often a solitary business. But, I found that I was never alone—even my cat, Lennie, was a sweet companion—while writing this book. Because of this, many are owed a debt of gratitude.

Colleagues at the University of Scranton supported my efforts. I am grateful to Dean Debra Pellegrino and my chairpersons, Lori Bruch and Lee-ann Eschbach. Many local colleagues reviewed chapters and made helpful comments including Chris Adonizio, Gerianne Barber, J. Timothy Cannon, John Deak, Candice Ricciardi, and Dominic Vangarelli. In addition, versions of these chapters were read by my students and they were honest in their reactions, suggesting word changes, preferred conceptualizations, and debating ideas. They helped to keep me honest. Ms. Abigail Rieder and my Graduate Assistant Emma Sommers provided valuable support.

A larger group of professional collaborators also provided support and valuable insight. Chief among these were Bruce K. Alexander and William L. White. Rob Anda, Kent Berridge, Craig Cashwell, Vincent Felitti, Keith Humphreys, Gabor Maté, and Lisa Najavits all made significant contributions. The publishers and editors at W. W. Norton, especially Louis Cozolino and Deborah Malmud, deserve special mention for encouraging me to undertake this project. Their staff has been wonderful to work with.

I am grateful to my clients over the years and particularly to my patients

243

at the Supportive Oncology Service for the past ten years. They were my primary and best teachers.

My editor, Candace Johnson, was a great gift at a crucial time and helped me to view the writing process more clearly. She also introduced me to my agent, Stephanie Evans.

My partner in all things, my wife Ellen, shouldered many responsibilities at home and freed me to explore this project. She encouraged me from the beginning, read and commented on the manuscript at crucial moments, and often reminded me that I am better than I believe . . . in many areas of living. My children's patience and support are remarkable and they stepped up at home when health issues became paramount for me during the writing.

All in all I am a lucky man, and a grateful one. This book is a collaborative effort. Thanks.

References

Adams, P. J. (2007). *Fragmented intimacy: Addiction in a social world.* New York: Springer Science+Business Media, LLC.

Ainsworth, M. D. S., Blehar, M. C., Waters, E., & Wall, S. N. (2015). *Patterns of attachment: A psychological study of the strange situation.* Psychology Press.

Alcoholics Anonymous (2002). *Alcoholics Anonymous: The Big Book* (Fourth Edition). New York: Alcoholics Anonymous World Services.

Alexander, B. K. (1987). The disease and adaptive models of addiction: A framework evaluation. *Journal of Drug Issues, 17*(1), 47–66.

Alexander, B. K. (2001). *The roots of addiction in free market society.* Vancouver, BC: Canadian Centre for Policy Alternatives.

Alexander, B. K. (2008/2011). *The globalization of addiction: A study in poverty of the spirit.* New York: Oxford University Press.

Alexander, B. K. (2014, July 3). *The rise and fall of the official view of addiction.* Bruce K. Alexander Official Website. Downloaded April 18, 2016.

Alexander, B.K. (2015). Eco-Crisis, Spirituality, and Addiction. Workshop presented at Healing Our World and Ourselves Conference. Vero Beach, Florida, February 21, 2014

Alexander, B. K. (2016). *Rat Park versus The New York Times.* www.brucekalexander .com/articles-speeches/281-rat-park-versus-the-new-york-times_Downloaded: May 2, 2016.

Alexander, B. K. & Hadaway, P. F. (1982). Opiate addiction: The case for an adaptive orientation. *Psychological Bulletin, 92*(2), 367–381.

American Society of Addiction Medicine (2001). *Definitions related to the use of opioids for the treatment of pain: Consensus statement of the American Academy of Pain Medicine, the American Pain Society, and the American Society of Addiction Medicine.*

245

American Academy of Pain Medicine, American Pain Society, and American Society of Addiction Medicine.

Anda, R. (2008). The health and social impact of growing up with adverse childhood experiences: The human and economic costs of the status quo. *Guest House Review, 2* (online journal of Guest House Institute. Lake Orion, MI). Retrieved January 26, 2009 from http://guesthouse.org/institute.php?page=Review

Anda, R. F., Felitti, V. J., Bremner, J. D., Walker, J. D., Whitfield, C., Perry, B. D., Dubé, S. R., & Giles, W. H. (2006). The enduring effects of abuse and related adverse experiences in childhood. A convergence of evidence from neurobiology and epidemiology. *European Archives of Psychiatry and Clinical Neuroscience. 256*(3):174–86. Epub 2005 Nov 29.

Babor, T. F., McRee, B. G., Kassebaum, P. A., Grimaldi, P. L., Ahmed, K., & Bray, J. (2007). Screening, Brief Intervention, and Referral to Treatment (SBIRT): Toward a public health approach to the management of substance abuse. *Substance Abuse, 28*(3), 7–30.

Badenoch, B. (2018). *The heart of trauma: Healing the embodied brain in the context of relationships.* New York: W. W. Norton & Company.

Bartholomew, K. & Shaver, P. R. (1998). Methods of assessing adult attachment: Do they converge? In Simpson, J. A. & W. S. Rholes, W. S. (Eds). *Attachment theory and close relationships.* (pp. 25–45). New York: The Guilford Press.

Bauer, G. (2014, September 27). DSM-5 and its use by chemical dependency professionals. NAADAC 2014 Annual Conference presentation. www.NAADAC.org.

Baylin, J. & Hughes, D. (2016). *The neurobiology of attachment-focused therapy: Enhancing connection and trust in the treatment of children and adolescents.* New York: W. W. Norton & Company.

Bazzano, M. (Ed.) (2018). *Re-visioning person-centered therapy: Theory and practice of a radical paradigm.* New York: Routledge.

Benoit, D. (2004). Infant-parent attachment: Definition, types, antecedents, measurement and outcome. *Paediatrics & Child Health, 9*(8), 541–545.

Bepko, C. & Krestan, J. A. (1985). *The responsibility trap: A blueprint for treating the alcoholic family.* New York: Free Press.

Berridge, K. C. (2012). From prediction error to incentive salience: Mesolimbic computation of reward motivation. *European Journal of Neuroscience, 35*(7), 1124–1143.

Berridge, K. C. (2017). Is addiction a brain disease? *Neuroethics, 10*(1), 29–33.

Berridge, K. C. & Kringelbach, M. L. (2015). Pleasure systems in the brain. *Neuron, 86*(3), 646–664.

Berridge, K. C. & Robinson, T. E. (2016). Liking, wanting, and the incentive-sensitization theory of addiction. *American Psychologist, 71*(8), 670–679.

Bertolero, M. A., Yeo, B. T. T., & D'Esposito, M. (2015). The modular and integrative functional architecture of the human brain. *Proceedings of the National Academy of Sciences of the United States of America, 112*(49), E6798–E6807.

Best, D., Beswick, T., Hodgkins, S., & Idle, M. (2016). Recovery, ambitions, and aspirations: An exploratory project to build a recovery community by generating a skilled recovery workforce. *Alcoholism Treatment Quarterly, 34*(1), 3–14.

Best, D. & deAlwis, S. (2017). Community recovery as a public health intervention: The contagion of hope. *Alcoholism Treatment Quarterly, 35*(3), 187–199.

Best, D., Edwards, M., Mama-Rudd, A., Cano, I., & Lehman, J. (2016, November 1). Measuring an individual's recovery barriers and strengths. *Addiction Professional Magazine*. www.addictionpro.com/article/special-populations/measuring-individuals -recovery-barriers-and-strengths.

Best, D., Irving, J., Collinson, B., Andersson, C., & Edwards, M. (2017). Recovery networks and community connections: Identifying connection needs and community linkage opportunities in early recovery populations. *Alcoholism Treatment Quarterly, 35* (1), 2–15.

Best, D. & Laudet, A. (2010). *The potential of recovery capital*. www.thersa.org/discover/ publications-and-articles/reports/the-potential-of-recovery-capital

Best, D. & Lubman, D. I. (2012). The recovery paradigm: A model of hope and change for alcohol and drug addiction. *Australian Family Physician, 41*(8), 593–597.

The Betty Ford Institute Consensus Panel (2007). What is recovery? A working definition from the Betty Ford Institute. [Special Section: Defining and Measuring "Recovery"]. *Journal of Substance Abuse Treatment, 33*, 221–228.

Blaszczynski, A. & Nower, L. (2002). A pathways model of problem and pathological gambling. *Addiction, 97*(5), 487–499.

Bloom, S.I. (2013). *Creating sanctuary, second edition*. New York: Routledge.

Boeck, C., Krause, S., Karabatsiakis, A., Schury, K., Gundel, H., Waller, C., & Kolassa, I. T. (2017, August). History of child maltreatment and telomere length in immune cell subsets: Associations with stress- and attachment-related hormones. *Development and Psychopathology, 30*(2) 539–551.

Bonn-Miller, M. O., Bucossi, M. M., & Tafton, J. A. (2012). The underdiagnosis of cannabis use disorders and other Axis-I disorders among military veterans within VHA. *Military Medicine, 177*(7), 786–788.

Bookchin, M. (1996). *Toward an ecological society*. Montreal, QC: Black Rose Books.

Bookchin, M. (2004). *Post-scarcity anarchism*. Chico, CA: AK Press (Working Classics series).

Bookchin, M. (2005). *The ecology of freedom: The emergence and dissolution of hierarchy*. Palo Alto, CA: Cheshire Books.

Bookchin, M. (2007). What is social ecology? In Bookchin, M. & Eiglad, E. (Eds.) *Social ecology and communalism*. (pp. 19–52). Oakland, CA: AK Press.

Boss, P. (1999). *Ambiguous loss: Learning to live with unresolved grief*. Cambridge, MA: Harvard University Press.

Boss, P. (2006). *Loss, trauma, and resilience: Therapeutic work with ambiguous loss.* New York: W. W. Norton & Company.

Boszormenyi-Nagy, I. & Spark, G. M. (1984). *Invisible loyalties: Reciprocity in intergenerational family therapy.* New York: Brunner/Mazel.

Bowen, S., Chawla, N., & Marlatt, G. A. (2011). *Mindfulness-based relapse prevention for addictive behaviors: A clinician's guide.* New York: The Guilford Press.

Bowlby, J. (1949). The study and reduction of group tensions in the family. *Human relations, 2*(2), 123–128.

Bowlby, J. (1958). The nature of the child's tie to his mother. *International Journal of Psycho-Analysis, 39*(5), 350–373.

Boyle, G. (2011). *Tattoos on the heart: The power of boundless compassion.* New York: Free Press.

Boyle, G. (2017). *Barking to the choir: The power of radical kinship.* New York: Simon & Schuster.

Bradshaw, G. A. & Schore, A. N. (2007). How elephants are opening doors: Developmental neuroethology, attachment and social context. *Ethology, 113*(5), 426–436.

Brady, K. T., McCauley, J. L., & Back, S. E. (2014, Nov 30). The Comorbidity of Post-Traumatic-Stress Disorder (PTSD) and Substance Use Disorders. In el-Guebaly, N., Carra, G., & Galanter, M. (Eds.) *Textbook of Addiction Treatment: International Perspectives* (pp.1986–2004). New York: Springer.

Bremner, J. D. (2002). *Does stress damage the brain? Understanding trauma-related disorders from a mind-body perspective.* New York: W. W. Norton & Company.

Bremner, J. D. (2016). (Ed.). *Posttraumatic stress disorder: From neurobiology to treatment.* New York: Wiley Blackwell.

Bretherton, I. (1990). Communication patterns, internal working models, and the intergenerational transmission of attachment relationships. *Infant Mental Health Journal, 11*(3), 237–252.

Bretherton, I. (1991a). The roots and growing points of attachment theory. In C. M. Parkes, J. Stevenson-Hinde, & P. Marris (Eds.) *Attachment across the life cycle* (pp. 9–32). New York: Routledge.

Bretherton, I. (1991b). Pouring new wine into old bottles: The social self as internal working model. In M. R. Gunnar & L. A. Sroufe (Eds.), *The Minnesota symposia on child psychology, Vol. 23. Self processes and development* (pp. 1–41). Hillsdale, NJ: Lawrence Erlbaum Associates.

Bronfenbrenner, U. (1981). *The ecology of human development: Experiments by nature and design.* Boston, MA: Harvard University Press.

Bronfenbrenner, U. (2004). *Making human beings human: Bioecological perspectives on human development.* New York: Sage.

Brous, K. (2018). *Don't Try This Alone: The Silent Epidemic of Attachment Disorder.* Available from https://attachmentdisorderhealing.com/about/

Brown, S. (1985). *Treating the alcoholic: A developmental model of recovery* (Vol. 109). Wiley-Interscience.

Brown, S. & Lewis, B. (1999). *The alcoholic family in recovery: A developmental model.* New York: The Guilford Press.

Brown, D. W., Riley, L., Butchart, A., Meddings, D. R., Kann, L., & Harvey, A. P. (2009). Exposure to physical and sexual violence and adverse health behaviors in African children: Results from the Global School-based Student Health Survey. *Bulletin of the World Health Organization, 87*(6), 447–455.

Bryant, R. S., O'Donnell, M. L., Creamer, M., McFarlane, A. C., & Silove, D. (2013, August). A multisite analysis of the fluctuating course of posttraumatic stress disorder. *JAMA Psychiatry, 70*(8), 839–846.

Burke, L. (2003). The impact of maternal depression on familial relationships. *International Review of Psychiatry, 15*(3), 243–255.

Byng-Hall, J. (1985). The family script: A useful bridge between theory and practice. *Journal of Family Therapy 7,* 301–305.

Byng-Hall, J. (1988). Scripts and legends in families and family therapy. *Family Process, 27*(2), 167–179.

Byng-Hall, J. (1991a). An appreciation of John Bowlby: His significance for family therapy. *Journal of Family Therapy, 13,* 5–16.

Byng-Hall, J. (1991b). The application of attachment theory to understanding and treatment in family therapy. In C.M. Parkes, J. Stevenson-Hinde, & P. Marris, (Eds.). (2006). Attachment across the life cycle (pp. 199–215). Routledge.

Byng-Hall, J. (1995). Creating a secure family base: Some implications of attachment theory for family therapy. *Family Process, 34*(1), 45–58.

Byng-Hall, J. (1998). *Rewriting family scripts: Improvisation and systems change.* Guilford Press.

Byng-Hall, J. (2008). The crucial roles of attachment in family therapy. *Journal of Family Therapy, 30,* 129–146.

Cacioppo, J. T., Berntson, G. G., & Decety, J. (2010). Social neuroscience and its relationship to social psychology. *Social Cognition, 28*(6), 675–685.

Camillus, J. C. (2008). Strategy as a wicked problem. *Harvard Business Review, 86*(5), 98.

Campaign for Trauma-Informed Policy and Practice (CTIPP). (2017, June). Trauma-informed approaches need to be part of a comprehensive strategy for addressing the opioid epidemic. *Policy Brief,* No. 1. www.ctipp.org. https://publichealth.gwu.edu/sites/default/files/downloads/Redstone-Center/CTIPP_OPB_final.pdf

Case, A. & Deaton, A. (2015). Rising morbidity and mortality in midlife among white non-Hispanic Americans in the 21st century. *Proceedings of the National Academy of Sciences, 112*(49), 15078–15083.

Case, A. & Deaton, A. (2017). Mortality and morbidity in the 21st century. *Brookings papers on economic activity,* 397.

Castonguay, L. G. & Hill, C. E. (2012). *Transformation in psychotherapy: Corrective experiences across cognitive behavioral, humanistic, and psychodynamic approaches.* American Psychological Association.

Chapman, D. P., Whitfield, C. L., Felitti, V. J., Dube, S. R., Edwards, V. J., & Anda, R. F. (2004). Adverse childhood experiences and the risk of depressive disorders in adulthood. *Journal of Affective Disorders, 82*(2), 217–225.

Childress, A. R. (2006). What can human brain imaging tell us about vulnerability to addiction and to relapse? In Miller, W. R. & Carroll, K. M. (Eds.), *Rethinking substance abuse: What the science shows, and what we should do about it* (pp. 46–60). New York: The Guilford Press.

Childress, A. R., Ehrman, R. N., Wang, A., Li, Y., Sciortino, N., et al. (2008). Prelude to passion: Limbic activation by "unseen" drug and sexual cues. *PLoS One, 3*(1), e1506.

Christakis, N. A. & Fowler, J. H. (2009). *Connected: The surprising power of our social networks and how they shape our lives.* New York: Little, Brown & Company.

Clark, L., Averbeck, B., Payer, D., Sescousse, G., Winstanley, C. A., & Xue, G. (2013). Pathological choice: The neuroscience of gambling and gambling addiction. *The Journal of Neuroscience, 33*(45), 17617–17623.

Cloud, W. & Granfield, W. (2004). Life course perspective on exiting addiction: The relevance of recovery capital in treatment. In P. Rosenquist, J. Blomquist, A. Koski-Jannes, & L. Ojesjo (eds). *Addiction and life course,* pp. 185–202. Helsinki, Finland: Nordic Council for Alcohol and Drug Research.

Cloud, W. & Granfield, W. (2009). Conceptualising recovery capital: Expansion of a theoretical construct. *Substance Use and Misuse, 42,* 12/13, 1971–1986

Cole, P. M. & Putnam, F. W. (1992). Effect of incest on self and social functioning: A developmental psychopathology perspective. *Journal of Consulting and Clinical Psychology, 60* (2), 174–184.

Commission on Social Determinants of Health (CSDH). (2008). *Closing the gap in a generation: Health equity through action on the social determinants of health.* Final Report, Executive Summary. www.who.int/social_determinants [WHO/IER/CSDH/08.1].

Connery, H. S. (2015). Medication-assisted treatment of opioid use disorder: Review of the evidence and future directions. *Harvard Review of Psychiatry, 23*(2), 63–75.

Conyers, B. (2003). *Addict in the family: Stories of loss, hope and recovery.* Center City, MN: Hazelden Publishing.

Conyers, B. (2018, May 14). *Five mindfulness practices to step up your recovery.* www.hazeldenbettyford.org

Cozolino, L. (2010/2002). *The neuroscience of psychotherapy: Healing the social brain* (Second Edition). New York: W. W. Norton & Company.

Cozolino, L. (2013). *The social neuroscience of education: Optimizing attachment and learning in the classroom* (The Norton Series on the Social Neuroscience of Education). W. W. Norton & Company.

Cozolino, L. (2014). *The neuroscience of human relationships: Attachment and the developing social brain* (Second Edition). New York: W. W. Norton & Company.

Cozolino, L. (2006). The social brain. *Psychotherapy in Australia, 12*(2), 12.

Cronholm, P. F., Forke, C. M., Wade, R., Bair-Merritt, M. H., Davis, M., Harkins-Schwarz, M., . . . & Fein, J. A. (2015). Adverse childhood experiences: Expanding the concept of adversity. *American Journal of Preventive Medicine, 49*(3), 354–361.

Daily, J. (2012). *Adolescent and young adult addiction: The pathological relationship to intoxication and the interpersonal neurobiology underpinnings.* Fair Oaks, CA: Recovery Happens.

Dallos, R. (2004). Attachment narrative therapy: Integrating ideas from narrative and attachment theory in systemic family therapy with eating disorders. *Journal of Family Therapy, 26*, 40–65.

Danese, A. & McEwen, B. S. (2012). Adverse childhood experiences, allostasis, allostatic load, and age-related disease. *Physiology & Behavior, 106*(1), 29–39.

Dayton, T. (2012). *The ACOA trauma syndrome: The impact of childhood pain on adult relationships.* Health Communications.

DeGrandpre, L. (2006/2010). *The cult of pharmacology: How America became the world's most troubled drug culture.* Duke University Press.

Dennis, M. & Scott, C.K. (2007). Managing addiction as a chronic condition. *Addiction Science and Clinical Practice, 4*(1), 45–55.

Devine, C. M., Jastran, M., Jabs, J., Wethington, E., Farell, T. J., & Bisogni, C. A. (2006). "A lot of sacrifices:" Work–family spillover and the food choice coping strategies of low-wage employed parents. *Social Science & Medicine, 63*(10), 2591–2603.

DeWall, C. N., MacDonald, G., Webster, G. D., Masten, C. L., Baumeister, R. F., Powell, C., . . . & Eisenberger, N. I. (2010). Acetaminophen reduces social pain: Behavioral and neural evidence. *Psychological Science, 21*(7), 931–937.

Diamond, G. S., Diamond, G. M., & Levy, S. A. (2014). *Attachment-based family therapy for depressed adolescents.* Washington, DC: American Psychological Association.

Dick, D. M., Agrawal, A., Keller, M. C., Adkins, A., Aliev, F., Monroe, S., . . . & Sher, K. J. (2015). Candidate gene-environment interaction research: Reflections and recommendations. *Perspectives on Psychological Science, 10*(1), 37–59.

DiClemente, C. C. & Velasquez, M. M. (2002). *Motivational interviewing and the stages of change.* In Rollnick, S. & Miller, W. R. (Eds.) *Motivational interviewing: Preparing people for change.* (Second Edition) (pp. 201–216). New York: The Guilford Press.

Doweiko, H. E. (1999). Substance use disorders as a symptom of a spiritual disease. In O. J. Morgan & M. Jordan (Eds.), *Addiction and spirituality: A multidisciplinary approach* (pp. 33–53). St. Louis, MO: Chalice Press.

Drury, S. S. (2015). Unraveling the meaning of telomeres for child psychiatry. *Journal of the American Academy of Child and Adolescent Psychiatry, 54*(7), 539.

Dubé, S. R., Anda, R. F., Felitti, V. J., Croft, J. B., Edwards, V. J., & Giles, W. H. (2001). Growing up with parental alcohol abuse: Exposure to childhood abuse, neglect, and household dysfunction. *Child Abuse & Neglect, 25*(12), 1627–1640.

Dubé, S. R., Felitti, V. J., Dong, M., Chapman, D, P., Giles, W. H., & Anda, R. F. (2003). Childhood abuse, neglect, and household dysfunction and the risk of illicit drug use: The Adverse Childhood Experiences Study. *Pediatrics. 111*(3):564–72.

Dunkelman, M. J. (2014). *The vanishing neighbor: The transformation of American community*. New York: W. W. Norton & Company.

DuPont, R. L., McLellan, A. T., Carr, G., Gendel, M., & Skipper, G. E. (2009). How are addicted physicians treated? A national survey of physician health programs. *Journal of Substance Abuse Treatment, 37*(1), 1–7.

DuPont, R. L., McLellan, A. T., White, W. L., Merlo, L. J., & Gold, M. S. (2009). Setting the standard for recovery: Physicians' Health Programs. *Journal of Substance Abuse Treatment, 36*(2), 159–171

Economic Innovation Group (2018). Distressed Communities Index. Washington, DC. https://eig.org/dci

Edwards, S. & Koob, G. (2010, May). Neurobiology of dysregulated motivational systems in drug addiction. *Future Neurology, 5*(3), 393–401.

Eisenberger, N. I. (2011). Why rejection hurts: What social neuroscience has revealed about the brain's response to social rejection. *Brain, 3*(2), 1.

Eisenberger, N. (2012a). Broken hearts and broken bones: A neural perspective on the similarities between social and physical pain. *Current Directions in Psychological Science, 21*(1), 42–47.

Eisenberger, N. (2012b). The neural bases of social pain: Evidence for shared representations with physical pain. *Psychosomatic Medicine, 74*(2), 126–135.

Eisenberger, N. (2015). Social pain and the brain: Controversies, questions, and where to go from here. *Annual Review of Psychology, 66*, 601–629.

Eisler, R. (2012). Economics as if caring matters. *Challenge, 55*(2), 58–86.

Erickson, C. K. (2018). *The science of addiction: From neurobiology to treatment* (Second Edition). New York: W. W. Norton & Company.

Everly, G. S. & Lating, L. M. (2013). *A clinical guide to the treatment of the human stress response*. (Third Edition). New York: Springer Science+Business Media, LLC.

Farrer, L., Marinetti, C., Cavaco, Y. K., & Costongs, C. (2015). Advocacy for health equity: A synthesis review. *Milbank Quarterly, 93*(2), 392–437.

Felitti, V. J. (2003). Origins of addictive behavior: Evidence from a study of stressful childhood experiences. *Praxis der Kinderpsychologie und Kinderpsychiatrie, 52*(8), 547–559.

Felitti, V. J., Anda, R. F., Nordenberg, D., Williamson, D. F., Spitz, A. M., Edwards, V., Koss, M. P., & Marks, J. S. (1998). Relationship of childhood abuse and household dysfunction to many of the leading causes of death in adults. The Adverse Childhood Experiences (ACE) Study. *American Journal of Preventive Medicine. 14*(4), 245–58.

Feliz, J. (2012, March). *Survey: Ten percent of American adults report being in recovery from substance abuse or addiction. Partnership for Drug Free Kids.* Downloaded on April 22, 2016. www.drugfree.org/newsroom/survey-ten-percent-of-american-adults -report-being-in-recovery-from-substance-abuse-or-addiction.

Field, T. (1998). Maternal depression effects on infants and early interventions. *Preventive Medicine, 27*(2), 200–203.

Field, T., Diego, M., & Hernandez-Reif, M. (2006). Prenatal depression effects on the fetus and newborn: A review. *Infant Behavior and Development, 29*(3), 445–455.

Finkelhor, D. and Browne, A. The traumatic impact of child sexual abuse: A conceptualization. *American Journal of Orthopsychiatry, 55*(4), [Trainer's Resource handout].

Firestone, R., Firestone, L. A., Catlett, J., & Love, P. (2002). *Conquer your critical inner voice: A revolutionary program to counter negative thoughts and live free from imagined limitations.* Oakland, CA: New Harbinger Publications.

First, L. R. & Kemper, A. R. (2018, June 20). *The effects of toxic stress and Adverse Childhood Experiences at our Southern border: Letting the published evidence speak for itself.* American Academy of Pediatrics (Journals Blog). www.aappublications.org/news/2018/06/20/the -effects-of-toxic-stress-and-adverse-childhood-experiences-eg-at-our-southern-border -letting-the-published-evidence-speak-for-itself-pediatrics-6-20-18

Fishbane, M. D. (2007). Wired to connect: Neuroscience, relationships, and therapy. *Family Process, 46*(3), 395–412.

Fisher, H. (2004). *Why we love: The nature and chemistry of romantic love.* New York: Henry Holt and Company, LLC.

Fletcher, K., Nutton, J., & Brend, D. (2015). Attachment, a matter of substance: The potential of attachment theory in the treatment of addictions. *Clinical Social Work Journal, 43*(1), 109–117.

Flores, P. J. (2004). *Addiction as an attachment disorder.* Jason Aronson.

Foster, H., Hagan, J., & Brooks-Gunn, J. (2008, June). Growing up fast: Stress, exposure and subjective "weathering" in emerging adulthood. *Journal of Health and Social Behavior, 49*, 162–177.

Fraley, R. C., & Shaver, P. R. (2000). Adult romantic attachment: Theoretical developments, emerging controversies, and unanswered questions. *Review of General Psychology, 4*(2), 132–154.

Framo, J. L. (1992). *Family-of-origin therapy: An intergenerational approach.* New York: Routledge

Garrett, J. & Landau, J. (2010). *ARISE to help your family member recover from alcohol, drug, and other addictions: A proven intervention and lifelong recovery guide for families*. Binghamton, NY: Taylor & Francis.

Gatzke-Kopp, L. M. (2011). The canary in the coalmine: The sensitivity of mesolimbic dopamine to environmental adversity during development. *Neuroscience & Biobehavioral Reviews, 35*(3), 794–803.

Gazzaniga, M. S. (2008). *Human: The science behind what makes your brain unique*. New York: Harper Perennial.

George, S. & Chima, C. (2014). Gambling addiction: What every doctor needs to know. *Internet Journal of Medical Update, 9*(1), 1–3.

Geronimus, A. T., Hicken, M., Keene, D., & Bound, J. (2006). "Weathering" and age patterns of allostatic load scores among blacks and whites in the United States. *American Journal of Public Health, 96*(5), 826–833.

Geronimus, A. T., Pearson, J. A., Linnenbringer, E., Schulz, A. J., Reyes, A. G., Epel, E. S., . . . & Blackburn, E. H. (2015). Race-ethnicity, poverty, urban stressors, and telomere length in a Detroit community-based sample. *Journal of Health and Social Behavior, 56*(2), 199–224.

Gill, R. (Ed.). (2014). *Addictions from an attachment perspective: Do broken bonds and early trauma lead to addictive behaviours?* London, UK: Karnac Books.

Gladwell, M. (2006). *The tipping point: How little things can make a big difference*. New York: Little, Brown & Company.

Glaser, G. (2015, April). The irrationality of Alcoholics Anonymous. *The Atlantic*. www.theatlantic.com/magazine/archive/2015/04/the-irrationality-of-alcoholics-anonymous/386255

Gold, M. S. & Frost-Pineda, K. (2006). Problem doctors: Is there a system level solution? *Annals of Internal Medicine, 44*, 861–862.

Goldstein, R. Z., & Volkow, N. D. (2011). Dysfunction of the prefrontal cortex in addiction: neuroimaging findings and clinical implications. *Nature Reviews Neuroscience, 12*(11), 652.

Goleman, D. (2006). *Emotional Intelligence: Why it can matter more than IQ*. New York: Bantam Books.

Goleman, D. (2006). *Social intelligence: The new science of human relationships*. New York: Bantam Books.

Goodman, A. (1995, March). Addictive disorders: An integrated approach: Part One—an integrated understanding. *Journal of Ministry in Addiction and Recovery, 2*(2), 33–76.

Goodman, A. (2008). Neurobiology of addiction: An integrative review. *Biochemical Pharmacology, 75*, 266–322.

Goodman, A. (2009, Aug 28). The neurological development of addiction: An overview. *Psychiatric Times, 26*(9), 1–14.

Gorski, T. T. & Miller, M. (1986). *Staying sober: A guide to relapse prevention.* SIDALC.net.

Goudriaan, A. E., Yücel, M., & van Holst, R. J. (2014). Getting a grip on problem gambling: what can neuroscience tell us? *Frontiers in Behavioral Neuroscience, 8,* 141.

Graham, C. & Pinto, S. (2018). Unequal hopes and lives in the USA: Optimism, race, place, and premature mortality. *Journal of Population Economics,* 1–69.

Graham, C., Pinto, S., & Juneau, J. (2017, July 24). *The geography of desperation in America.* Brookings Institution report.

Granfield, R. & Cloud, W. (1996). The elephant that no one sees: Natural recovery among middle-class addicts. *Journal of Drug Issues, 26*(1), 45–61.

Granfield, R. & Cloud, W. (2001). Social context and "natural recovery": The role of social capital in the resolution of drug-associated problems. *Substance Use & Misuse, 36*(11), 1543–1570.

Grant, R. (1996). *Way of the wound: A spirituality of trauma and transformation.* Oakland, CA: Self-Published.

Grinage, B. D. (2003, Dec 15). Diagnosis and management of post-traumatic stress disorder. *American Family Physician, 68*(12):2401–2409.

Guilford, G. (2017, December 30). The 100-year capitalist experiment that keeps Appalachia poor, sick, and stuck on coal. *Quartz.*

Gunnar, M. R. (1992). Reactivity of the hypothalamic-pituitary-adrenocortical system to stressors in normal infants and children. *Pediatrics, 90*(3), 491–497.

Hamoudi, A., Murray, D. W., Sorensen, L., & Fontaine, A. (2015, February). *Self-regulation and toxic stress: A review of ecological, biological, and developmental studies of self-regulation and stress* (Vol. 30). OPRE Report #2015–30, Washington, D.C., Office of Planning, Research and Evaluation, Administration for Children and Families, U.S. Department of Health and Human Services.

Hari, J. (2017, January 12). What's really causing the prescription drug crisis? Op. Ed., *Los Angeles Times.*

Hari, J. (2015). *Chasing the scream: The first and last days of the War on Drugs.* New York: Bloomsbury USA.

Hari, J. (2015, June). *Everything you think you know about addiction is wrong.* TEDGlobalLondon. www.ted.com/talks/johann_hari_everything_you_think_you_know_about_addiction_is_wrong Retrieved January 01, 2016.

Harris, N. B. (2018). *The deepest well: Healing the long-term effects of childhood adversity.* New York: Houghton Mifflin Harcourt.

Hart, C. (2014). *High price: A neuroscientist's journey of self-discovery that challenges everything you know about drugs and society.* New York: Harper Perennial.

Hart, S. (2011). *The Impact of Attachment.* W. W. Norton & Company.

Hart, S. (2008). *Brain, Attachment. Personality: An Introduction to Neuroaffective Development.* London: Karnac.

Haynes, S. N. & O'Brien, W. H. (1990). Functional analysis in behavior therapy. *Clinical Psychology Review, 10*(6), 649–668.

Heather, N. & Robertson, I. (1983). Why is abstinence necessary for the recovery of some problem drinkers? *Addiction, 78*(2), 139–144.

Heatherton, T. F. (2011). Neuroscience of self and self-regulation. *Annual Review of Psychology, 62*, 363–390.

Heatherton, T. F. & Wagner, D. D. (2011). Cognitive neuroscience of self-regulation failure. *Trends in Cognitive Sciences, 15*(3), 132–9.

Heckman, J. J. (2007, November 18). "The Technology and Neuroscience of Capacity Formation." Presented at the Economic Causes and Consequences of Population Aging, Robert Fogel 80th Birthday Celebration.

Heckman, J. J. (2008, July). Schools, skills, and synapses. *Economic Inquiry, 46*(3), 289–324. Presidential Address, Western Economic Association International.

Heilig, M., Epstein, D. H., Nader, M. A., & Shaham, Y. (2016, September). Time to connect: Bringing social context into addiction neuroscience. *Nature Reviews Neuroscience, 17*(9), 592–599.

Herman, J. (2015). *Trauma and recovery: The aftermath of violence—From domestic abuse to political terror* (First Revised Edition). New York: Basic Books.

Heyman, G. M. (2010). *Addiction: A disorder of choice.* Cambridge, MA: Harvard University Press.

Hingson, R. W., Zha, W., & White, A. M. (2017). Drinking beyond the binge threshold: Predictors, consequences, and changes in the U.S. *American Journal of Preventive Medicine, 52*(6), 717–727.

Hoge, E. A., Chen, M. M., Orr, E., Metcalf, C. A., Fischer, L. E., Pollack, M. H., . . . & Simon, N. M. (2013). Loving-kindness meditation practice associated with longer telomeres in women. *Brain, Behavior, and Immunity, 32*, 159–163.

Holton R. & Berridge KC. (2013). Addiction between compulsion and choice. In: Levy N, editor. Addiction and Self-Control: Perspectives from Philosophy, Psychology, and Neuroscience. New York, NY: Oxford University Press; p. 239–268.

Hser, Y. I., Evans, E., Grella, C., Ling, W., & Anglin, D. (2015). Long-term course of opioid addiction. *Harvard Review of Psychiatry, 23*(2), 76–89.

Hsu, S. H., Grow, J., & Marlatt, G. A. (2008). Mindfulness and addiction. In Galanter, M. & Kaskutas, L. A. *Recent developments in alcoholism: Research on Alcoholics Anonymous and spiritualism in addiction recovery* (Vol. 18) (pp. 229–250). New York: Springer Science+Business Media, LLC.

Hsu, D. T., Sanford, B. J., Meyers, K. K., Love, T. M., Hazlett, K. E., Wang, H., . . . & Zubieta, J. (2013). Response of the μ-opioid system to social rejection and acceptance. *Molecular Psychiatry, 18*(11), 1211–1217.

Hughes, D. (2007). *Attachment-focused family therapy*. New York: W. W. Norton & Company.

Hughes, D. (2017). *Building the bonds of attachment: Awakening love in deeply trauma-tized children* (Third Edition). New York: W. W. Norton & Company.

Hughes, D. A., Golding, K. S., & Hudson, J. (2019). *Healing Relational Trauma with Attachment-Focused Interventions: Dyadic Developmental Psychotherapy with Children and Families*. New York: W. W. Norton & Company.

Huizink, A. C., Mulder, E. J., & Buitelaar, J. K. (2004). Prenatal stress and risk for psychopathology: Specific effects or induction of general susceptibility? *Psychological Bulletin, 130*, 115–142.

Humphreys, K., Malenka, R. C., Knutson, B., & MacCoun, R. J. (2017). Brains, environments, and policy responses to addiction. *Science, 356*(6344), 1237–1238.

Humphreys, K., Moos, R. H., & Finney, J. W. (1995). Two pathways out of drinking problems without professional treatment. *Addictive Behaviors, 20*, 427–441.

Insel, T. R., Winslow, J. T., Wang, Z., & Young, L. J. (1998). Oxytocin, vasopressin, and the neuroendocrine basis of pair bond formation. In *Vasopressin and oxytocin* (pp. 215–224). Springer, Boston, MA.

Institute of Medicine. (2001). *Crossing the quality chasm: A new health system for the 21st century*. Washington, DC: The National Academies Press.

Institute of Medicine. (2004). *Crossing the quality chasm: Adaptation to mental health and addictive disorders: Quality Chasm Series*. National Academy of Sciences. Downloaded: June 28, 2016.

Institute of Medicine. (2005, November 1). *Improving the quality of health care for mental and substance-use conditions: Quality Chasm Series*. National Academy of Sciences. Downloaded: June 28, 2016 from https://www.ncbi.nlm.nih.gov/pubmed/20669433.

Iton, A. (2016, May 3). *Building healthy communities by tackling social determinants*. Drexel University Urban Health Collaborative Distinguished Speaker Series. http://drexel.edu/dornsife/news/latest-news/2016/May/iton-tackles-social-determinants

Jackson, J. S., Knight, K. M., & Rafferty, J. A. (2010). Race and unhealthy behaviors: Chronic stress, the HPA axis, and physical and mental health disparities over the life course. *American Journal of Public Health, 100*(5), 933–939.

Jacobs, T. L., Epel, E. S., Lin, J., Blackburn, E. H., Wolkowitz, O. M., Bridwell, D. A., . . . & King, B. G. (2011). Intensive meditation training, immune cell telomerase activity, and psychological mediators. *Psychoneuroendocrinology, 36*(5), 664–681.

Jacobsen, L. K., Southwick, S. M., & Kosten, T. R. (2001). Substance use disorders in patients with posttraumatic stress disorder: A review of the literature. *The American Journal of Psychiatry, 158*(8), 1184–1190.

James, O. (2006). *They f*** you up: How to survive family life*. New York: Marlowe & Company.

James, O. (2008). *Affluenza*. New York: Random House.

James, O. (2013). *The Selfish Capitalist:Origins of Affluenza*. New York: Vermillion.

Johnson, S. B., Riley, A. W., Granger, D. A., & Riis, J. (2013, February). The science of early life toxic stress for pediatric practice and advocacy. *Pediatrics, 131(2),* 319–327.

Kalant, H. (2009). What neurobiology cannot tell us about addiction. *Addiction, 105,* 780–789.

Karr-Morse, R. (2012). *Scared sick: The role of childhood trauma in adult disease.* New York: Basic Books.

Karr-Morse, R. & Wiley, M. S. (2013). *Ghosts from the nursery: Tracing the roots of violence,* (New and Revised Edition). New York: Atlantic Monthly Press.

Kaskutas, L. A. (2009). Alcoholics Anonymous effectiveness: Faith meets science. *Journal of addictive diseases, 28*(2), 145–157.

Katehakis, A. (2016). *Sex addiction as affect dysregulation: A neurobiologically informed holistic treatment.* New York: W. W. Norton & Company.

Kazak, A. E., Alderfer, M., Rourke, M. T., Simms, S., Streisand, R., & Grossman, J. R. (2004). Posttraumatic stress disorder (PTSD) and posttraumatic stress symptoms (PTSS) in families of adolescent childhood cancer survivors. *Journal of Pediatric Psychology 29*(3) pp. 211–219.

Kazak, A.E., Barakat, L,P,, Meese K., et al. (1997). Posttraumatic stress, family functioning, and social support in survivors of childhood leukemia and their mothers and fathers. *Journal of Consulting and Clinical Psychology, 65,* 120–129.

Kazak, A. E., Kassam-Adams, N., Schneider, S., Zelikovsky, N., Alderfer, M. A., & Rourke, M. (2006). An integrative model of pediatric medical traumatic stress, *Journal of Pediatric Psychology 31*(4) pp. 343–355.

Kelly, J. F., Bergman, B., Hoeppner, B., Vilsaint, C., & White, W. L. (2017) Prevalence, pathways, and predictors of recovery from drug and alcohol problems in the United States population: Implications for practice, research, and policy. *Drug and Alcohol Dependence, 181,* 162–169.

Kelly, J. F. & Hoeppner, B. (2014). A biaxial formulation of the recovery construct. *Addiction Research and Theory* (Early Online).

Kenny, P. J. (2011). Common cellular and molecular mechanisms in obesity and drug addiction. *Nature Reviews Neuroscience, 12*(11), 638–651.

Khantzian, E. J. & Albanese, M. J. (2008). *Understanding addiction as self medication: Finding hope behind the pain.* New York: Rowman & Littlefield Publishers, Inc.

Kinner, S. A. & Borschmann, R. (2017, August). Inequality and intergenerational transmission of complex adversity. *Lancet Public Health, 2,* e 342–343.

Klingemann, H. & Sobell, L. C. (2007). *Promoting self-change from addictive behaviors: Practical implications for policy, prevention and treatment.* New York: Springer Science+Business Media, LLC.

Klingemann, H., Sobell, M. A. & Sobell, L. C. (2010). Continuities and changes in self-change research. *Addiction, 105*, 1510.

Kolodny, A., Courtwright, D. T., Hwang, C. S., Kreiner, P., Eadie, J. L., Clark, T. W., & Alexander, G. C. (2015). The prescription opioid and heroin crisis: A public health approach to an epidemic of addiction. *Annual Review of Public Health, 36*, 559–574.

Koob, G. F. (2009a). Neurobiological substrates for the dark side of compulsivity in addiction. *Neuropsychopharmacology, 56* (Supplement 1), 18–31. NIH Public access, Author manuscript.

Koob, G. F. (2009b). Dynamics of neuronal circuits in addiction: Reward, antireward, and emotional memory. *Pharmacopsychiatry, 42*(S 01), S32–S41.

Koob, G.F. & Le Moal, M. (2005). Plasticity of reward circuitry and the "dark side" of drug addiction. *Nature Neuroscience, 8*(11), 1442–1444.

Koob, G. F. & Le Moal, M. (2008). Addiction and the brain antireward system. *Annual Review of Psychology, 59*, 29–53.

Korhonen, M. J., Halonen, J. I., Brookhart, M. A., et al., (2015). Childhood adversity as a predictor of non-adherence to statin therapy in adulthood. *PLoS One, 10*(5), e0127638.

Kross, E., Berman, M. G., Mischel, W., Smith, E. E., & Wager, T. D. (2011). Social rejection shares somatosensory representations with physical pain. *Proceedings of the National Academy of Sciences, 108*(15), 6270-6275.

Kubicek, K. R., Morgan, O. J., & Morrison, N. C. (2002). Pathways to long-term recovery from alcohol dependence: Comparison of spontaneous remitters and AA members. *Alcoholism Treatment Quarterly, 20*(2), 71-81.

Landale, S. & Roderick, M. (2014). Recovery from addiction and the potential role of sport: Using a life-course theory to study change. *International Review for the Sociology of Sport, 49*(3–4), 468–484.

Landau, J. & Garrett, J. (2008). Invitational intervention: The ARISE model for engaging reluctant alcohol and other drug abusers in treatment, In Morgan, O. J. & Litzke, C.H. (Eds.) *Family intervention in substance abuse: Current best practices* (pp. 147–168). Binghamton, NY: The Haworth Press.

Landau, J., Garrett, J., Shea, R. R., Stanton, M. D., Brinkman-Sull, D., & Baciewicz, G. (2000). Strength in numbers: The ARISE method for mobilizing family and network to engage substance abusers in treatment. *The American journal of drug and alcohol abuse, 26*(3), 379–398.

Larimer, M. E., Palmer, R. S., & Marlatt, G. A. (1999). Relapse prevention an overview of Marlatt's cognitive-behavioral model. *Alcohol Research & Health, 23*(2), 151–151.

Lawford, C. K. (2010). *Moments of clarity: Voices from the front lines of addiction and recovery.* New York: Harper Luxe.

Lewis, M. (2013). *Memoirs of an addicted brain: A neuroscientist examines his former life on drugs.* New York: PublicAffairs.

Lewis, M. (2015). *The biology of desire: Why addiction is not a disease*. New York: PublicAffairs.

Lieberman, M. D. (2013). *Social: Why our brains are wired to connect*. New York: Crown Publishers.

Linehan, M. M. (2018). *Cognitive-behavioral treatment of borderline personality disorder*. The Guilford Press.

Lupien, S. J., McEwen, B. S., Gunnar, M. R., & Heim, C. (2009). Effects of stress throughout the lifespan on the brain, behavior, and cognition. *Nature Reviews Neuroscience, 10*(6), 434–445.

Magura, S. & Laudet, A. B. (1996). Parental substance abuse and child maltreatment: Review and implications for intervention. *Children and Youth Services Review, 18*(3), 193–220.

Main, M. & Goldwyn, R. (1988). *Adult attachment classification system*. (Version 3.2.) Unpublished manuscript, University of California, Berkeley.

Main, M, Siegel, D. et al. (2010). Video by Dr. Mary Main, Dr. Erik Hesse, Dr. Daniel J. Siegel, Dr. Marion Solomon. Available at https://www.youtube.com/watch?v=YJTGbVc7EJY

Marlatt, G. A. & Donovan, D. M. (Eds.). (2005). *Relapse prevention: Maintenance strategies in the treatment of addictive behaviors*. The Guilford Press.

Marmot, M. G. & Bell, R. (2009). Action on health disparities in the United States: Commission on social determinants of health. *The Journal of the American Medical Association, 301*(11), 1169–1171.

Marmot, M., Friel, S., Bell, R., Tanja, A. J. H., & Taylor, S. (2008). Closing the gap in a generation: Health equity through action on the social determinants of health. *Lancet, 372*, 1661–1669.

Martín-Baró, I. (1994). *Writings for a liberation psychology*. Cambridge, MA: Harvard University Press.

Maté, G. (2010). *In the realm of hungry ghosts: Close encounters with addiction*. New York: North Atlantic Books.

Mayou, R., Bryant, B., & Ehlers, A. (2001, August). Prediction of psychological outcomes one year after a motor vehicle accident. *The American Journal of Psychiatry, 158*(8), 1231–8.

McEwen, B. S. (2004). Protection and damage from acute and chronic stress: Allostasis and allostatic overload and relevance to the pathophysiology of psychiatric disorders. *Annals of the New York Academy of Sciences, 1032*(1), 1–7.

McFarlane, A. C. (2016). How PTSD affects mind, brain and biology. [Conference Presentation]. Bessel van der Kolk's Intensive Trauma Treatment Course. Boston, MA. PESI.

McFarlane, A.C. & van der Kolk, B. (1996). Trauma and its challenge to society. In van der Kolk, B. A., McFarlane, A. C., & Weisaeth, L. (Eds). *Traumatic stress: The effects of overwhelming experience on mind, body, and society* (pp. 24–46). New York: The Guilford Press.

McKay, J. R. (2006). Continuing care in the treatment of addictive disorders. *Current Psychiatry Reports, 8*(5), 355–362.

McKay, J. R. (2009a). *Treating substance use disorders with adaptive continuing care.* Washington, DC: American Psychological Association.

McKay, J. R. (2009b). Continuing care research: What we have learned and where we are going. *Journal of Substance Abuse Treatment, 36*(2), 131–145.

McLellan, A. T. (2010). *A new demand reduction strategy: Prevention, intervention, treatment & recovery.* Executive Office of the President of the United States. Office of National Drug Control Policy. https://cabhp.asu.edu/sites/default/files/lastplendary_mclellanthedrugwarisover.pdf

McLellan, A. T. (2011, 30 August). "Through the Maze: Making Treatment Better." 2011 Drug Policy Symposium, Wellington, NZ. Available at www.youtube.com/watch?v=ofJ8Zpk1J8M. Downloaded: March 13, 2015.

McLellan, A. T., Lewis, D. C., O'Brien, C. P., & Kleber, H. D. (2000). Drug dependence, a chronic medical illness: Implications for treatment, insurance, and outcomes evaluation. *The Journal of the American Medical Association, 284*(13), 1689–1695.

McLellan, A. T., McKay, J. R., Forman, R., Cacciola, J., & Kemp, J. (2005). Reconsidering the evaluation of addiction treatment: From retrospective follow-up to concurrent recovery monitoring. *Addiction, 100*(4), 447–458.

McNeill, J. R. (2009, November–December). Runaway change. *American Scientist, 97*(6), Scientists' Nightstand.

Mennis, J., Stahler, G. J., & Mason, M. J. (2016). Risky substance use environments and addiction: A new frontier for environmental justice research. *International Journal of Environmental Research and Public Health, 13*(6), 607.

Merlo, L. J. & Gold, M. S. (2008). Prescription opioid abuse and dependence among physicians: Hypotheses and treatment. *The Harvard Review of Psychiatry,* 16, 181–194.

Merlo, L. J. & Gold, M. S. (2009, August 28). Successful treatment of physicians with addiction. *Psychiatric Times, 26*(9).

Miller, W. R. & Caddy, G. R. (1977). Abstinence and controlled drinking in the treatment of problem drinkers. *Journal of Studies on Alcohol, 38*(5), 986–1003.

Miller, W. R. & Carroll, K. M. (eds). (2006). *Rethinking substance abuse: What the science shows and what we should do about it.* New York: The Guilford Press.

Miller, W. R. & Rollnick, S. (2012). *Motivational interviewing: Helping people change.* New York: The Guilford Press.

Moos, R. H. & Moos, B. S. (2006). Rates and predictors of relapse after natural and treated remission from alcohol use disorders. *Addiction, 101*(2), 212–222.

Morgan, O. J. (1992). *In a sober voice: A psychological study of long-term alcoholic recovery with attention to spiritual dimensions.* [The Graduate School, Boston University]. Ann Arbor, MI: University Microfilms. Dissertation Abstracts.

Morgan, O. J. (1995a). Extended length of sobriety: The missing variable. *Alcoholism Treatment Quarterly, 12*(1), 59–71.

Morgan, O. J. (1995b). Recovery-sensitive counseling in the treatment of alcoholism. *Alcoholism Treatment Quarterly, 13*(4), 63–73.

Morgan, O. J. (1999). "Chemical comforting" and the theology of John C. Ford: Classic answers to a contemporary problem. *Journal of Ministry in Addiction and Recovery, 6*(1), 29–66.

Morgan, O. J. (2007). "They come to us vulnerable": Elements of the sacred in spiritually sensitive counseling. In *Counseling and spirituality: Views from the profession* (pp. 25–44). Boston, MA: Wadsworth, Cengage Learning.

Morgan, O. J. (2017, September 7). Coming to grips with adversity. *Counseling Today.* Downloaded January 23, 2019 from https://ct.counseling.org/2017/09/coming-grips-childhood-adversity/

Morgan, O. J. & Jordan, M. (Eds.). (1999). *Addiction and spirituality: A multidisciplinary approach.* St. Louis, MO: Chalice Press.

Morgan, O. J. & Litzke, C. H. (Eds.). (2008). *Family interventions with substance abuse: Current best practices.* Binghamton, NY: Haworth. Re-printed "special issue" of *Alcoholism Treatment Quarterly, 26*(12).

Morgen, K & Morgan, O.J. (in press). Chapter 15: Twelve Step Spirituality in Cashwell & Young, *Integrating Spirituality and Religion into Counseling: A Guide to Competent Practice*, 3rd edition. American Counseling Association.

Morrill, E. F., Brewer, N. T., O'Neill, S. C., Lillie, S. E., Dees, C., Carey, L. A., & Rimer, B. K. (2008). The interaction of post-traumatic growth and posttraumatic stress symptoms in predicting depressive symptoms and quality of life. *Psycho-Oncology, 17*, 948–953.

Murray, D. W., Rosanbalm, K. D., Christopoulos, C., & Hamoudi, A. (2015, January). *Self-regulation and toxic stress: Foundations for understanding self-regulation from an applied developmental perspective.* OPRE Report #2015-21, Washington, DC, Office of Planning, Research and Evaluation, Administration for Children and Families, U.S. Department of Health and Human Services.

Najavits, L.M. (2017). *Recovery from trauma, addiction, or both.* New York: Guilford.

Najavits, L. M. (2007). Seeking Safety: An evidence-based model for substance abuse and trauma/PTSD. In Witkiewitz, K. A. & Marlatt, G. A. (eds.) *Therapist's guide to evidence based relapse prevention: Practical resources for the mental health professional* (pp.141–167). San Diego, CA: Academic Press.

Najavits, L. M., Weiss, R. D., Shaw, S. R., & Muenz, L. R. (1998). "Seeking safety":

Outcome of a new cognitive-behavioral psychotherapy for women with posttraumatic stress disorder and substance dependence. *Journal of Traumatic Stress, 11*(3), 437–456.

Nakazawa, D. J. (2015). *Childhood disrupted: How your biography becomes your biology, and how you can heal.* New York: Atria Books.

National Addiction Centre (2003). *Dangerousness of drugs: A guide to the risks and harms associated with drug misuse.* Retrieved 18 Feb. 2015.

National Child Traumatic Stress Network (NCTSN). (2008, June). *Making the connection: Trauma and substance abuse: Understanding the links between adolescent trauma and substance abuse.* NCTSN.

National Institute on Alcohol Abuse and Alcoholism. (2006, October). National Epidemiologic Survey on Alcohol and Related Conditions. Alcohol Alert 70. Downloaded: June 28, 2016. http://pubs.niaaa.nih.gov/publications/AA70/AA70.pdf National Institute on Drug Abuse. (2010). From the Director . . . Research Report Series. Comorbidity: Addiction and other mental illnesses. U.S. Department of Health and Human Services. NIH Publication Number 10-5771.

National Institute on Drug Abuse (NIDA). (2012). *Principles of drug addiction treatment: A research-based guide.*

National Scientific Council on the Developing Child (2007). *The timing and quality of early experiences combine to shape brain architecture: Working Paper #5.* www.developingchild.net

Neff, K. (2015). *Self-compassion: The proven power of being kind to yourself.* New York: William Morrow.

Nelson, E. E. & Panksepp, J. (1998). Brain substrates of infant–mother attachment: Contributions of opioids, oxytocin, and norepinephrine. *Neuroscience & Biobehavioral Reviews, 22*(3), 437–452.

Noll, J. G., Trickett, P. K., Harris, W. W., & Putnam, F. W. (2009). The cumulative burden borne by offspring whose mothers were sexually abused as children. Descriptive results from a multigenerational study. *Journal of Interpersonal Violence, 24*(3), 424–449.

Nurius, P. S., Green, S., Logan-Greene, P., Longhi, D., & Song, C. (2016). Stress pathways to health inequalities: Embedding ACEs within social and behavioral contexts. *International Public Health Journal, 8*(2), 241.

Ogden, P., Minton, K., Pain, C., & van der Kolk, B. (2006). Trauma and the body: A sensorimotor approach to psychotherapy (Norton Series on Interpersonal Neurobiology). W. W. Norton & Company.

Olds, D. (2008, December). Preventing child maltreatment and crime with prenatal and infancy support of parents: The nurse-family partnership. *Journal of Scandinavian Studies in Criminology and Crime Prevention, 9.* www.researchgate.net/publication/47157432

Olds, D. L., Henderson, C. R., Chamberlin, R., & Tatelbaum, R. (1986). Preventing child abuse and neglect: A randomized trial of nurse home visitation. *Pediatrics, 78*(1), 65–78.Olds, D. L., Eckenrode, J., Henderson, C. R., Kitzman, H., Powers, J., Cole, R., . . . & Luckey, D. (1997). Long-term effects of home visitation on maternal life course and child abuse and neglect: Fifteen-year follow-up of a randomized trial. *The Journal of the American Medical Association, 278*(8), 637–643.Ouimette, P. & Brown, P. J. (2003). (Eds.). *Trauma and substance abuse: Causes, consequences, and treatment of comorbid disorders* (pp. 91–110). Washington, DC: American Psychological Association.

Ouimette, P. C., Brown, P. J., & Najavits, L. M. (1998). Course and treatment of patients with both substance use and posttraumatic stress disorders. *Addictive Behaviors, 23*(6), 785–795.

Panksepp, J. (2003). Feeling the pain of social loss. *Science, 302*(5643), 237–239.

Park, M., Verhoeven, J. E., Cuijpers, P., Reynolds III, C. F., & Penninx, B. W. (2015). Where you live may make you old: The association between perceived poor neighborhood quality and leukocyte telomere length. *PloS One, 10*(6), e0128460.

PolicyLink, The California Endowment. (2007). *Why place matters: Building a movement for healthy communities.* Oakland, CA: The California Endowment.

Pope Francis. (2015, June 18). *Laudato si . . . On care for our common home.* Rome: Vatican.

Porges, S. W. (2004). Neuroception: A subconscious system for detecting threats and safety. *Zero to Three (J), 24*(5), 19–24.

Porges, S. W. (2011). *The polyvagal theory: Neurophysiological foundations of emotions, attachment, communication, and self-regulation* (First Edition). New York: W. W. Norton & Company.

Porges, S. W. (2017). Vagal pathways: portals to compassion. *The Oxford handbook of compassion science,* 189.

Prendergast, M., Podus, D., Finney, J., Greenwell, L., & Roll, J. (2006). Contingency management for treatment of substance use disorders: A meta-analysis. *Addiction, 101*(11), 1546–1560.

Prochaska, J. O., Norcross, J., & DiClemente, C. (1994). *Changing for good: A revolutionary six-stage program for overcoming bad habits and moving your life positively forward.* New York: William Morrow.

Putnam, R. D. (2001). *Bowling alone: The collapse and revival of American community.* New York, NY: Simon & Schuster.

Reinarman, C. & Granfield, R. (2015). *Expanding addiction: Critical essays.* New York: Routledge.

Rivera, L. M. (2014). Ethnic-racial stigma and health disparities: From psychological theory and evidence to public policy solutions. *Journal of Social Issues, 70*(2), 198–205.

Roberts, L. J. & McCrady, B. S. (2003). *Alcohol problems in intimate relationships: Identification and intervention: A guide for marriage and family therapists.* American Association for Marriage and Family Therapy.

Robinson, T. E. & Berridge, K. C. (2008). The incentive sensitization theory of addiction: Some current issues. *Philosophical Transactions of the Royal Society B: Biological Sciences, 363*(1507), 3137–3146.

Rogers, C. (1951). *Client-centered therapy.* New York: Houghton Mifflin.

Rohsenow, D. J., Monti, P. M., Martin, R. A., Colby, S. M., Myers, M. G., Gulliver, S. B., . . . & Abrams, D. B. (2004). Motivational enhancement and coping skills training for cocaine abusers: Effects on substance use outcomes. *Addiction, 99*(7), 862–874.

Roisman, G. I., Padrón, E., Sroufe, L. A., & Egeland, B. (2002). Earned–secure attachment status in retrospect and prospect. *Child Development, 73*(4), 1204–1219.

Roman, P. M., Abraham, A. J., & Knudsen, H. K. (2011). Using medication-assisted treatment for substance use disorders: Evidence of barriers and facilitators of implementation. *Addictive Behaviors, 36*(6), 584–589.

Rush, B., & Urbanoski, K. (2019). Seven core principles of substance use treatment system design to aid in identifying strengths, gaps, and required enhancements. *Journal of Studies on Alcohol and Drugs, Supplement, (s18),* 9–21.

Samorini, G. (2002). *Animals and psychedelics: The natural world and the instinct to alter consciousness.* New York: Park Street Press.

Sanger-Katz, M. (2018, August 15). Bleak New Estimates in Drug Epidemic: A Record 72,000 Overdose Deaths in 2017. *The New York Times,* Upshot.

Sapolsky, R.M. (2004). *Why zebras don't get ulcers* (Revised and Updated). New York: St. Martin's

Satel, S. & Lilienfeld, S. O. (2013a). *Brainwashed: The seductive appeal of mindless neuroscience.* New York: Basic Books.

Satel, S. & Lilienfeld, S. O. (2013b). Addiction and the brain-disease fallacy. *Frontiers in Psychiatry, 4,* 141.

Satel, S. & Lilienfeld, S.O. (2017, June 22). Calling it 'brain disease' makes addiction harder to treat. *The Boston Globe.* Ideas. Downloaded: July 5, 2017. www.bostonglobe.com/ideas/2017/06/22/calling-brain-disease-makes-addiction-harder-treat/ehaJs5ZYIXpPottG89KOGK/story.html

Scaer, R. (2005). *The trauma spectrum: Hidden wounds and human resiliency.* New York: W. W. Norton & Company.

Schaler, J. (2002). *Addiction is a choice.* New York: Open Court Publishing.

Scheffer, M. (2009). *Critical transitions in nature and society* (Vol. 16). Princeton University Press.

Schepis, T. S., Rao, U., Yadav, H., & Adinoff, B. (2011). The limbic-hypothalamic-pituitary-adrenal axis and the development of alcohol use disorders in youth. *Alcoholism, Clinical and Experimental Research, 35*(4), pp. 595–605.

Schmid, J. & Brown, S. (2008). Beyond "happily every after:" Family recovery from alcohol problems. In Morgan, O. J. & Litzke, C. *Family intervention in substance abuse: Current best practices* (pp. 31–58). Binghamton, NY: Haworth Press.

Schore, A. N. (1994). *Affect regulation and the origin of the self: The neurobiology of emotional development.* Hillsdale, NJ: Lawrence Erlbaum Associates, Inc.

Schore, A. N. (1996). The experience-dependent maturation of a regulatory system in the orbital prefrontal cortex and the origin of developmental psychopathology. *Development and Psychopathology, 8,* 59–87.

Schore, A. N. (2000). Attachment and the regulation of the right brain. *Attachment & human development, 2*(1), 23–47.

Schore, A. N. (2001). Effects of a secure attachment relationship on right brain development, affect regulation, and infant mental health. *Infant Mental Health Journal, 22*(1–2), 7–66.

Schore, A. N. (2002). The neurobiology of attachment and early personality organization. *Journal of Prenatal & Perinatal Psychology & Health, 16*(3), 249.

Schore, A. (2003a). *Affect regulation and disorders of the self.* New York: W. W. Norton & Company.

Schore, A. (2003b). *Affect regulation and the repair of the self.* New York: W. W. Norton & Company.

Schore, A. N. (2005). Attachment, affect regulation, and the developing right brain: Linking developmental neuroscience to pediatrics. *Pediatrics in Review, 26*(6), 204–217.

Schore, A. N. (2014). The right brain is dominant in psychotherapy. *Psychotherapy, 51*(3), 388–397.

Schore, A. N. (2016). *Affect regulation and the origin of the self: The neurobiology of emotional development.* (Classic Edition). New York: Routledge.

Schore, J. R. & Schore, A. N. (2008). Modern attachment theory: The central role of affect regulation in development and treatment. *Clinical Social Work Journal. 36*(1). https://link.springer.com/article/10.1007/s10615-007-0111-7 Downloaded June 02, 2017.

Schwartz, R. (2017). *Internal Family Systems skills training manual: Trauma-informed treatment for anxiety, depression, PTSD & substance abuse.* New York: PESI.

Senay, E. C. (1985). Methadone maintenance treatment. *International Journal of the Addictions, 20*(6&7), 803–821.

Shonkoff, J. P. & Garner, A. S. (2012, January). The lifelong effects of early childhood adversity and toxic stress. *Pediatrics, 129*(1), 232–246.

Siegel, D. J. (1999). *The developing mind: Toward a neurobiology of interpersonal experience.* New York: The Guilford Press.

Siegel, D. J. (2001a). Toward an interpersonal neurobiology of the developing mind: Attachment relationships, "mindsight," and neural integration. *Infant Mental Health Journal, 22*(1–2), 67–94.

Siegel, D. J. (2001b). Memory: An overview, with emphasis on developmental, interpersonal, and neurobiological aspects. *Journal of the American Academy for Child and Adolescent Psychiatry, 40*(9), 997–1011.

Siegel, D. J. (2010). *Mindsight: The new science of personal transformation.* New York: Bantam Books.

Siegel, D. J. (2006). An interpersonal neurobiology approach to psychotherapy. *Psychiatric Annals, 36*(4), 248–256.

Siegel, D. J. (2007). *The mindful brain: Reflections and attunement in the cultivation of well-being.* New York: W. W. Norton & Company.

Siegel, D. J. (2010). *The mindful therapist: A clinician's guide to mindsight and neural integration.* New York: W. W. Norton & Company.

Siegel, D. J. (2016). *Wheel of Awareness.* www.drdansiegel.com/resources/wheel_of_ awareness. Retrieved December, 28, 2016.

Siegel, D.J. (2018). *Aware: The Science and Practice of Presence--The Groundbreaking Meditation Practice.* New York: TarcherPerigree.

Siegel, D.J. (2018). "What's going on in the brain when the inner critic is active." Question and answer responses in an online webinar, *How to work with clients who struggle with an inner critic.* National Institute for the Clinical Application of Behavioral Medicine (NICABM). At NICABM.com

Siegel, D. J., & Hartzell, M. (2003). *Parenting from the inside out.* New York: Jeremy P. Tarcher.

Siegel, R. K. (1989). *Intoxication: Life in pursuit of artificial paradise.* New York: E. P. Dutton.

Siegel, R. K. (2005). *Intoxication: The universal drive for mind-altering substances* (Third Edition). New York: Park Street Press.

Sinha, R. (2007). The role of stress in addiction relapse. *Current Psychiatry Reports, 9*(5), pp. 388–395.

Sinha, R. (2008). Chronic stress, drug use, and vulnerability to addiction. *Annals of the New York Academy of Sciences, 1141,* 105–130. http://doi.org/10.1196/annals.1441.030

Sinha, R., & Jastreboff, A. M. (2013). Stress as a common risk factor for obesity and addiction. *Biological psychiatry, 73*(9), 827–835.

Slade-Sawyer, P. (2014, November–December). Is health determined by genetic code or ZIP code? Measuring the health of groups and improving population health. *North Carolina Medical Journal, 75*(6), 394–397.

Sobell, L. C., Cunningham, J. A., & Sobell, M. R. (1996). Recovery from alcohol problems with and without treatment: Prevalence in two population surveys. *American Journal of Public Health, 86*(7), 966–972.

Solomon, G. M., Morello-Frosch, R., Zeise, L., & Faust, J. B. (2016). Cumulative environmental impacts: science and policy to protect communities. *Annual review of public health, 37*, 83–96.

Spinelli, C. & Thayer, B. A. (2017). Is recovery from alcoholism without treatment possible? A review of the literature. *Alcoholism Treatment Quarterly, 35*(4), 426–444.

Stein, D. J., van Honk, J., Ipser, J., Solms, M., & Panksepp, J. (2007). Opioids: From physical pain to the pain of social isolation. *CNS Spectrums, 12*(9), 669–674.

Stein, M. D., Conti, M. T., Kenney, S., Anderson, B. J., Flori, J. N., Risi, M. M., & Bailey, G. L. (2017). Adverse childhood experience effects on opioid use initiation, injection drug use, and overdose among persons with opioid use disorder. *Drug & Alcohol Dependence, 179*, 325–329.

Steinglass, P., Bennett, L. A., Wolin, S. J., & Reiss, D. (1987). *The alcoholic family*. Basic Books.

Stephens, M. A. C., McCaul, M. E., & Wand, G. S. (2014). The potential role of glucocorticoids and the HPA axis in alcohol dependence. In Noronha, A. B. C., Cui, C., Harris, R. A., & Crabbe, J. C. (Eds.) *Neurobiology of Alcohol Dependence* (pp. 429–450). London, UK: Academic Press.

Stuber, M. L., Kazak, A. E., Meeske, K., & Barakat, L. (1998). Is posttraumatic stress a viable model for understanding responses to childhood cancer? *Child and Adolescent Psychiatric Clinics of North America, 7*(1), 169–182.

Stuber, M. L., Meeske, K. A., Krull, K. R., Leisenring, W., Stratton, K., Kazak, A. E., . . . & Robison, L. L. (2010). Prevalence and predictors of posttraumatic stress disorder in adult survivors of childhood cancer. *Pediatrics, 125*(5), e1124–e1134.

Szalavitz, M. (2016). *Unbroken brain: A revolutionary new way of understanding addiction*. New York: St. Martin's Press.

Taylor, S. E. (2006). Tend and befriend biobehavioral bases of affiliation under stress. *Current Directions in Psychological Science, 15*(6), 273–277.

Taylor, S. E. & Master, S. L. (2011). Social responses to stress: The tend-and-befriend model. *The handbook of stress science: Biology, Psychology, and Health*, 101–109.

Teicher, M. H. (2000). Wounds that time won't heal: The neurobiology of child abuse. *Cerebrum: The Dana Forum on Brain Science, 2*(4).

Teicher, M. H. (2002). Scars that won't heal: The neurobiology of child abuse. *Scientific American, 286*(3), 68–75.

Teicher, M. H. & Samson, J. A. (2016, March). Annual research review: Enduring neurobiological effects of childhood abuse and neglect. *Journal of Child Psychology and Psychiatry, 57*(3), 241–266.

Tilson, E. C. (2018). Adverse Childhood Experiences (ACEs): An important element of a comprehensive approach to the opioid crisis. *North Carolina Medical Journal, 79*(3), 166–169.

Tomer, J. F. (2016). *Integrating human capital with human development: The path to a more productive and humane economy.* New York: Palgrave Macmillan.

Tryon, M. S., Carter, C. S., DeCant, R., & Laugero, K. D. (2013). Chronic stress exposure may affect the brain's response to high calorie food cues and predispose to obesogenic eating habits. *Physiology & Behavior, 120,* 233–242.

U.S. Department of Health and Human Services (HHS), Office of the Surgeon General. (2016, November). *Facing addiction in America: The Surgeon General's report on alcohol, drugs, and health.* Washington, DC: HHS.

Vance, J. D. (2016). *Hillbilly elegy: A memoir of a family and culture in crisis.* New York: HarperCollins.

Van der Kolk, B. A. (1994). The body keeps the score: Memory and the evolving psychobiology of posttraumatic stress. *Harvard Review of Psychiatry, 1*(5), 253–265.

Van der Kolk, B. A. (2003). *Psychological trauma.* American Psychiatric Pub.

Van der Kolk, B.A., McFarlane, A.C., & Weisaeth, L. (Eds.), (1996). *Traumatic stress: The effects of overwhelming experience on mind, body, and society.* New York: Guilford.

Van der Kolk, B. (2007). The complexity of adaptation to trauma: Self-regulation, stimulus discrimination, and characterological development. In Van der Kolk, B. A., McFarlane, A. C. & Weisaeth, L. (Eds.), *Traumatic stress: the effects of overwhelming experience on mind, body, and society* (pp. 3–23). New York: The Guilford Press.

Van der Kolk, B. (2014). *The body keeps the score: Brain, mind, and body in the healing of trauma.* New York: Penguin Books.

Van der Kolk, B. A. & McFarlane, A. C. (2006). The black hole of trauma. In Van der Kolk, B. A., McFarlane, A. C. & Weisaeth, L. (Eds.), *Traumatic stress: the effects of overwhelming experience on mind, body, and society* (pp. 3–23). New York: The Guilford Press.

Van der Kolk, B. A., McFarlane, A. C., & Weisaeth, L. (Eds.). (2007). *Traumatic stress : The effects of overwhelming experience on mind, body, and society.* New York: The Guilford Press.

Volkow, N. (2014, May 14). America's addiction to opioids: Heroin and prescription drug abuse. Hearing: Senate Caucus on International Narcotics Control. NIDA.

Volkow, N. D., Fowler, J. S., & Wang, G. J. (2003). The addicted human brain: insights from imaging studies. *The Journal of Clinical Investigation, 111*(10), 1444–1451.

Volkow, N. D. & Koob, G. (2015). Brain disease model of addiction: Why is it so controversial? *Lancet Psychiatry, 2,* 677–679.

Volkow, N. D., Koob, G. F., & McLellan, A. T. (2016, January 28). Neurobiologic advances from the brain disease model of addiction. *New England Journal of Medicine, 374*(4), 363–371.

Volkow, N. D. & Li, T. K. (2004). Drug addiction: the neurobiology of behaviour gone awry. *Nature Reviews Neuroscience, 5*(12), 963.

Von Cheong, E., Sinnott, C., Dahly, D., & Kearney, P. M. (2017). Adverse childhood experiences (ACEs) and later-life depression: perceived social support as a potential protective factor. *BMJ open, 7*(9), e013228.

Wagner, D. D. & Heatherton, T. F. (2012). Self-regulatory depletion increases emotional reactivity in the amygdala. *Social Cognitive and Affective Neuroscience, 8*(4), 410–417.

Weinhold, B. K. & Weinhold, J. B. (2015). *Developmental trauma: The game changer in the mental health profession.* Colorado Springs, CO: CICRCL Press.

White, W. L. (2007a). Addiction recovery: Its definition and conceptual boundaries. *Journal of Substance Abuse Treatment, 33*(3), 229–241.

White, W. L. (2007b). The new recovery advocacy movement in America. *Addiction, 102*(5), 696–703.

White, W. L. (2008). *Recovery management and recovery-oriented systems of care: Scientific rationale and promising practices.* Northeast Addiction Technology Transfer Center, the Great Lakes Addiction Technology Transfer Center, and the Philadelphia Department of Behavioral Health/Mental Retardation Servicers.

White, W. L. (2009). The mobilization of community resources to support long-term addiction recovery. *Journal of Substance Abuse Treatment, 36,* 146–158.

White, W.L. (2011, April). Circles of Recovery: An interview with Keith Humphreys, PhD. Posted at www.williamwhitepapers.com; to be published in abridged form in Pioneer Series in Counselor, *12*(6), 48–52.

White, W. L. (2012). *Recovery/remission from substance use disorders: An analysis of reported outcomes in 415 scientific studies, 1868–2011.* Chicago: Great Lakes Addiction Technology Transfer Center (ATTC); Philadelphia Department of Behavioral Health and Developmental disAbility Services; Northeast Addiction Technology Transfer Center.

White, W. (2016, March 18). Rethinking the characterization of addiction as a "relapsing condition." William White Papers Blog. www.williamwhitepapers.com/blog. Downloaded: April 22, 2016.

White, W. L. (2017). *Recovery rising: A retrospective of addiction treatment and recovery advocacy.* Amazon Edition.

White, W., Boyle, M., & Loveland, D. (2003). Addiction as chronic disease: From rhetoric to clinical application. *Alcoholism Treatment Quarterly, 3–4,* 107–130.

White, W., Boyle, M., & Loveland, D. (2005 Recovery from addiction and recovery from mental illness: Shared and contrasting lessons. In Ralph, R. & Corrigan, P. (Eds.) *Recovery and mental illness: Consumer visions and research paradigms* (pp. 233–258). Washington DC: American Psychological Association.

White, W. & Cloud, W. (2008). Recovery capital: A primer for addictions professionals. *Counselor, 9*(5), 22–27.

White, W. L., DuPont, R. L., & Skipper, G. E. (2007). Physicians health programs: What counselors can learn from these remarkable programs. *Counselor, 8*, 42–47.

White, W., Kelly, J., & Roth, J. (2012). New addiction recovery support institutions: Mobilizing support beyond professionals addiction treatment and recovery mutual aid. *Journal of Groups in Addiction and Recovery, 7*(2–4), 297–317.

White, W. & Kurtz, E. (2006a). The varieties of recovery experience: A primer for addiction treatment professionals and recovery advocates. *International Journal of Self Help and Self Care, 3*(1/2), 21–61.

White, W. & Kurtz. E. (2006b). *Linking addiction treatment & communities of recovery: A primer for addiction counselors and recovery coaches.* Pittsburgh, PA: IRETA and Northeast ATTC, the Addiction Technology Transfer Center Network.

White, W. L., & McClellan, A. T. (2008). Addiction as a chronic disorder. *Counselor: The Magazine for Addiction Professionals*, 8.

White, W. L. & Mojer-Torres, L. (2010). *Recovery-oriented methadone maintenance.* Chicago, IL: Great Lakes Addiction Technology Transfer Center.

White, W., Parrino, M., & Ginter, W. (2011). A dialogue on the psychopharmacology in behavioral healthcare: The acceptance of medication-assisted treatment in addictions. Commissioned briefing paper for: SAMHSA Dialogue on Psychopharmacology in Behavioral Healthcare, 11–12.

White, W. & Savage, B. (2005). All in the family: Alcohol and other drug problems, recovery, advocacy. *Alcoholism Treatment Quarterly, 23*(4), 3–38.

Wilkinson, M. (2010). *Changing minds in therapy: Emotion, attachment, trauma, and neurobiology.* New York: W. W. Norton & Company.

Wilkinson, R. G. & Marmot, M. (Eds.). (2003). *Social determinants of health: The solid facts.* Geneva, Switzerland: World Health Organization.

Williams, G. (2013). *The anonymous people: A ground-breaking documentary on addiction and recovery.* Alive Mind Cinema: 4th Dimension Productions.

Williams, G. (2016). *Generation found.* Gathr Films.

Wilson, E.O. (1998). *Consilience: The unity of science.* New York, NY: Knopf.

Wimberly, E. T. (2009). *Nested ecology: The place of humans in the ecological hierarchy.* Baltimore, MD: Johns Hopkins University Press.

Winnicott, D. W. (2012). *The Family and Individual Development.* New York: Routledge.

Woo, C. W., Koban, L., Kross, E., Lindquist, M. A., Banich, M. T., Ruzic, L., . . . & Wager, T. D. (2014). Separate neural representations for physical pain and social rejection. *Nature Communications, 5*, 5380.

Yau, Y. H. & Potenza, M. N. (2013). Stress and eating behaviors. *Minerva Endocrinologica, 38*(3), 255.

Young, K. A., Franklin, T. R., Roberts, D. C. S., Jagannathan, K., Suh, J. J., Wetherill, R. R., Wang, Z., Kampman, K. M., O'Brien, C. P., & Childress, A. R. (2014).

Brief communications: Nipping cue reactivity in the bud: Baclofen prevents limbic activation elicited by subliminal drug cues. *The Journal of Neuroscience, 34*(14), 5038–5043.

Zebrack, B. J. (1999). *Living beyond the sword of Damocles: The quality of life of long-term survivors of leukemia and lymphoma* (Doctoral dissertation). https://deepblue.lib .umich.edu/handle/2027.42/132283

Zeltzer, L. K., Recklitis, C., Buchbinder, D., Zebrack, B., Casillas, J., Tsao, J. C. I., Lu, Q., & Krull, K. (2009, May 10). Psychological status in childhood cancer survivors: A report from the Childhood Cancer Survivor Study. *Journal of Clinical Oncology, 27*(14), 2396–2404.

Zemestani, M. & Ottaviani, C. (2016). Effectiveness of mindfulness-based relapse prevention for co-occurring substance use and depression disorders. *Mindfulness, 7*(6), 1347–1355.

Zemore, S. E., Liu, C., Mericle, A., Hemberg, J., & Kaskutas, L. A. (2018).A longitudinal study of the comparative efficacy of Women for Sobriety, LifeRing, SMART Recovery, and 12-step groups for those with AUD. *Journal of Substance Abuse Treatment, 88, 18–26.*

Zschucke, E., Heinz, A., & Ströhle, A. (2012, May 3). Exercise and physical activity in the therapy of substance use disorders. *The Scientific World Journal,* 2012. Downloaded March 12, 2018. https://www.ncbi.nlm.nih.gov/pmc/articles/PMC3354725/

Notes

PREFACE

1. First heard in his TED Talk, "Everything You Think You Know About Addiction Is Wrong." TEDGlobalLondon. Filmed Jun 2015. Downloaded: March 20, 2016. www.ted.com/talks/johann_hari_everything_you_think_you_know_about _addiction_is_wrong

2. Economic Innovation Group. (2017). Distressed Communities Index. Washington, DC. http://eig.org/dci

CHAPTER 1

1. Working with "Joe" in individual and family therapy came at a pivotal moment in my own rethinking about addiction. My work now echoes what I learned. The case is a composite of several persons I worked with during that time. Details but not the substance of this case have been changed for purposes of confidentiality.

2. Those interested in addressing this dynamic may go to https://awakeningrecovery center.com/addiction-treatment-blog/self-talk-voice-inner-critic, for resources that can help.

3. Readers may wish to consult the Center on the Developing Child at Harvard University for further information. https://developingchild.harvard.edu4. The SBIRT website at the Substance Abuse and Mental Health Services Administration has a wealth of information. www.samhsa.gov/sbirt

4. Those who may wish to learn more should examine the "internal family systems" model of working with clients. See (Schwartz, 2017). Dr. Ruth Buczynski, founder of the National Institute for the Clinical Application of Behavioral Medicine (NICABM), has organized a number of online workshops for practitioners who

wish to learn research-based treatment strategies. A recent workshop is titled, "How to Work with Clients Who Struggle with an Inner Critic." Go to www.nicabm .com.

5. Kristin Neff's work on self-compassion is essential reading for counselors working with struggling addicts. http://self-compassion.org/the-three-elements-of-self -compassion-2

CHAPTER 2

1. This was what Alan Marlatt called an "apparently irrelevant decision" or AID (Marlatt & Donovan, 2005). It facilitates drinking/using while the person remains "unaware" of triggering it.

2. Readers who wish to learn more should consult the mindfulness-based relapse prevention (MBRP) website, at www.mindfulrp.com.

3. The work of Marsha Linehan on dialectical behavior therapy (2018) provides a treasure-trove of methods for mindful practice.

4. Pioneered by psychologist G. Alan Marlatt and his colleagues, cognitive-behavioral and mindfulness-based relapse prevention are now standard in addiction treatment. They are also powerful tools in working with trauma, depression, and other mental illnesses (Larimer, Palmer, & Marlatt, 1999; Marlatt & Donovan, 2005).

5. Siegel (www.drdansiegel.com) discusses his Wheel of Awareness, a tool for seeking greater mindful awareness.

6. Seeking Safety is well-supported by research and voluminous publications, and trainings, video presentations, and consultations with the founder, Dr. Najavits, are available. The program is laid out in detail in her book (2002), *Seeking Safety: A Treatment Manual for PTSD and Substance Abuse*. New York: Guilford Press.

CHAPTER 3

1. www.asam.org

2. As I write this chapter, the World Health Organization (WHO) has classified gaming disorder and compulsive sexual behavior disorder in its diagnostic *International Classification of Diseases* (ICD 11). The American *Diagnostic and Statistical Manual of Mental Disorders* (DSM) often follows suit.

3. Taken from "Demand Reduction in the 2010 Drug Control Strategy: Prevention, Intervention, Treatment & Recovery." Executive Office of the President of the United States. Office of National Drug Control Policy. It is in the public domain. Available at: https://slideplayer.com/slide/3911045

4. Recent reports indicate that approximately 32 million American adults drink dangerously high levels of alcohol, according to the *American Journal of Preventive Medicine* (Hingson, Zha, & White, 2017). Alcohol is the most commonly used intoxicant in the U.S.

5. To put these numbers in context, roughly 26 million patients struggled with diabetes in 2010 and 86 million were estimated to have "pre-diabetes." As with diabetics, those struggling with harmful and addictive drug use can benefit from some kind of intervention or help. Of the pre-diabetics (one in every three people) nine out of ten do not know that they have a serious condition. Many "harmful" users of alcohol and other drugs (more than 93 million people) are in the same boat.

6. The reader should consult the DSM-5 for further information.

7. It is interesting to note that approximately 85 percent of marriage and family therapists treat clients with primary or secondary alcohol problems. In a collaboration of AAMFT and NIAAA, published in 2003, "Alcohol Problems in Intimate Relationships: Identification and Intervention," Roberts and McCrady detailed a family systems approach to alcohol and other drug problems.

8. The interested reader can explore Daily's perspective through YouTube. Several video presentations are available, including "The Interpersonal Neurobiology of Addiction" (2014, May 16). California Southern University. www.youtube.com/watch?v=ypNLGG8Twly

9. The interested reader should consult Morgan and Litzke, in *Family Intervention in Substance Abuse: Current Best Practices* (Haworth Press, 2008). Chapters on the ARISE intervention and Community Reinforcement and Family Training (CRAFT) programs present this perspective in more detail.

10. This is the term used by Dr. Pam Peeke in her TEDxWall Street talk, "Hooked, Hacked, Hijacked: Reclaim Your Brain from Addictive Living." Downloaded: October 13, 2015. www.youtube.com/watch?v=aqhzFd4NUPI

11. A YouTube production, "The Business of Recovery" (Greg Horvath Productions, 2015) documents the failures and challenges of organized recovery. www.thebusinessofrecovery.com

12. The National Epidemiologic Survey on Alcohol and Related Conditions (NESARC) was published in October 2006 by NIAAA, in their *Alcohol Alert 70*.

13. Over the years, as a professor, consultant, and board member to several treatment centers, I would ask the clinical directors how they understood the "revolving door" and the patients who seemed unable to stick with recovery. In other words those at greatest risk for multiple relapse. One clinical director spoke for the rest when I asked how many of his patients who had multiple relapse also had a history of trauma. He smiled and said, "Every single one."

CHAPTER 4

1. A "common pathological process" underlying addiction does not negate the diversity of activities that are triggered in neural systems due to various specific drugs of abuse or compulsive behaviors. A view of common process and variety of mechanisms can be advocated simultaneously.

2. Professor Robert Sapolsky of Stanford University explains this phenomenon of anticipatory reward and dopamine in a 2009 lecture entitled, *The Uniqueness of Humans*. TED Talk, April 11, 2014. Downloaded: November, 2016. www.ted .com/talks/robert_sapolsky_the_uniqueness_of_humans

3. Vivitrol is an injectable form that needs applications once a month.

4. Suboxone is the brand name. Methadone is another useful medication.

5. https://www.drugabuse.gov/publications/principles-drug-addiction-treatment -research-based-guide-third-edition/principles-effective-treatment

6. The short-acting sympatho-adrenomedullary (SAM) axis—activating the adrenal glands (adrenaline) and locus coeruleus in the brain (noradrenaline)—is also part of our complex reactions to stress (Harris, 2018). The vagal complex is involved as well (Porges, 2012, 2017).

7. A number of local affiliations are emerging, including organizations such as The Phoenix (formerly Phoenix Multisport). Interested readers should consult www .stand-together.org or Google "sober living cities" for information about local affiliations in your location.

8. Psychologist Jon Allen (2013) from The Menninger Clinic describes an experiment in which spouses who can hold hands lessen the experience of pain through attachment connection. "What We All Need to Know About Attachment." www.youtube .com/watch?v=RdCBip-8pC8

9. In his TED Talk, "Addiction in the Age of Brain Science" (March 21, 2016), Dr. Markus Heilig addresses the current research on the insula as a brain mechanism that is central to understanding physical pain, social marginalization/ exclusion, and the connection to craving for relief or reward. www.youtube.com /watch?v=4un3XxMqN3I

CHAPTER 5

1. The interested reader can discover a world of insight into these dynamics by consulting the website for the Center on the Developing Child at Harvard University, http://developingchild.harvard.edu

2. Attachment Theory (AT) discusses the role of mothers at length. Observations of parent/child interactions have made it clear that, while infants can relate with many human actors, they prefer deep bonding interactions with a very few caregivers, although they can be flexible if need be. Most often, this primary bonding occurs in our culture with the mother, and I will use this as shorthand for a wider range of caregiving. Speaking of "mother" is less cumbersome than "mothering figure." It is also clear that, as the forms of family life in our society become more diverse, fathers, grandparents, even older siblings can and do fulfill this role. This is an extension of normal family-based and clan dynamics (Schore, 1994, 2003a & b).

3. May Benatar. (2011, May 16). "The Healing Power of a Personal Narrative." *Huffington Post Blog.* www.huffingtonpost.com/may-benatar-phd-lcsw/personal -narrative-healing_b_862285.html

4. See also Daniel J. Siegel (2010), *Mindsight: The New Science of Personal Transformation.*

5. Tools from mindfulness practice, Seeking Safety and dialectical behavior therapy (DBT) can be very helpful.

CHAPTER 6

1. DSM-5 lists several other diagnostic categories, such as reactive attachment disorder and adjustment disorders under the larger classification of Trauma and Stressor-Related Disorders. However, following Bremner (2002, 2016), I list additional stress-related disorders as well.

2. Glucocorticoids (GCs), especially cortisol, are primary instigators of the stress response in the short-term, but over the longer term can dampen the stress response, a mechanism that restores the animal to homeostasis. With continuous, serial, or hyper-activation, there is dysregulation of the HPA axis, changes in gene expression, and persistent increase of glucocorticoids, which can be toxic in many different brain areas and functions, including immunological and inflammatory systems.

3. "Killer Stress" is a National Geographic video presentation that examines stress and its social and hierarchical dynamics. www.youtube.com/watch?v=AytXzf2TvA8

4. See "Why Don't Zebras Get Ulcers? Why Do We?" Episode 1 of "Stress and Your Body Series." The Great Courses. Downloaded: September 13, 2017. www.kanopy .com/product/why-dont-zebras-get-ulcers-why-do-we

5. The website for the Center on the Developing Child contains a wealth of important information about human development, stress, and coping resources. See http:// developingchild.harvard.edu. See also Harris, 2018.

6. The term "toxic stress" is most often used in the context of childhood stress, developmental trauma, and their aftermath. We will explore this in more detail in the next chapter.

7. The reader should consult the DSM-5 diagnostic criteria for PTSD.

8. To understand the serious long-term implications of developmental adversity, the reader should consult http://developingchild.harvard.edu.

9. A phrase attributed to developmental psychologist Urie Bronfenbrenner.

10. According to the National Cancer Institute, with access to contemporary therapies, approximately 80 percent of children diagnosed with cancer are expected to survive.

11. Serious and debilitating chronic health conditions, impacting function, activity, and health status, called "late effects," can be seen even decades after treatment.

Surveillance, multidisciplinary follow-up, targeted education, family therapy, and prevention are recommended. www.cancer.gov

12. The Childhood Cancer Survivor Study began in 1994 and is ongoing. Basic information can be gleaned from the web at www.cancer.gov/types/childhood-cancers /ccss.

13. National Highway Traffic Safety Administration estimates that approximately every 10 seconds someone in the U.S. is injured in a motor vehicle accident. Of those, as many as one-third may have a diagnosed case of PTSD. The numbers of those with subclinical, stress-related symptoms is not known.

14. In a recent publication, "Drug Addiction in America," *The Guardian* explores the dimensions of the opioid and prescription drug crisis in Appalachia. (www .theguardian.com/society/series/addiction-in-america) The article, "America's opioid addiction: 'I ended up selling all my valuable stuff to buy pills' " (May 9, 2016) is a worthwhile read.

15. Homeboy Industries is listed by the National Gang Center as a model and "promising" program of gang intervention services for inner-city youth. www .nationalgangcenter.gov/SPT/Programs/86

16. For more on Father Boyle and Homeboy Industries see www.homeboyindustries .org

17. Boyle's second book, *Barking to the Choir: The Power of Radical Kinship* (Simon & Schuster, 2017), is a follow-up to *Tattoos*, describing changes to the neighborhood and the transforming power of kinship and community.

18. http://ourohiorenewal.com

CHAPTER 7

1. Quoted in Stevens (2012), *The Adverse Childhood Experiences Study—The Largest Public Health Study You Never Heard Of, Part Three*, Nadine Burke Harris, MD, describes how ACEs facilitate a trauma-informed pediatric practice. Her TED Talk, "How Childhood Trauma Affects Health Across a Lifetime," can be seen at www.youtube.com/watch?v=95ovIJ3dsNk

2. The ACE score measures an individual's dose and exposure to 10 categories of childhood adverse experiences. This score is correlated to medical, psychiatric, and behavioral outcomes in adulthood. It is a simple frequency count (scale: 0–10) of exposure to adversity (physical, verbal, or sexual abuse, neglect, or household dysfunction, such as mental illness in the home or divorce), not occurrences. Multiple instances of neglect, for example, count as only one category. This likely underestimates the burden of adversity an individual carries.

3. For more information, readers can go to ACE Science 101 at https://acestoohigh .com/aces-101.

4. Editors at the American Academy of Pediatrics have written recently about the practice of family separation at the U.S. southern border as an "adverse childhood experience" (First and Kemper, *Journals Blog*, AAP, June 20, 2018.) With these and other additions, it is likely that the scoring regime will be revised soon.

5. Interested readers can consult the BRFSS website from the CDC at www.cdc.gov /brfss/index.html

6. Taken from the World Health Organization website. Downloaded: September 26, 2017. www.who.int/violence_injury_prevention/violence/activities/adverse _childhood_experiences/en

7. J. D. Vance & Rosen, A. (2017, April.) "Opioid Addiction Is Like 'A Nuclear Bomb' Going Off In The Family." *Huffington Post*. www.huffingtonpost.com/entry/jd -vance-opioid-addiction-is-like-a-nuclear-bomb_us_59022f2fe4b0768c2682e40e

8. Pioneers in this area include the Center on the Developing Child at Harvard University (https://developingchild.harvard.edu) and the *ACEs Connection* (www .acesconnection.com).

9. www.nursefamilypartnership.org/about/program-history. A brief review of Olds's work can be seen at: Kitzman, et al., 1997; Olds, et al., 1986; Olds, et al., 1997; Olds, 2008)

10. The campaign is part of the Milliken Institute School for Public Health at George Washington University.

11. The medical practice established by Nadine Burke Harris, MD, and the child/family programs operating in connection with that practice (Center for Youth Wellness at https://centerforyouthwellness.org) present another model of community-based care. See Harris, 2018.

12. Morgan, O. J. (September 7, 2017). "Coming to grips with child adversity." *Counseling Today*.

13. The Center on The Developing Child and National Scientific Council on the Developing Child have published a number of reports and working papers that flesh out proposals to achieve these ends. https://developingchild.harvard.edu

CHAPTER 8

1. Readers can discover some sense of the strength and exhilaration in the recovery advocacy movement by watching the documentary film, "The Anonymous People" (Williams, 2013).

2. Another documentary film by Williams (2016), "Generation Found," is publicizing the advantages and supportive institutions of recovery for millennials and other recovering young people.

3. The Connecticut Community for Addiction Recovery (CCAR, http://ccar.us) is one example. It is an online and local recovery community organization that rec-

ognizes and sponsors recovery community centers and telephone recovery support, promotes recovery coaching (sponsorship), and maintains resources for education, recovery housing, employment opportunities, and other services. It is a catalyst for a recovery ecology.

4. See the HBO series on "Addiction," produced in partnership with The Robert Wood Johnson Foundation, the National Institute on Drug Abuse (NIDA), and the National Institute on Alcohol Abuse and Alcoholism (NIAAA). See particularly, the stories of Justin and Amanda at Acadia Healthcare Comprehensive Treatment Centers.

5. See also White (2012).

6. The work of Connections CSP in Delaware is testimony to the effectiveness of this approach on a broad spectrum of social challenges. They are integrating medical, behavioral health, and correctional medical services to fight opioid addiction. www.connectionscsp.org

7. This phrase was first used in a letter of Dr. Karl Menninger to Dr. Thomas Szasz, quoted in *Bulletin of the Menninger Clinic* (July 1989). The reference is to recovery in both the addiction and mental health fields

8. See the Guide to Mutual Aid Resources, sponsored by Faces & Voices of Recovery, for a listing of diverse peer support groups at https://facesandvoicesofrecovery.org/resources/mutual-aid-resources/mutual-aid-resources.html

9. One such recovery group resource is "Phoenix Multisport," reviewed in her TEDx-Boulder presentation (2013), www.youtube.com/watch?v=gzpTWaXshfM, "Transcending addiction and redefining recovery" by Jacki Hillios. An alternative is "Rebound," founded by Byron Thompson out of Milwaukee, WI. www.facebook.com/rebound2008

10. For a broader and concrete sense of the variety of activities and organizations that may emerge locally, see White, Kelly, & Roth (2012).

11. ARC is a 50-item instrument (25 questions relate to personal recovery capital; 25 relate to social recovery capital) with 10 subscales and strong reliability, consistency, and concurrent validity. ARC complements the Recovery Group Participation Scale (RGPS), a 14-item survey assessing the individual's recovery group participation. In a transatlantic partnership REC-CAP, a battery of recovery assessments combining ARC and RGPS with other scales that measure recovery supports, barriers, needs, life-satisfaction, and well-being, has been constructed and administered. All this data, imbedded in a single instrument and located within a matrix of recovery theory, is geared toward recovery capital planning. For ease of administration it is now available online through the Advanced Recovery Management System (ARMS) website: REC-CAP Assessment & Recovery Planning Tool.(www.recoveryoutcomes.com/rec-cap) ARMS also offers a full menu of services in sup-

port of recovery, including training in the REC-CAP for clinicians, navigators, and mentors, confidential login for self-administering the instrument and receiving reports, information and referrals for job support, employment, recovery housing, and other supports.

12. The Centers for Disease Control and Prevention (CDC) has begun working with communities to improve data collection as well as to implement evidence-based intervention and prevention. Project Lazarus in western North Carolina, for example, is but one of many community-based approaches.

CHAPTER 9

1. These traditions are echoed even in our modern cinema and art. Think of Yoda's admonition to young Anakin Skywalker in *Star Wars*, "train yourself to let go" of all (disordered) attachments as temptations toward the Dark Side.

2. Dayton, T. (2009, June 28). "Money addiction." *Huffington Post Blog*.

3. Neuroscientist Bruce McEwen, in an interview published in *Time* magazine (February 20, 2013) speaks about the social environment, toxic stress, allostatic load, and the impact on physiologic systems, and vulnerability to adverse health. "How Stress Gets Under the Skin," http://healthland.time.com/2013/02/20/how-stress-gets-under-the-skin-qa-with-neuroscientist-bruce-mcewen

4. http://social-ecology.org/wp/1986/01/what-is-social-ecology

5. In relation to addiction, this interpretation is not a throwback to old moralistic notions of drunkenness as sinful behavior. Rather, it points to a deeper state of existential (sinful) breach from relationship that can spawn behavioral outcomes (Morgan, 1999).

6. See Luis Rivera in *Psychology Today*, "Ethnic-racial Health Disparities are Social Justice Issues" (April 16, 2018),

7. See "The Tale of Two Zipcodes" from the California Endowment at www.facebook.com/CalEndow/videos/a-tale-of-two-zip/1019122714790021

8. Iton's TEDx Talk can be accessed through The California Endowment at www.calendow.org/news/tces-tony-itons-tedx-talk-changing-odds-health

9. Gail Christopher, "Should Your Zip Code Determine How Long you Live?" *Huffington Post Blog* (February 14, 2013). www.huffingtonpost.com/dr-gail-christopher/socioeconomic-status-health_b_2678553.html. See also Anne Li and Shayla Klein "Your Zip Code has more to do with Drug Addiction than the Quality of Healthcare Does." *Appalachia Health News* (November 7, 2016). www.wvpublic.org/post/your-zip-code-has-more-do-drug-addiction-quality-healthcare-does#stream/0 and Hilmers et al. "Neighborhood Disparities in Access to Healthy Foods and their Effects on Environmental Justice." *American Journal of Public Health* (September, 2012).

10. A most recent posting by Graham "Premature mortality and the long decline of hope in America" (May 10, 2018), Brookings.edu points squarely at loss of hope as a critical factor in premature "deaths of despair."

11. Graham and her colleagues continue this research with a series of articles, including "Unequal hopes and lives in the USA: Optimism, race, place, and premature mortality" (Graham & Pinto, 2018).

12. American Society of Addiction Medicine website. Downloaded: October 20, 2017.

13. Harvard Business Review. "Strategy as a Wicked Problem" by John C. Camillus. From the May 2008 issue. Camillus is Professor of Strategic Management at the University of Pittsburgh's Graduate School of Business. https://hbr.org/2008/05/strategy-as-a-wicked-problem.

14. See posting from The Farley Center at Williamsburg Place, Virginia about the work of Dr. Jonathan Lee: https://farleycenter.com/node/626.

15. SBIRT is an evidence-based, early intervention protocol for at-risk substance users. It helps providers to assess the severity of substance use, raise awareness in patients and motivate them toward behavioral change, and identify needed next steps (Babor et al., 2007). www.integration.samhsa.gov/clinical-practice/sbirt

16. Recently several exposés have appeared examining the inadequacies of the addiction treatment industry. A very well-researched video presentation titled, "The Business of Recovery" is available online from multiple sources. It is produced by Greg Horvath. www.thebusinessofrecovery.com

17. The Institute of Medicine's reports, "Crossing the Quality Chasm: A New Health System for the 21st Century" (2001) and "Improving the Quality of Health Care for Mental Health and Substance-use Conditions" (2005), make this case.

18. The stories of international successes, using holistic methods, is told well by Johann Hari in his book, *Chasing the Scream: The Opposite of Addiction is Connection* (2016). National Public Radio covers the essentials of Portugal's story, in a report aired on April 18, 2017: "In Portugal, Drug Use Is Treated As A Medical Issue, Not A Crime."

19. For deeper exploration of these efforts, see Chris Branch, "What The U.S. Can Learn From Portugal About Decriminalizing Drugs." Huffington Post Video. Updated February 03, 2015. See also Glenn Greenwald , *Drug Decriminalization in Portugal: Lessons for Creating Fair and Successful Drug Policies*, Cato Institute (2009). As well as "Swiss recipe for dealing with drug addiction proves a success" from *The Sydney Morning Herald* (June 24, 2013).

CHAPTER 10

1. Dr. Alexander tells this story about the perils of social dislocation and need for social change in an interview at www.youtube.com/watch?time_continue=33&v=DcV_pEcuIS4

Index

Note: Italicized page locators refer to figures.

283

Why Therapy Works: Using Our Minds to Change Our Brains
Louis Cozolino

From Axons to Identity: Neurological Explorations of the Nature of the Self
Todd E. Feinberg

Loving with the Brain in Mind: Neurobiology and Couple Therapy
Mona DeKoven Fishbane

Body Sense: The Science and Practice of Embodied Self-Awareness
Alan Fogel

The Healing Power of Emotion: Affective Neuroscience, Development & Clinical Practice
Diana Fosha, Daniel J. Siegel, Marion Solomon

Healing the Traumatized Self: Consciousness, Neuroscience, Treatment
Paul Frewen, Ruth Lanius

The Neuropsychology of the Unconscious: Integrating Brain and Mind in Psychotherapy
Efrat Ginot

10 Principles for Doing Effective Couples Therapy
Julie Schwartz Gottman and John M. Gottman

The Impact of Attachment
Susan Hart

*Art Therapy and the Neuroscience of Relationships, Creativity,
and Resiliency: Skills and Practices*
Noah Hass-Cohen and Joanna Clyde Findlay

Affect Regulation Theory: A Clinical Model
Daniel Hill

Brain-Based Parenting: The Neuroscience of Caregiving for Healthy Attachment
Daniel A. Hughes, Jonathan Baylin

Sex Addiction as Affect Dysregulation: A Neurobiologically Informed Holistic Treatment
Alexandra Katehakis

*The Interpersonal Neurobiology of Play: Brain-Building
Interventions for Emotional Well-Being*
Theresa A. Kestly

Self-Agency in Psychotherapy: Attachment, Autonomy, and Intimacy
Jean Knox

The Neurobehavioral and Social-Emotional Development of Infants and Children
Ed Tronick

The Haunted Self: Structural Dissociation and the Treatment of Chronic Traumatization
Onno Van Der Hart, Ellert R. S. Nijenhuis, Kathy Steele

*Prenatal Development and Parents' Lived Experiences: How Early Events
Shape Our Psychophysiology and Relationships*
Ann Diamond Weinstein

Changing Minds in Therapy: Emotion, Attachment, Trauma, and Neurobiology
Margaret Wilkinson

For all the latest books in the series, book details (including sample chapters), and to
order online, please visit the Series webpage at wwnorton.com/Psych/IPNB Series